★ ★ ★ ★ ★ ★ ★ ★ Between Authority & Liberty

In all governments, there is a perpetual
intestine struggle, open or secret, between
AUTHORITY and LIBERTY; and neither of
them can ever absolutely prevail in the
contest. A great sacrifice of liberty must
necessarily be made in every government;
yet even the authority, which confines liberty, can never, and perhaps ought never,
in any constitution, to become quite entire
and uncontroulable.

—David Hume

"Of the Origin of Government"

Marc W. Kruman

The University of North Carolina Press

Chapel Hill & London

Between

★ ★ ★ State Constitution Making

Authority

★ ★ ★ in Revolutionary America

& Liberty

The paper in this book meets the guidelines for
permanence and durability of the Committee on
Production Guidelines for Book Longevity of the
Council on Library Resources.

Library of Congress Cataloging-in-Publication Data
Kruman, Marc W.
Between authority and liberty : state constitution
making in revolutionary America / by Marc W.
Kruman.   p. cm.   Includes bibliographical
references and index.
ISBN 0-8078-2302-3 (cloth: alk. paper)
ISBN 0-8078-4797-6 (pbk.: alk. paper)
1. Representative government and representation
—United States—History. 2. United States—
Constitutional history. 3. United States—Politics
and government—1775–1783. 4. Political science
—United States—History. I. Title.
JK2484.K78   1996   96-11615
320.473—dc20   CIP

03 02 01 00 99   6 5 4 3 2

For my parents,
Martin and Florence Kruman,
with love

★ ★ ★ ★ ★ ★ ★ ★ ★ ★ ★ ★ ★ Contents

This book originated as a study of the right to vote in the United States from the Revolution to Reconstruction. I began, logically enough, with the revolutionary state constitutions. Because of the availability of several recent studies of revolutionary constitutionalism, especially Gordon Wood's magnificent *The Creation of the American Republic*, I expected to devote little time to revolutionary-era documents. I supposed that my work in primary sources would simply confirm Wood's findings. Generally, Wood argues that the revolutionary republican belief in a homogeneous people virtuously committed to the common good precluded attention to voting rights—the embodiment, after all, of atomistic self-interest. In the states, the interests of the representative and his constituency were presumed to be the same. What benefited or injured one, supposedly benefited or injured the other. Therefore, the disfranchised were as well represented as the electors. Only when wartime conflict drowned out consensus did Americans exalt voting and direct representation.

Because Wood's arguments are elegant and based upon considerable evidence, I was surprised when my own research led me in other directions. Rather than believing in 1776 that the legislature embodied the popular will, revolutionary republicans often treated legislators as mistrusted delegates to a potentially tyrannical government. They expected the people to watch carefully over the actions of their representatives through broad suffrage eligibility and annual elections.

Such is the power of Wood's brilliant work that I resisted my own conclusions. In my initial draft of the suffrage book's first chapter, now mercifully buried in the hard drive of my computer, I managed to stuff my incompatible research into Wood's framework. But my dissatisfaction with the resulting mess compelled further inquiry.

I soon discovered other important areas of disagreement with Wood. He contends, for example, that revolutionary Americans' faith in legislators as their representatives encouraged them to permit the legislatures or the quasi-legislative provincial congresses to write constitutions. Moreover, they viewed constitutions not as permanent documents that established and defined the limits of government power, but as expressions of legislative will subject to legislative revision. Aiming to restrain the magistrate, Wood continues, constitution makers entrusted almost all power to themselves as members of the legislatures. Because they successfully restricted gubernatorial powers in their constitutions, they paid scant attention to declarations of rights. In the declarations they did write, they further sought to constrain governors.

My research suggested otherwise. The constitution makers (outside of South Carolina in 1778) were not legislators, but members of provincial congresses (institutions very different from legislatures) or constitutional conventions. They perceived the constitutions, and the declarations of rights with which many were prefaced, as permanent documents designed to create the structures of government and to establish behavioral guidelines for men in power. From the first, the framers assumed the need to restrain all government—legislators no less than magistrates.

I also came to disagree with Wood's explanation for the emergence of bicameral legislatures. In his estimation, bicameralism initially represented a continuation of the tradition that different parts of government represented different social estates. Ordinary Americans participated in government through the lower house of the legislature, as had ordinary Englishmen in the House of Commons. The people's sovereignty was embodied in state legislatures. Only later, as Americans came to fear untrammeled legislative power, did they conclude that bicameralism checked the arbitrary exercise of power by legislators. My reading of the evidence suggested, to the contrary, that, although constitution makers sometimes aimed to create some form of mixed government, they worried primarily about curbing the legislature. This was true in states adopting bicameral *and* unicameral legislatures.

From the earliest days of the Revolution, patriot leaders largely rejected the notion of an organic polity in favor of a "mechanical polity."[1] In the organic polity, representatives selflessly embodied and defended the whole people; in the mechanical polity, they hungered after power, endangered the people's liberties, and were curbed by a vigilant citizenry at the polls. The mechanical polity depended upon a large and incorruptible electorate and deep-seated veneration of the right to vote. As revolutionaries abandoned the organic polity, they made voting the measure of legitimate representation. If representatives were potential tyrants, then the people needed to define and limit their authority through constitutions and declarations of rights.

Revolutionaries summarily rejected the idea that legislators might create the documents designed to restrain themselves. Instead, they lodged authority to write constitutions in temporary and extraordinary provincial congresses and constitutional conventions. Because representatives, like all men, yearned for ever greater power, they had to be hemmed in tightly by ensuring that the legislature represented all parts of a state, that representatives be elected annually, and that they live in the districts they represented. As a further consequence, lawmakers had to be constrained through mechanical devices such as a separation of powers, which parceled out power among different government branches and prevented the consolidation of power in any one branch, including the legislature. Also, in most states, constitution makers inhibited the legislatures' accumulation of unlimited power by dividing legislative power into two houses. Even in states with unicameral legislatures, the framers constructed numerous devices to restrain those assemblies.

In many respects, the ideas underlying the mechanical polity I describe in these chapters resemble Gordon Wood's portrait of an American science of politics after 1789. I find the portrait fully developed at the beginning of the Revolution; he finds it bubbling up from the cauldron of revolutionary and postindependence political strife and wholly formed only in 1789. Because Professor Wood identifies the establishment of an American science of politics with "the origins of liberal America," readers might conclude that I have joined the "liberal" camp. I have not. Indeed, I hope to transcend the increasingly fruitless debate over whether late-eighteenth- and early-nineteenth-century America was "republican" or "liberal." The unfortunate result of the debate (in which, I confess, I have participated) is to create a bipolar, fictionalized, and rarefied understanding of revolutionary America. If America was "republican," then it was not "liberal." We are presented with an "either/or" choice, one perhaps suitable for the formal analytical categories of political philosophers, but not for historians.[2]

Historians who have become uncomfortable with bipolar formulations of revolutionary political ideologies have responded in several ways, some of which I find more valuable than others. One, in effect, finds in the body politic republican hearts and heads and liberal hands and feet. Thus, Peter Onuf and Cathy Matson conclude that "even as liberal capitalism triumphed in America, Americans continued to invoke the language of classical republicanism."[3] Another path, taken by Robert Shalhope, is to locate different political traditions in different social groups. According to Shalhope, Jeffersonian Republicans resolved ideological conflict by successfully synthesizing the republican and liberal traditions.[4]

My interpretation follows more closely, yet departs from, the path first marked by James Kloppenberg and Lance Banning. Banning, for example, counters the idea that liberalism and republicanism were mutually exclusive ideologies with his notion of "liberal republicanism." The term has significant advantages. It allows him to lay the two categories side by side and then identify and integrate those parts of the classical republican and liberal traditions embraced by Americans in the late eighteenth century. Nevertheless, I remain troubled by the term. As Gordon Wood persuasively argues, classical republicanism "was not a clearly discernible body of thought" in revolutionary America; and "Lockean liberalism was even less manifest and less palpable."[5] The term "liberal republican," therefore, is problematic.

Instead, I have used the simple term "republican." I do not mean to imply that eighteenth-century Americans were "classical republicans." They were not. But they thought of themselves as creators and citizens of republics and, therefore, were republicans. They disagreed about the meaning of their republicanism well into the nineteenth century, but they always thought of themselves as republicans.

In the year of independence, patriots shared what modern scholars term a "liberal" commitment to the preservation of individual rights—a commitment indebted as much to English constitutionalism as to any political philosophy. They proclaimed that commitment in newspapers, pamphlets, constitutions, and declarations of rights. Yet, in their defense of individual rights, they did not repudiate "republican" concerns about civic virtue, the public good, citizens' obligations to the polity, or the corrupt exercise of power. Indeed, the pervasive fear of arbitrary power, which built upon but reformulated many ideas central to English constitutionalism, fused the liberal and republican traditions into the distinctly American alloy transmitted into the age of Jefferson and Jackson.

In the preparation of this book, I have accumulated many debts. At the outset, David Herbert Donald, Michael F. Holt, Richard L. McCormick, Joel H. Silbey, J. Mills Thornton III, and C. Vann Woodward offered especially warm encouragement. Vann Woodward's example emboldened me, as one trained in nineteenth-century American political history, to tackle the constitutional history of revolutionary America. My concerns were allayed by the training I received from two splendid teachers, Michael G. Kammen and Edmund S. Morgan. Richard L. McCormick, Suzanne Lebsock, and Harry L. Watson offered welcome advice at crucial moments in the writing of this book. Alan Raucher begged me to finish this book so that I could succeed him as chair of the Wayne State University history department.

I am grateful to the National Endowment for the Humanities, which funded the initial research for the suffrage book. I hope that the staff will not be disappointed by the change in topic. (I promise to return now to the suffrage project.) I also appreciate Wayne State University's considerable research support, in the form of a sabbatical leave and a faculty research award. A grant from the university's new humanities center enabled me to complete the manuscript. A Richard Barber fellowship from the university's Center for Legal Studies gave me the time to revise the manuscript. My research assistants, James Schwartz and Bonnie Speck, helped perform the thankless tasks of checking citations, making the index, and proofreading. Gayle McCreedy assisted in countless ways.

I am greatly indebted to the staff of the University of North Carolina Press. Executive Editor Lewis Bateman was the ideal editor. He offered encouragement, prodding, and silence in just the right measure at just the right times. Managing Editor Ron Maner and manuscript editor Randall Chase did fine work shepherding the manuscript into print.

I owe special thanks to Gordon Wood and his extraordinary book *The Creation of the American Republic*. Without *Creation*, the present volume could not have been written. I offer this book as my contribution to the exciting conversation about revolutionary constitutionalism that he and his mentor, Bernard Bailyn, initiated more than twenty-five years ago.

Several historians have read parts or all of the manuscript. Kermit Hall and Linda Kerber offered valuable and perceptive critiques of an early and brief version of the suffrage chapter. Jeffrey J. Crow read the manuscript with great care and gave superb advice about revisions. Chris Johnson and the students in his research methods seminar at Wayne State University, especially Rick Weiche and Ken Garner, compelled me to reconsider some of the arguments made in Chapter 2. Chris also brought to a reading of an early draft of the entire manuscript the perspective of a superb historian of France. The two anonymous readers for the University of North Carolina Press offered perceptive and enormously valuable evaluations of the manuscript.

I owe my greatest intellectual debt to my colleague and friend, Sandra F. VanBurkleo. A legal and constitutional historian, she welcomed me into her field and served as my mentor in the study of constitutional history. She concluded that I had something significant to say about revolutionary constitutionalism and persuaded me to write this book. She has read the entire manuscript and left her intellectual imprint on virtually every page.

My greatest debt is to my family. My wife, Randie, and my children—Sarah, Elizabeth, and Benjamin—reminded me daily about the most important things in life. Without their loving support, I would not have written this book. Randie has been a steady, tender optimist through the inevitable, manic highs and lows that authors experience. More than anyone else, she made the writing of this book, as she makes my life, worthwhile. My children have provided an endless source of pleasure and distraction. One of the wonderful aspects of an academic job is the flexible schedule. It has allowed me the inestimable privilege of sharing the burdens and joys of child rearing. I will always be grateful for the time my children spent with me when I could have been writing and they could have been with their friends. Were it not for them, I might have completed this book some time ago. But good books are published often; children are once-in-a-lifetime opportunities.

With love, I dedicate this book to my parents, Florence and Martin Kruman, as a token of thanks for a lifetime of love and support.

★ ★ ★ ★ ★ ★ ★ ★ Between Authority & Liberty

★ ★ ★ ★ ★ ★ ★ ★ ★ ★ ★   Nearly in the

Old Channel?

English Constitutionalism,

Imperial Crisis, and

State Formation in

Revolutionary America

1

On May 10 and 15, 1776, the Continental Congress ordered the suppression of "the exercise of every kind of authority under the . . . crown" and urged that "all the powers of government, [be] exerted under the authority of the people of the colonies."[1] Congressional delegates viewed state government formation as both a cause and an effect of revolution. Leaders like John Adams saw the creation of state governments as de facto state declarations of independence: the mere existence of independent state governments would sever American ties to Great Britain. But urgency about the need for governments increased when royal authority collapsed after Lexington and Concord. Provincial congresses and conventions filled the governmental breach left by departing royal officials, but because political leaders perceived these bodies as temporary, extralegal expedients, they hastened to establish regular governments to secure civil order and foster independence.

Past experience seemed to dictate the shape of the new governments. "The great outlines of our future government, are to be found in our former," averred one New Yorker.[2] An "Independent Whig" agreed: "Some of the Colonies have their modes of Government, so agreeable to the voice and suited to the rights of the people, and which they have been so long habituated to, that an attempt to alter them would only occasion confusion."[3] A worried Virginian urged each colony to adopt "a Constitution . . . as nearly resembling the old one as Circumstances, and the Merit of that Constitution will admit of."[4] Another writer saw great opportunities in impending independence: "The British constitution may be immediately restored to each colony, with the great and necessary improvements of a Governor and Council chosen by the people."[5]

Many contemporaries, and subsequent historians, believed that the framers of the state constitutions had drafted such documents based on the British model. "This form is much approved of, as matters are expected to go on nearly in the old channel," one Charlestonian wrote appreciatively of South Carolina's temporary constitution of 1776.[6] In general, historians have seen marked continuities between the new state constitutions and the royal past. They have been struck especially by the presence of bicameral legislatures and governors, a structure that "closely resembled the old governments," which in turn had reflected English ideas about good government.[7]

The extent to which Americans attempted to maintain constitutional continuity may be measured by examining the fate of Carter Braxton's plan for a Virginia constitution. As delegates to the Virginia convention debated a plan of government for the colony, they received advice from different quarters. From Philadelphia, Thomas Jefferson offered one of his three drafts of a state constitution to the convention for its consideration.[8] Jefferson's recommendations influenced enough delegates to change some portions of the constitution. But Carter Braxton's constitutional model attracted more attention, and abuse.

Writing under the pseudonym "A Native," Braxton offered an English Radical Whig diagnosis of the ills besetting the British constitution and prescribed for Virginia a constitution resistant to such political diseases. Because the British constitution approached perfection, he argued, Virginians ought to emulate it. But he also found room for improvement. The king had used his patronage and fiscal policies to destroy the independence of both houses of Parliament. Following the Radical Whig insistence that frequent elections would ensure legislative independence, Braxton proposed that Virginia replace the septennial election of parliamentarians in England with the triennial election of assemblymen by the traditional electorate of freeholders. He also urged that the constitution prohibit representatives from holding posts of profit.

Otherwise, Braxton recommended a British system similar in structure to Virginia's colonial government. The assembly would elect a governor for a term of good behavior and a council of twenty-four members for life. By suggesting such terms of office, Braxton came remarkably close to proposing kingship and lordship based, however tenuously, upon direct or indirect popular election. To be sure, the match with British practice was imperfect. Councillors and the governor could not bequeath offices to their heirs. Representatives and councillors could remove the governor from office. As in England, the governor and a privy council would make military and judicial appointments, but the assembly would appoint the state treasurer, secretary, and other "great officers."[9]

Because Braxton's essay came as close as any revolutionary tract to proposing a constitution faithful to English tradition, its repudiation by well-placed Virginians is revealing. Richard Henry Lee, for one, dismissed it as a "contemptible little Tract."[10] "A silly Thing. . . . The whole performance [is] an Affront and Disgrace to this Country," scoffed Patrick Henry.[11] The convention punished Braxton by denying him reelection to the Continental Congress.[12] But the most telling commentary came from the Virginia state constitution itself. The constitution included only two of Braxton's recommendations: the uncontroversial maintenance of existing suffrage requirements and the innovative exclusion of officeholders from the legislature. Otherwise, the authors of the state constitution implicitly repudiated Braxton's proposal. Voters elected members of the lower house annually and of the upper house quadrennially. The same electorate chose members of both houses, who possessed no special social or economic distinctions, thereby undermining the tenets of mixed government. Together, the two houses elected the nearly powerless governor (with no veto and minimal appointive power) for a one-year term, not the stuff of which monarchs—even republican monarchs—were made. And the short terms of legislators, dependent upon popular election in a society in which more than half of the free white adult males could vote, meant constitution makers feared unlimited power in the hands of any man or group of men. Moreover, in an effort to limit the powers of legislators as well as those of the governor, the framers carefully separated the branches of government by forbidding individuals to hold office in more than one branch.

The fate of Braxton's proposals reveals how many American revolutionaries dismissed out of hand any consideration of retaining the colonial constitutional order. Despite talk about continuity and the need to pre-serve familiar governmental structures in a time of public unrest, the framers of the first constitutions were determined to "new-modell" state governments.[13]

How did Americans do this? The most important and influential study of the state constitutions, Gordon Wood's *Creation of the American Republic*, argues, on the one hand, that the revolutionaries of 1776 maintained traditional English Whig notions about representation, government, and constitutionalism but, on the other hand, that their deep fear of the magistracy caused them to write constitutions strikingly at odds with those beliefs. At the beginning of the Revolution, Wood contends, medieval political categories shaped the constitutional thought and practice of the revolutionary political leadership.[14] American Whigs envisioned a political society in which the magistrate protected the people's liberties and received, in return, their allegiance. But because people holding power always lusted for more, politics became "a perpetual battle" between potentially tyrannical rulers and the people (who participated in public life mainly by electing assemblymen) protecting their liberty.

British imperial policy after the Seven Years' War seemed to validate Whig political theory. Leaders of the American resistance blamed oppressive British policies on the king's ministers, who, they charged, manipulated the House of Commons in order to establish an arbitrary government. The House of Commons, no longer a bulwark of popular liberty but a tool of the ministry, supposedly had passed unconstitutional, oppressive legislation effective both at home and abroad. As a consequence of the persistence of medieval political theory and its validation after the Stamp Act crisis, Americans wrote constitutions that enfeebled governors and situated virtually all governmental power in the hands of enlarged legislatures more entirely representative of the people.

As revolutionaries launched their experiment in republicanism, the responsibilities of public men increased. Republicanism, according to Wood, demanded "the sacrifice of individual interests to the greater good of the whole."[15] Underpinning republican governments were the related assumptions that a common good existed "prior to and distinct from the various private interests that made up the community" and that the people "were a homogeneous body" capable of discerning and expressing commonalities.[16]

Both republican ideology and fear of a powerful magistracy, Wood explains, shaped revolutionaries' understanding of political society. These factors influenced conceptions of a constitution, the composition of political society, membership in and representation of the political community, the extent of governmental powers, and the distribution of those powers.

The idea of a constitution, for example, supposedly emerged slowly. By 1776, in response to the imperial debate, American theorists concluded that every government had to be based upon some written document.[17] They were concerned primarily with fashioning a document that restrained the magistracy. Building upon the notion that all government originated in a contract between the ruler and the ruled, they believed that, in return for allegiance, the magistracy owed the people protection. The revolutionaries distinguished between fundamental and statutory law, but only at a "somewhat theoretical" level. Constitutions restrained magistrates, not legislatures. As the people's "legitimate representatives," legislatures could revise a constitution at will, at least until Americans developed "a new conception of representation."[18] By limiting the magistracy, the constitutions presumably would restrain the only part of government that potentially endangered historic rights. Thus, declarations of rights were inessential; to the extent they were deemed necessary, they aimed to restrict the magistracy further.[19]

Similarly, revolutionaries assumed that state legislatures, as bodies representing the people, possessed exclusive authority to draft constitutions. They viewed conventions as "legally deficient legislature[s]," in contrast to the modern notion of a constitutional convention as the embodiment of the sovereign people.[20]

The same obsessive fear of the magistrate's powers, according to Wood, also molded revolutionary thinking about constitutional doctrines like the separation of powers. Among American patriots, separation of powers did not mean the partitioning of governmental functions among different parts of the government. After all, colonial assemblies had been usurping and restraining executive power throughout the eighteenth century. Rather, the doctrine called to mind the elimination of executive meddling in legislative affairs.[21]

During the Revolution, however, traditional beliefs about representation crumbled, compelling Americans to view the legislatures not as embodiments of the popular will, but as threats to their liberty. Consequently, they developed new, modern understandings of constitutional conventions, constitutions, bills of rights, the separation of powers doctrine, and bicameralism.[22]

While revolutionaries jettisoned the British notion of virtual representation (i.e., that every member of Parliament represented all members of the empire) in their argument with Britain, they retained it at home. They could move in seemingly opposite directions simultaneously because of their adherence to the concept of interest. Virtual representation explained the proper functioning of representation only if the legislator and the people shared the same interests. But, they declared, the concerns of England and the British North American colonies diverged markedly. Only in colonial assemblies did the interests of the representative and his constituents converge: what benefited or injured one, benefited or injured the other. So long as local assemblies remained active and vital, colonists rarely contemplated the act of or qualifications for voting; the disfranchised were as well represented as the electors because the interests of all were the same.[23]

Thus, Wood argues, constitution makers in 1776 and 1777 largely ignored voting rights. Instead, they strengthened and expanded the legislature and weakened the power of the magistrate. In most states, patriots curbed or eliminated the governor's patronage and veto powers to prevent him from corrupting the legislature. They also adopted annual legislative elections and expanded the size of legislatures to prevent long-sitting legislators from being corrupted by magistrates.[24] After making these changes, Wood contends, "Americans in 1776 were hopeful and confident that their representative assemblies, now definitely free from magisterial contamination, could be fair and suitable embodiments of the people-at-large."[25]

Soon, however, the citizenry, especially political conservatives, lost faith in legislative action as the embodiment of popular will. As legislatures seemed to divide into factions and enacted laws endangering the security of private property, some observers increasingly perceived the *legislature* as the primary threat to liberty. Viewing the legislature as an adversary, Americans found a new appreciation of voting. Only through deliberate, sometimes punitive use of elections could the citizenry protect itself from a hostile legislature. "Everywhere," Wood writes, "politicians and writers put more and more emphasis on the explicitness of consent: on equal electoral districts, on a broadened suffrage, on residence requirements for both the elected and the electors, on the strict accountability of representatives to the local electorate, indeed, on the closest possible ties between members and their particular constituents."[26]

Whereas in 1776 the people participated in government through the "democratical" branch of government, the lower house of the legislature, by the late 1770s and early 1780s they had rejected this traditional notion of representation. Instead, they effectively withdrew from government. Sovereignty came to rest in the people at large, not in the legislature, and "the only criterion of representation left was election." When election became "the sole basis and measure of representation," traditional understandings of mixed government collapsed. Once, the people had been coextensive with the democratic lower house of the assembly; now, "the several branches of the government began to seem indistinguishable." Public officers came to be viewed "as equally trusted or mistrusted agents of the people."[27] Therefore, "in the 1780s the Americans' inveterate suspicion and jealousy of political power, once concentrated almost exclusively on the Crown and its agents, was transferred to the various state legislatures."[28]

The present study reaches conclusions almost diametrically opposed to Wood's. It finds already in place in 1776 an American theory of constitutionalism that Wood sees emerging only in the 1780s in response to the chaos of revolutionary politics. From the beginning of the Revolution, American patriots insisted upon written state constitutions drafted by temporary political bodies, such as provincial congresses or constitutional conventions, with no permanent institutional interest in the forms of government. Framers wrote constitutions, which they often prefaced or interlaced with declarations of rights, to protect enumerated individual rights from governmental encroachment and to place restrictions on all branches of government, including the legislatures. They assumed that all political communities in a state required direct representation in the legislature and that citizens needed to restrain their representatives through frequent elections, residential qualifications, and (in some states) public and published legislative proceedings. Many also demanded an altered and broadened electorate that conceivably included propertyless taxpayers, free black men, and women and that excluded propertied Loyalists or neutrals. Constitution makers also expected the constitutions to implement a doctrine of separation of powers that restricted both legislative and executive power and to establish legislatures (usually bicameral) constructed to restrain legislative tyranny. Framers attempted to restrict those elements of government vested with primary responsibility for preserving the commonwealth—the legislature and the executive.

The American commitment to "new-modelling" constitutions drew upon an inheritance of traditional English constitutionalism and a reconsideration of that heritage. During the prerevolutionary decade, American Whigs refined their constitutional thinking as they considered two interrelated but separate constitutional issues: Parliament's authority over the colonies and the nature of the charters granted by the Crown to the colonists. Colonists linked the two because arguments about the nature of the charters raised questions about Parliament's authority to alter them. Did the English constitution impose limits on parliamentary authority, or did Parliament, through its actions, define the constitution? Was there a fundamental law, in other words, apart from acts of Parliament that restricted parliamentary power? These questions provoked others: were colonial charters fundamental laws unalterable except by agreement of both the Crown and the colonists? were the charters therefore constitutions limiting the prerogatives of the Crown and the powers of Parliament? or were they merely royal grants of right that could be amended or revoked as the monarch (or king-in-Parliament) wished?

The answers Americans gave to these questions flowed from their understanding of English constitutionalism. Historians John Phillip Reid and Jack P. Greene have compelled a reconsideration of traditional American historical interpretations of British constitutionalism and parliamentary authority. Americanists often have assumed that, at least since the Glorious Revolution, sovereignty rested in the king-in-Parliament. There was no "constitution of legal restraint" because Parliament alone determined the limits of its own power. Therefore, Americans, believing that the ancient English constitution constrained Parliament and denied its authority to tax and legislate for the colonies, offered a novel constitutional doctrine, in effect inventing the notion of higher law.

On the contrary, says Reid, colonists established no new constitutional ideas. They built their case upon "old law, the not yet quite passé law of Magna Carta, the Petition of Right, and the English Bill of Rights."[29] Most colonial lawyers and many of their British colleagues believed the constitution constrained Parliament. Indeed, as Reid observes, "The American constitutional case against the authority of Parliament to legislate for the internal police of the colonies depended to a large extent on the illegitimacy of arbitrary power in English and British constitutional theory."[30] American Whigs and a substantial number of English constitutional lawyers thought Parliament's power was limited in numerous ways: by custom, by the trust the sovereign people of Britain placed in its conservators, by the constitutional contract that lay at the foundation of all governments, by the balanced constitutional government of king, Lords, and Commons, and by the rule of law.[31]

Only Parliament could restrain itself because no institutional impediments prevented it from acting arbitrarily. Although Parliament might not have the constitutional *authority* to act despotically, as the supreme legislature it possessed unlimited power and therefore could act in any way its members wished. Yet most contemporaries assumed Parliament would stay within the bounds laid out, however vaguely, by England's customary constitution. When colonists insisted that the constitution restrained Parliament, they spoke in the language of the customary constitution.[32]

Alongside the constitution of customary restraint lay the emerging constitution of Parliament's sovereign command. Some imperialists asserted that the Glorious Revolution had established Parliament's sovereignty by fusing the Crown and Parliament. As sovereign, king-in-Parliament held absolute and unrestrained power and therefore governed by command. The constitution was whatever the composite sovereign determined it to be. By the 1760s, the constitution of sovereign command gained the support of some members of Parliament, but it did not dominate English constitutional thought and practice until the nineteenth century.[33]

During the imperial crisis, Americans came to believe that Parliament endorsed a constitution of sovereign command, which meant for the colonies the end of constitutional government and the beginning of tyranny. American apprehensions rested on the conviction that Parliament—especially the House of Commons, which historically had defended popular liberties in England's mixed government—had become oppressive. In traditional English constitutional thought, the House of Commons, as the embodiment of the people, checked the monarch's propensity for tyranny. It consented to taxes to help government defray its expenses and presented the people's grievances to the monarch. Its role as the embodiment of the people was entirely defensive; at least in theory, the accumulation of power in the Commons threatened not to establish tyranny, but to unleash the licentiousness of ungoverned people.

In the years after 1763, American Whigs maintained, the Commons abandoned its defensive role and attained so much power that it threatened oligarchy, not anarchy. In their eyes, the Commons had become part of the ministerial conspiracy against liberty; the lower house now was the enemy of the people, not their protector. Corrupted by ministerial manipulation of Crown patronage, members of the Commons obsequiously followed orders from their masters, the king's ministers.[34]

Although leaders of the resistance often saved their most venomous attacks for the English cabinet, they also reexamined Parliament's authority to govern them. The source of Parliament's unconstitutional behavior may have been the ministry, but it was the behavior of Parliament itself that was unconstitutional. Thus, American Whigs denounced Parliament, as well as rotten ministers, for aiming to establish tyrannical government and destroy the liberties of the people of England and the colonies. By the end of 1774, they had rejected Parliament's authority over the colonies on the ground that "the British government—the *King*, *Lords*, and *Commons*—have laid a regular plan to enslave America."[35]

Colonists reached these conclusions gradually in the wake of the Stamp Act of 1765, the Declaratory Act of 1766, and, ultimately, the Coercive Acts of 1774. When Parliament attempted to impose a stamp tax exclusively on the American provinces in 1765, colonists denounced it as an unconstitutional abandonment of tradition. The English constitution had long been predicated upon customary practice. Since the founding of the colonies, whenever the Crown sought revenue from the colonies, it asked provincial assemblies for voluntary contributions. The customary constitution also required uniform taxation throughout the realm, unless the tax demonstrably benefited only those taxed. Parliament's assertion of a right to tax colonists, and only North American colonists, repudiated these long-standing practices, colonists contended, and so breached the constitution.[36]

Amid this challenge to the constitutionality of parliamentary taxation, colonists sidestepped the question of Parliament's general power to legislate for them.[37] Instead, they focused on taxation to avoid escalation of the conflict and to resolve the immediate constitutional issue. As good common lawyers, which most of the revolutionary leaders were, they chose to deal with the narrowest constitutional issue and avoid broader questions. As good politicians, which they also were, they knew that a challenge to Parliament's legislative authority imperiled the colonial relationship, a crisis few wished to invite.

Colonial Whigs maintained this strategy even after Parliament passed the Declaratory Act of 1766 and repealed the Stamp Act. The Declaratory Act asserted that Parliament "had, hath, and of right ought to have, full power and authority to make laws and statutes of sufficient force and validity to bind the colonies and people of *America*, subjects of the crown of *Great Britain*, in all cases whatsoever." In case any questions remained, it voided all colonial "resolutions, votes, orders, and proceedings" denying that authority.[38] Many who led the resistance to the Stamp Act ignored the Declaratory Act. In part, their silence may be attributed to a lawyerlike decision not to contest issues unnecessarily. But, more specifically, they concluded that the Declaratory Act itself would jeopardize liberty only if Parliament used the act to justify oppressive legislation in the future.[39] Colonists read the act as a face-saving formality issued by a Parliament that had capitulated to American demands. Why protest a claim of authority when the concrete expression of that authority, the Stamp Act, had been repealed? Instead of using the act as the basis for further assaults on colonial autonomy, Parliament seemed to be retreating from its vision of a new imperial order.[40]

This combination of legal and political caution and constitutional argument dictated the pattern of later American resistance to English imperial policies. Colonists construed each subsequent incident in the narrowest possible terms, but as Parliament gradually cast a wider constitutional net, American Whigs responded with a broader constitutional argument. They were not shifting constitutional ground; rather, they made the same arguments on an ever broader stage, moving from narrow opposition to Parliament's authority to tax to broadly gauged protests against its authority to legislate. From the beginning of the dispute, they had rejected Parliament's legislative authority in internal colonial affairs. When the English shifted gears—from the use of customs duties to raise revenues to passage of legislation designed to break the colonists' will—the colonists accordingly attacked the constitutionality of each new measure.

In 1774, Parliament reasserted the principles enunciated in the Declaratory Act in the form of the Coercive Acts. American anxiety about parliamentary tyranny now materialized; soldiers streamed into port cities. The actual exercise of arbitrary power, not amorphous fears about unconstitutional exercise of power, drove Americans to revolution. When, in the American Whig view, Parliament turned unconstitutional principles into sustained, unconstitutional, and oppressive political acts, Americans rebelled. The Coercive Acts signaled to them the death knell of two constitutions: the colonial constitutions, composed of customary political practices and of charters for each colony that delineated the rights and obligations of the Crown and the colonists, and the customary English constitution that restrained Parliament.

Parliament employed the Coercive Acts to punish Massachusetts for the Boston Tea Party and to commence reforms in colonial government long desired by imperial bureaucrats. All of the acts—from closing Boston harbor until the town paid for tea to allowing trials in England for government officials in Massachusetts accused of capital crimes committed while enforcing acts of Parliament—involved meddling in the internal affairs of a colony and put flesh on the skeleton of the Declaratory Act.[41]

American towns and colonies responded with resolutions denouncing not only the Coercive Acts but also the eight-year-old Declaratory Act.

One Rhode Island town attacked the Declaratory Act as "inconsistent with the natural, constitutional and charter rights and privileges of the inhabitants of this colony."[42] A writer from Hampshire County, Massachusetts, insisted that the crucial question was "whether the British Parliament has a right to bind us by her laws in all cases; and of consequence, to tax us, not only without our consent, but directly in the face of our most solemn and unanimous protestations." These questions, not a few pence tax on tea, were "the bone of contention."[43] A Pennsylvania farmer similarly denounced "the claims . . . of the *British* Parliament of a power to bind us in all cases whatsoever, to give away our property in what measure and for what purpose they please, and to dispose of our lives as they think proper, when we have no voice in the legislation, nor constitutional power allowed us to check their most violent proceedings." In his judgment, British usurpations were "not of the nature of Government, but in the true and strict sense of the word, Tyranny."[44] When Henry Laurens, president of the South Carolina committee of safety, showed the Declaratory Act to several jailed neutrals, their incredulous spokesman condemned the English desire "'to bind us in all Cases whatsoever?['] 'Why then how can we be free? We are as bad off as the Negroes.'"[45] The Declaration of Independence also denounced parliamentarians for "declaring themselves invested with power to legislate for us in all cases whatsoever."

Repeated denunciations of the Declaratory Act expressed the well-developed American belief that the English constitution restrained Parliament and the Declaratory Act violated the customary constitution. If members of Parliament legitimately could claim authority to make any laws they wished for the colonists, then they legitimately could tyrannize the colonies, effectively abolishing local assemblies.

None of the Coercive Acts angered Americans more than the Massachusetts Government Act, which abrogated the Bay Colony Charter of 1691. Provincial councillors had been elected annually by the lower house; now, the king appointed them. The governor no longer needed the house's approval to appoint and dismiss inferior court judges and sheriffs. Towns required gubernatorial permission for any town meeting, excepting only the one held to conduct annual elections. Finally, all grand jurors were to be chosen by the sheriff, rather than elected by enfranchised townsmen.[46]

Americans generally viewed the colonial charters not merely as royal grants to the colonists but as contracts between the ruler and the ruled that could be amended neither by Parliament, which was not a party to the agreement, nor by the king, who ruled by consent of the colonists.[47] The charters, which Americans repeatedly termed their "constitutions," purportedly were agreements between the colonists and the king as monarch, not as the king-in-Parliament or (as Grenville had it) as a private aristocrat with landholdings in the New World. Hence, when Parliament overturned one charter and, by implication, jeopardized the rest, it violated constitutional protections afforded to Americans by their charters.

Nothing animated colonial writers more than the possibility of charter abrogation. As one Massachusetts writer explained: "A charter abrogatable at pleasure, is no charter at all, with respect to the purposes of granting it; the very design and idea of which, is to secure to the grantees, the thing granted. What security have they in that which depends upon the whim and caprice of another? They have none; they are slaves. . . . Any people who depend upon the caprice, and are subjected to the unlimitted power of another, are in a state of servitude."[48] The Massachusetts town of Leicester resolved, "Charters have become bubbles—empty shadows without any certain stability or security."[49] The Maryland convention denounced Parliament for "assuming a power to alter the Charters, Constitutions, and internal polity of the Colonies without their consent."[50] Gouverneur Morris worried that one of the resolutions he had drafted to provide security for the New York legislature "may raise an Idea that Britain has some Right to the Power of altering Colony Constitutions which is in American Politicks a most damnable Position."[51] If Parliament could destroy the Massachusetts charter, then financial ruin would soon follow. "What security can we have for our lands and improvements, and privileges which we hold under these Charters?" asked several Presbyterian ministers. "Certainly if they can disannul Province Charters, they can disannul all our deeds and patents for lands or for any other privileges."[52]

As colonists moved toward independence, they justified their decision partly on the ground that Parliament had altered the Massachusetts charter arbitrarily. The Declaration of Independence denounced the king-in-Parliament for trying "to subject us to a jurisdiction foreign to our constitution; . . . for taking away our charters, . . . and altering fundamentally the forms of our governments." John Jay, then chief justice of New York, blamed "the infatuated sovereign of Britain" for "destroying our former constitutions."[53] The citizens of Buckingham County, Virginia, defended independence on the grounds that the king and Parliament "violated the faith of Charters, the principles of the Constitution, and attempted to destroy our legal as well as natural rights."[54] In South Carolina, Chief Justice William Henry Drayton's first charge to a grand jury explained that South

Carolinians championed independence because Parliament had rendered "the *American* Charters of no validity, having annulled the most material parts of the Charter of the *Massachusetts-Bay*."[55]

More generally, state constitution makers attacked the constitutionality of the Declaratory Act and all the Coercive Acts. As the authors of Maryland's declaration of rights put it, colonists formed independent state governments because "the parliament of Great Britain" had "assumed a right to make laws to bind the Colonies in all cases" and had dispatched an army to ensure "an unconditional submission to their will and power."[56] The preamble to the South Carolina constitution of 1776 maintained that, if not resisted, the unconstitutional Declaratory Act "would at once reduce [white South Carolinians] from the rank of freemen to a state of the most abject slavery"—that is, as subjects deprived of security of liberty.[57] New Jersey's constitutional preamble contended that George III had "by assenting to sundry acts of the British parliament, attempted to subject [colonists] to the absolute dominion of that body."[58] Georgia's preamble censured "the legislature of Great Britain" for claiming "a right to raise taxes upon the people of America, and to make laws to bind them in all cases whatsoever, without their consent."[59]

The framers of state constitutions condemned the Coercive Acts and Declaratory Act in their documents in the language of customary English constitutionalism, which hedged Englishmen against the threat of arbitrary government, and in terms of recent political experience, which tied the threat of tyranny to representative assemblies and magistrates. Thomas Jefferson synthesized those views in 1774, when he reminded colonists that "history has informed us that bodies of men as well as individuals are susceptible of the spirit of tyranny."[60] Constitution makers planned to thwart tyranny, whether it appeared in the executive, the legislature, or in some grotesque combination of the two. No part of government could be trusted with unlimited power; government needed to be hemmed in at every turn. As a consequence, delegates attempted to write constitutions that delineated the limits of government powers, identified individual rights that lay beyond the reach of government, ensured equal representation of white male freeholders in state legislatures, enabled citizens to thwart arbitrary executive and legislative behavior through frequent elections and a broad franchise, and prevented the consolidation of power by means of the separation of governmental powers and bicameralism. In the process, state constitution makers abandoned much of "the old channel" of English and colonial government and "new-modelled" republican constitutions.

★ ★ ★ ★ ★ ★ ★ ★ ★ ★ The Present Business

of All America

Constitution Making

in the Revolutionary

States

2

For generations, historians of revolutionary state constitution making have been obsessed with the Massachusetts constitution of 1780, casting earlier frames of government as prologues to the "Massachusetts moment" of 1779–80, when the General Court of Massachusetts and the state's free male inhabitants instantly transformed American constitutional development. The general court broadened the electorate to include all free men and empowered them to elect delegates to a special convention, the sole task of which was to draft a constitution to be ratified by the same extensive electorate.

The sovereign people thus called into being new governments through their embodiment, the constitutional conventions. According to R. R. Palmer, this method addressed a crucial need: how "to 'constitute' new governments" and "to find a constituent power." The constitutional convention, which "embodied the sovereignty of the people," created a new government and then dissolved itself. This Massachusetts model, "revolutionary in origin, soon became institutionalized in the public law of the United States" and around the world.[1]

Implicit, and sometimes explicit, in scholarly analyses is the notion that the Massachusetts model was and is the *correct* way for a state to draft a constitution. When revolutionary framers adopted a different method, they embraced a premodern conception of organic law and political establishment.[2] Writing in the shadow of Massachusetts, historians treat the framing of other state constitutions as the work of legislatures. In this view, these representatives of the people lacked a modern understanding of constitutions as fundamental law that created and restrained government. They also lacked a clear conception of a constitutional convention as a temporary political body convened separately and lawfully to write a constitution. In effect, they have echoed Thomas Jefferson, who complained that the framers attending Virginia's constitutional convention "received in their creation no powers but what were given to every legislature before and since."[3] Donald Lutz asserts that the first "constitutions were written by the legislature."[4] For Gordon Wood, constitutions "were created by the legislatures, when they were still sitting, or by revolutionary congresses considered to be legally imperfect legislatures."[5] "So complete was the assumption of legislative power by the [colonial] Assemblies," writes J. R. Pole, "that their immediate successors, the provincial conventions based on the same electorates, exercised their authority to form new, independent Constitutions for their States."[6] Willi Paul Adams similarly associates constitution writing with ordinary lawmaking.[7]

This interpretation of state constitutional development rests on relatively solid ground. In 1776, for example, the provincial congresses of South Carolina and New Hampshire adopted temporary constitutions, which in turn reconstituted the congresses as the lower houses of new state legislatures. The South Carolina provincial congress, observed its president Henry Laurens, "metamorphosed in the twinkling of an eye into a General Assembly."[8] Two years later, the South Carolina *legislature* adopted a new constitution, which could be "altered by the legislative authority."[9] In Connecticut and Rhode Island, the charters of 1662 already provided for popular elections of governors and bicameral legislatures; legislators simply declared their states independent, adding in the case of Connecticut that the "form of civil government in this State shall continue to be as established by Charter received from Charles the second, King of England, so far as an adherence to the same will be consistent with an absolute independence of this State on the Crown of Great Britain."[10]

Virginia and North Carolina congressmen adopted state constitutions, according to one historian, in the same manner that legislators enacted ordinary statutes.[11] In 1783, New Jersey's legislature amended the state constitution with a simple statute. Whereas the state constitution of 1776 required a legislator to reside for one year in his constituents' county, lawmakers in 1783 also demanded two years' state residence and seven years' United States citizenship.[12] Finally, Vermont assemblymen, doubting the legitimacy of the state's 1777 founding document, twice passed statutes to incorporate and authenticate it "as part of the laws of this State."[13]

This preoccupation with the kindredness of constitution making and ordinary lawmaking understates genetic dissimilarities. In order to understand those differences, several questions need to be answered. Did framers consider state constitutions analogous to statutory law? Did legislatures, defective legislatures, or something else draft and adopt republican plans of government? How were those entities constituted? And how did framers execute the framing process? Did they simply follow the usual forms and procedures of statutory adoption so that the passage of constitutions resembled that of other "laws"?

As they located themselves in history, members of the revolutionary generation thrilled at the prospect of forming their own governments.[14] Calling for a constitutional convention, delegates to Pennsylvania's provincial congress reminded voters, "Divine Providence is about to grant you a favour which few people have ever enjoyed before, the privilege of choosing Deputies to form a Government under which you are to live. . . . Your liberty, safety, happiness, and everything that posterity will hold dear to them, to the end of time, will depend upon their deliberations."[15] Awestruck by the magnitude of the enterprise, "A Lover of His Country" declared that a constitution "equally and wisely formed, is of more importance to the public safety in these States, where freedom and liberty is its groundwork, than any can express or imagine." A good constitution "cements and unites a people to their rulers, and rulers to a people, whereby civil happiness becomes mutual; it saves from uneasiness, discords and complaints wrath and anger, envy and ill-will; it encourageth diligence and frugality; it disposeth men to undertake the most dangerous enterprises, with intrepidity and magnanimity of heart; as well as in many other cases serves the good end of society."[16] During the election of delegates to Delaware's constitutional convention, one speaker asserted that no previous colonial poll had been "half so interesting as the present."[17] The Massachusetts house, in a call for the election of delegates to a general court that also would frame the state government, advised voters that few of "the Multitude of Mankind who have lived and the variety of people who have succeeded each other in the several ages of the world . . . have ever had an oppertunity [*sic*] of choosing and forming a Constitution of Government for themselves."[18] For many, the moment was sacred. Two young South Carolinians, watching a procession of newly elected officials in Charleston, reported that it was "beheld by the People with Transports and Tears of Joy. The People gazed at them, with a Kind of Rapture."[19]

The publication of innumerable essays about both the framing and the texts themselves spoke eloquently to the special importance Americans attached to the documents. Newspapers regularly printed the entire constitutions of other states, and essayists closely scrutinized them.[20] Constitution makers themselves carefully examined the handiwork of other states. One representative of the New York committee of safety subscribed to a variety of newspapers in order to aid the provincial congress with word of developments elsewhere.[21]

Congressional delegates longed for home so that they could assist in drafting their states' constitutions. Pennsylvania's Robert Morris remarked sourly, "Mr. *Johnston*, and indeed all the *Maryland* Delegates, are at home, forming a constitution. This seems to be the present business of all *America*, except the army."[22] But delegates from states further from Philadelphia than Maryland could not easily return home. No congressional delegate yearned for his home province more keenly than did Thomas Jefferson. In May, he described the new governments as "the whole object of the present controversy; for should a bad government be instituted for us in future it had been as well to have accepted the bad one offered to us from beyond the water without the risk and expense of contest."[23] Even as the revolutionary crisis climaxed in the Continental Congress, Jefferson authored three versions of a state constitution.[24]

The framers were certain that new constitutional governments would profoundly affect the prospects of republicans for decades to come. North Carolina congressional delegate William Hooper ached to be in Halifax to help draft "the rule of conduct which is to be prescribed to him, and under the influence of which he is destined to spend the remainder of his days, & be happy or miserable."[25] As John Adams reminded readers in his influential *Thoughts on Government*, "the divine science of politicks is the science of social happiness, and the blessings of society depend *entirely* on the constitutions of government."[26]

Few observers doubted the extraordinary, almost millenial, character of the establishment process. When the Pennsylvania conference of committees of inspection called for a popularly elected convention to write a state constitution, it reminded voters "of the importance of the trust you are about to commit to them. Your liberty, safety, happiness, and everything that posterity will hold dear to them, to the end of time, will depend upon their deliberations."[27] One writer declared constitution making "the most important [affair] that has been transacted in any nation for some centuries past. If our civil Government is well constructed and well managed, *America* bids fair to be the most glorious State that has ever been on earth. We should now, at the beginning, lay the foundation right."[28] "A Watchman" warned the people of Massachusetts that careless construction of a new constitution might unintentionally impose tyranny on future ages.[29] Their decisions would shape "the Inter[e]st & happiness of themselves & posterity."[30] As Massachusetts towns considered the draft constitution of 1778, an "Old Roman" cautioned that a constitution "will effect not only a day, a year or a century, but unborn ages; therefore it is a matter of great delicacy."[31] A year later, James Bowdoin, president of the Massachusetts constitutional convention of 1779, implored delegates to attend the deliberations because "the business before the Convention is not of a transient but permanent nature, and is designed for the benefit of the remotest ages of the Commonwealth."[32]

Concerns for posterity betrayed the widespread belief that constitutions were permanent, portentous documents, wholly unlike ordinary legislation—visible manifestations of the idea of security of liberty. When Richard Henry Lee sent a copy of the Virginia state constitution to General Charles Lee, he happily reported that it "will shew you that this Country has in view a permanent system of Liberty."[33] Likewise, the North Carolina committee of safety urged voters to give special attention to the election of delegates to the congress that would write the state constitution because "it is the Corner Stone of all Law, so it ought to be fixed and permanent."[34] To be sure, the framers of the earliest state constitutions did not devise methods that future generations would find satisfactory for establishing organic law; nevertheless, they understood that they were writing law fundamentally different from statutory law. As one Massachusetts writer explained: "The *constitution* . . . is the rule which those in power ought at *all times* to observe; government is that by which they actually do govern at any *particular time*."[35] In 1777, the town of Pittsfield, Massachusetts, expressed the widely shared belief "that government is founded in compact, and originates in the people." Hence, townsmen concluded, "there is an essential distinction to be observ'd between the fundamental constitution of a free state, and the powers of legislation." The "fundamental constitution" established "the basis and ground work of legislation." But it did much more. It "ascertains the rights, franchises, immunities and liberties of the people; how and how often officers, civil and military, shall be elected by the people and circumscribing and defining the power of the rulers; and so affording a sacred barrier against tyranny and despotism."[36]

The movement to draft new state constitutions began when New Hampshire and South Carolina attempted to establish legitimate and effective governments in the wake of their governors' departures. Neither province wished to undermine the union of the colonies by acting prematurely, so both asked the Continental Congress for authorization to write temporary constitutions.[37] After gaining approval in November 1775, the provincial congresses quickly adopted constitutions, the authority of which ended when "an accommodation of the differences between Great Britain and America shall take place."[38]

But on May 10 and 15, 1776, the Continental Congress squelched thoughts of reconciliation when it passed what John Adams called "the most important Resolution, that ever was taken in America."[39] The resolution, and its crucial preamble, ordered power transferred from governments resting on the Crown's sovereignty to those based upon popular authority. The preamble demanded "that the exercise of every kind of authority under the . . . Crown should be totally suppressed."[40]

As the revolutionary congresses commenced state making, delegates assumed that the formation of new governments required special popular sanction. Instead of simply writing constitutions, the congresses or their committees of safety generally called for special elections to new congresses or conventions that would draft the constitutions. Among states that wrote constitutions, only Virginia and South Carolina failed to hold such elections.

By conducting extraordinary elections, congresses and committees further clarified distinctions between fundamental and statutory law. The votes signified that the provincial congresses and conventions would not be granting constitutions and liberties to the people, as the king had granted charters and privileges to the colonists. Nor would they be parties to contracts between rulers and the ruled. Rather, the congresses explicitly located sovereignty in the people, who, in turn, would instruct a political body to act on their behalf to form governments. The Maryland convention called for "a new convention [to] be elected for the express purpose of forming a new government, by the authority of the people only."[41] New Jersey's provincial congress authorized an election for delegates to a new congress that might form "a new mode of government, or enter . . . fully into an independence upon Great Britain." It urged "that when the people are collected together for said election, that . . . the electors" vote directly on those issues or instruct "their deputies . . . to act with freedom and full power." [42]

New York followed the trail blazed by New Jersey. The provincial congress admitted that "doubts have arisen whether this Congress are invested with sufficient power and authority to deliberate and determine on so important a subject as the necessity of erecting and constituting a new form of Government." Because the right to establish government rested "in the people," the congress urged voters to determine whether they desired a new republican constitution. If "the majority of the Counties, by their Deputies in Provincial Congress, shall be of opinion that such new Government ought to be instituted and established," then the new congress would be authorized to create a text. [43] In effect, the congress called for a referendum on whether New York should write a new constitution, and which political body should be entrusted with it. [44] As if to emphasize the weight it placed upon popular approval for a constitution, the new congress refused seats to the Kings County delegation because its credentials had not stipulated "whether any or what powers are given to the Representatives . . . when . . . the said Representatives ought to be expressly authorized to assist in forming and establishing a new form of Government." [45]

The congresses did not conduct special elections simply to gather a better understanding of the public's views on vital public questions. [46] Rather, they held them to gain popular approval for the extraordinary acts of framing and founding constitutions, and to enable the people to decide who would shape their political communities. When the North Carolina committee of safety called an election of delegates to a new provincial congress, it urged voters "to have particularly in view this important Consideration. That it will be the Business of the Delegates then Chosen not only to make Laws for the good Government of, but also to form a Constitution for this State, that this last . . . as it is well or ill Ordered . . . tend in the first degree to promote the happiness or Misery of the State." [47] Congressional delegates looked to this popular mandate for authority to act. In the constitution's preamble, they asserted that the representatives of freemen, "elected and Chosen for that particular Purpose in Congress assembled," had approved the result of their deliberations. [48]

Having acknowledged the people as the animating force behind state constitutions, delegates then lodged the power to write constitutions in provincial congresses or constitutional conventions but, emphatically, not ordinary legislatures. Larger, more representative, more powerful, and decidedly less permanent than colonial assemblies, the provincial congresses bore only faint resemblance to colonial legislatures. On July 2, 1776, for example, the New Jersey provincial congress made itself dizzy traversing the boundaries of executive, legislative, and judicial powers, and acting as a constitutional convention. During that heady day, it first received a report on a proposed state constitution from the committee of the whole. Then, acting as the executive, delegates accepted Captain Henry Waddell's resignation because of gout. The congress also ordered the arrest of fourteen disaffected men (an executive act), the judicial disposition of whom would be determined by the provincial congress or its creation, the committee of safety. The congress then amended and accepted the constitution.[49]

Some historians point to the behavior of congressional delegates like New Jersey's to prove that framers little understood the distinction between fundamental and statutory law.[50] After all, the congresses simultaneously wrote constitutions and carried on regular government activities. Yet such actions stemmed less from an inability to discriminate between fundamental and statutory law than from the exigencies of war. In the face of an imminent British invasion, for instance, many members of the New Jersey provincial congress abandoned the assembly for home. The remaining delegates responded in June 1776 by lowering the quorum to twenty "to transact any business, except such as may respect the formation of the Constitution."[51] Authorship of the state's fundamental law required full attendance. In all but one state, war compelled congresses and constitutional conventions to defend their states and the United States. Only Massachusetts, which delayed writing its constitution until long after the war had shifted far to the south, had the luxury of creating a formalized, impenetrable barrier between constitutional and statutory enactments.

Congresses and conventions seemed to be ideal assemblies to write constitutions because they were temporary political bodies with no vested institutional interest in the form of government. Unlike a legislature, a provincial congress would be dissolved with the adoption of a state constitution. Contrary to the general view, congresses did not simply perpetuate their power by assuming control of the new governments or transforming themselves into all or part of their states' legislatures. The only states whose congresses assumed the powers of the lower houses of the legislatures were New Hampshire, South Carolina, and Virginia—the first two of which explicitly wrote temporary constitutions. Each of those three provincial congresses possessed the province's entire legislative, executive, and judicial powers. Importantly, when they became lower houses of state legislatures, they drastically curtailed their own power. Their bills no longer automatically had the force of law, but needed approval from newly created legislative councils or senates. They also surrendered executive power. Delegates recognized just how much they had reduced their own power and work loads. A relieved and exhausted Henry Laurens, president of both South Carolina's provincial congress and its committee of safety, reported to his son that, under the new constitution, "If I am dragged in to any service again it must be attended with less fatigue as business will be more divided."[52] Had they been committed to the idea that they, as members of legislatures, represented the popular will, or had they been anxious to maintain extraordinary powers, they might have adopted unicameral governments. But the delegates understood that they were acting unusually, for posterity; *they* might not abuse their authority, but future generations of legislators surely might.

When congresses did extend their authority, they did so only until the next legislative elections, which loomed mere weeks or months away. The South Carolina provincial congress became the general assembly after adopting the constitution on March 26, 1776, but only until October, when voters elected a new assembly.[53] New Hampshire's provincial congress simply resolved to "assume the name, power and authority of a house of Representatives or Assembly" and elected a council; but it, too, served only until December, when members were replaced by men elected on November 1.[54] Virginia's convention adopted the state constitution on June 29, elected a governor and privy council, and passed a flurry of resolutions before it adjourned on July 5. It acted as a convention until October, when it became the House of Delegates. Voters elected the new senate.[55]

Beyond those three states, the congresses and conventions adjourned immediately or soon after they adopted constitutions. The constitutional conventions of Pennsylvania and Delaware both temporarily performed some of the ordinary functions of government, but dissolved after adopting state constitutions. The New York convention adopted a constitution on April 20, 1777, then adjourned. Delegates authorized the election of a governor and bicameral legislature in June; New Yorkers established the new government in September. In Georgia, the convention adopted the state's fundamental law on February 5, 1777, and dissolved soon thereafter. In order to implement the constitution, the committee of safety appointed a president. He, in turn, called for popular elections to the House of Assembly, which met on the second Tuesday in May.[56]

New Jersey's and North Carolina's provincial congresses tried to ease the transition to constitutional government. After adopting the constitution on July 2, 1776, the New Jersey provincial congress continued to function in the same capacity until July 17, when it ratified the Declaration of Independence. The next day, the congress renamed itself the Convention of the State of New Jersey. It governed until August 21 but never resolved itself into a legislature; rather, the new assembly, elected on August 2, met four weeks later.[57] North Carolina's provincial congress adopted the state constitution on December 5, 1776, but continued to act in its capacity as an extralegal political body until December 23. Before adjourning, members authorized elections to be held on March 10, 1777, for the legislature, which convened on April 2.[58]

Revolutionary Americans plainly thought of provincial congresses as extraordinary political bodies. They also assumed that only such assemblies—not legislatures—could write constitutions, which, after all, aimed to restrict governmental powers. Indeed, no ordinary legislature wrote any of the first state constitutions. In June 1776, three provinces still had regular, sitting legislatures. The Massachusetts General Court operated under the Charter of 1691, and the Pennsylvania and Delaware assemblies functioned initially under proprietary authority and later under the congressional resolution and preamble of May 10 and 15. All three provinces explicitly rejected legislative authorship of founding texts. Instead, each relied upon a constitutional convention whose primary, if not always exclusive, task was to draft a state constitution.

Not surprisingly, Pennsylvanians illustrated these sentiments in bold relief. The Pennsylvania assembly's opposition to independence spurred its radical supporters of independence to circumvent and ultimately destroy the royal assembly. The need for action intensified after May 1, 1776, when anti-independence candidates won seats in special Philadelphia elections. However, support for continued dependence on the Crown soon dwindled. On May 7, Philadelphians learned that the British government had sent foreign mercenaries to subdue the rebellious colonies and that a British naval vessel was sailing up the Delaware River toward the city.[59]

Philadelphia radicals received help from the Continental Congress in resolving Pennsylvania's crisis of authority. John Adams, working in tandem with them, drafted a resolution, passed by Congress on May 10, that declared that in all provinces without a "government sufficient to the exigencies of their affairs," representatives should establish such a government. Pennsylvania's moderates and conservatives were undaunted. Such a resolution surely did not apply to Pennsylvania's assembly, argued loyalists, for it functioned well during the crisis. But Adams's draft of the resolution's preamble undermined the assembly's claim to legitimate power. The preamble asserted that "the exercise of every kind of authority under the . . . crown should be totally suppressed, and all the powers of government, exerted under the authority of the people of the colonies."[60]

Several hours after Congress approved the preamble, Philadelphia radicals had mapped their strategy. The next day, they determined to hold a convention to establish a government "under the authority of the people." Because the assembly still governed under the authority of the king, radicals argued, Pennsylvanians needed a new government, and the assembly was legally incapable of providing it. Only a specially elected constitutional convention could perform such a task. On May 21, the city's committee of observation announced a provincial conference to plan the convention and invited all county committees to send delegates to Philadelphia on June 18.[61] It was not that Pennsylvania's radicals understood better than other revolutionaries the purpose of a constitution or a constitutional convention. Rather, the assembly's heated and protracted resistance to independence forced them to develop and fully articulate their views about the origins of legitimate government.

Defenders of a constitutional convention argued that, because constitutions defined and limited governmental powers, only a special, temporary convention with no permanent institutional interests should undertake the task. One author defended a convention with the customary explanation "that individuals by agreeing to erect forms of government, (for the better security of themselves) must give up some part of their liberty for that purpose." In a constitution, which settled the form of government and circumscribed its powers, the people decided "*how much* they shall give up." Therefore, he concluded, "all the great rights which man never mean, nor ever ought, to lose, should be *guaranteed*, not *granted*, by the Constitution."[62] An assembly could not draft a constitution, another writer argued, for a constitution "is an act which can only be *done to them*, but cannot be done *by them*." If the assembly could "suppress" the Crown's authority and write a constitution, then it could, "by continually making and unmaking themselves at pleasure, leave the people at last no right at all."[63]

Radical cries for a constitutional convention, and the Continental Congress's May 15 preamble, undermined the authority of the legislature, which reassembled on May 22. Assemblymen tried to evade the preamble by eliminating the oath to the king for new members only, but, paralyzed by factional conflict, they failed to act. On June 8, under mounting popular pressure, the assembly permitted (but did not require) its congressional delegates to vote for independence. Conservative assemblymen then attempted unsuccessfully to establish a constitutional convention under the legislature's auspices, thereby acknowledging that only a popularly elected assembly, not the Pennsylvania legislature, possessed the authority to form a new government.[64]

Unlike the assembly's plan for a constitutional convention, which never bore fruit, the Philadelphia committee's call for a provincial conference inspired committeemen throughout the province to participate in founding a new state. Even those counties least inclined to independence, such as Quaker-dominated Bucks County, sent representatives. The most basic organizational and procedural questions were taken to be portentous. The conference had to decide, for example, how to constitute the convention. Which citizens would be eligible to vote for delegates? How many representatives would be drawn from counties? How many persons would be permitted to attend? Conference delegates probably imagined themselves in a Lockean world where the people would determine a form a government and relinquish some of the rights they possessed in a state of nature. They would protect other rights by carefully restricting government's power. Therefore, the people required full and fair representation at the assembly of framers.

The conference created a generous electorate, increasing the number of eligible voters from about 50 to 75 percent of the free adult men to more than 90 percent. Whereas colonial laws enfranchised men who possessed fifty-acre freeholds or property worth fifty pounds, clear of debts, the conference opened the convention election to all adult taxpaying associators who had lived in Pennsylvania for a year, and to men qualified to vote under colonial statutes who took an oath of allegiance.[65] The conference also enfranchised Germans, most of whom had been ineligible to vote under the old regime. Because loyalty was the key to political participation, the conference disfranchised any man—even though he met the property qualification—who had "been published by any committee of inspection, or the committee of safety, in this province, as an enemy to the liberties of America," and had "not been restored to the favor of his country."[66]

Delegates then moved to distribute representatives among the counties. They agreed that representation ought to be distributed according to the number of taxable inhabitants in a county, but they lacked ready access to those figures. Believing erroneously that the number of taxables varied little among the counties, conference delegates divided representation equally among the counties and the city of Philadelphia. Though not attained, their goal was to realize the revolutionary ideal of "equal representation."[67]

The conference's distribution of delegates among counties and cities broke sharply with Pennsylvania tradition. In 1774, the colony's original three counties elected a majority of the forty-member legislature, the city of Philadelphia selected two representatives, and the eight newer counties chose fourteen—a number that had remained unchanged despite enormous population growth in those counties.[68] So zealously did the conference redress that imbalance that it created another one, underrepresenting the conservative counties of Bucks, Chester, and Philadelphia.

Conference delegates also sought to make the convention more representative by making it much larger than the assembly. They established a limit of ninety, more than twice the size of the 1774 assembly. Even that body, which acknowledged the problem of western underrepresentation, had raised its membership in 1776 to seventy-two by admitting more members from the newer counties.[69]

Conference delegates assumed that the convention was a temporary body whose sole responsibility was to draft a constitution. They recognized that it inevitably would play a temporary governing role during the wartime interregnum, but they hoped to restrict the convention's governmental functions to the election of the provincial committee of safety and of delegates to the Continental Congress.

But the governmental vacuum created by the expiration of the provincial assembly and the exigencies of war compelled the convention, which assembled on July 15, to play a greater role than anticipated. In addition to drafting the constitution, it passed ordinances authorizing two companies of associators to defend the citizenry against Indian attacks. It also defined and punished treason, established more rigorous enforcement of regulations for disarming nonassociators, appointed a council of safety to govern the state between the adjournment of the convention and the formation of the new state government, extended the terms of members of local committees of inspection and observation, appointed county justices of the peace, and fined nonassociators.[70]

Nevertheless, convention delegates remained extremely sensitive to the distinction between the writing of fundamental law and the enactment of ordinary legislation. In the convention's report on its proceedings and on the constitution, it apologized for its quasi-governmental actions: "The pressing necessity of the times, and urgent application of public bodies and men in publick stations, induced the Convention to enter into certain resolves, as will appear to every one who examines their minutes."[71]

As in Pennsylvania, Delaware's electorate rejected legislative authorship of organic law and commissioned a convention to write the state constitution. The political situation in Delaware differed from Pennsylvania's because the assembly did not resist the decision for independence; the province's Whigs, therefore, did not need extralegal institutions to circumvent an obstructionist assembly. Indeed, the assemblymen themselves doubted their own authority to draft a constitution and handed over responsibility to a special convention.

Delaware Whigs responded happily to the Continental Congress's resolution and preamble of May 10 and 15. A state with a substantial Loyalist population like Delaware's, they believed, required a vigorous government to maintain order and prosecute the war. The old assembly's authority was tenuous at best. As Caesar Rodney, one of Delaware's congressional delegates and speaker of the assembly, observed: "The Continuing to Swear Allegiance to the power that is Cutting our throats, and attesting jurors to keep the Secrets and Try offenders against the peace of our Sovereign Lord the King &c is Certainly absurd."[72]

On June 14, the assembly approved the congressional resolution. The next day, it asserted that Delaware required a "temporary authority . . . adequate to the exigencies of their affairs." Following the directive from the Continental Congress, it resolved that all officeholders should perform their duties "in the name of the Government of the Counties of *New Castle, Kent*, and *Sussex*, upon *Delaware*," not for King George III. The assemblymen, who assumed they had no authority to act as a permanent government or write a state constitution, agreed to hold power only "until a new Government can be formed."[73]

After Congress declared independence, the assembly moved to establish a permanent government. Significantly, legislators, "not thinking themselves authorized by their constituents to execute this important work," refused to draft a constitution. Instead, they urged "the good people of the several Counties in this Government to choose a suitable number of Deputies to meet in Convention, there to order and declare the future form of Government for this State."[74]

Assemblymen pronounced themselves incompetent to write a constitution. When the extralegal congresses in other states determined to write a constitution, they called for special elections to new congresses, but when the regular Delaware assembly accepted the need for a new constitution, it did *not* call for elections for a new assembly. Legislators deemed such a method unacceptable, for it would empower the legislature to write and amend a document designed to restrict legislative and other governmental power. Instead, the assembly proposed a special, temporary constitutional convention, to be dissolved at labor's end.

The experience of Delaware clearly challenges the usual scholarly view of state constitution making during the Revolution. The usual formulation is to say that the congresses of the different revolutionary states were simply legislatures writing constitutions. Rather, Delawareans' rejection of legislative authorship suggests that the extraordinary, extralegal, and temporary nature of those congresses—not their resemblance to legislatures—gave them the authority to write a constitution, which, in turn, surrounded and surmounted statutory law.

Many of Delaware's Whigs were unhappy about the results of the delegate selection process. They were especially appalled by the electoral defeat of Caesar Rodney and other Whig leaders. Conservatives so dominated the convention that one Whig denounced it as "our T—y Convention." The political complexion of the convention encouraged Whig delegates to limit its activities to drafting the constitution. No delegate was more adamant about this limitation than Thomas McKean, on leave from the Continental Congress. McKean feared that if the convention conducted any ordinary business, delegates would "hold it out as a president [*sic*] for their taking upon them some other matters." The convention seemed to confirm his worst fears. He denounced the proposed removal of the capital to Dover as an invasion of the authority of the legislature. Delegates, he said, "were not vested with the legislative power, being expressly chosen for the purpose of 'ordaining and declaring the future form of government for this State,' which being a special purpose excluded an Idea of any other being delegated, as no other was mentioned." He argued further "that the Sovereign power of the state resided in the people collectively, and they had delegated a certain portion to us, which if we exceeded we were usurpers & tyrants."[75]

Although McKean lost that particular vote and feared convention tyranny, delegates generally accepted his analysis of the limits of the convention's authority. Like their counterparts in Pennsylvania, delegates devoted virtually all of their time and attention to drafting a constitution, but the war compelled them to assume military obligations unconnected to the constitution-making process. In the end, they fulfilled Caesar Rodney's prediction, made midway through the session, that the convention "will attempt nothing but Barely the framing a plan of Government Except what may be necessary for dispatching the flying Camp Battalion." The

delegates appointed a committee to evaluate the condition of the province's battalion, to borrow money to sustain the battalion, and to devise
methods for paying off the resulting debt. Then, the convention approved
committee recommendations. Otherwise, the delegates concentrated on
the constitution.[76]

In this context, the Massachusetts experience looks less pathbreaking
and more typical than historians have suggested. In 1775, following the advice of the Continental Congress, the general court restored the charter of
1691, elected a new council, and feigned the governor's temporary absence.[77] Concerned about the legitimacy of its authority, the general court
considered the task of constitution making, a task completed or in
progress in every other state. As one of only two legislatures sitting after
the Declaration of Independence, the court evidently worried about its authority to write fundamental law for the state.

The Massachusetts House of Representatives turned to the towns for
advice. In September, it asked the towns whether the house, "together
with the Council if they consent, in One Body with the House, and by
equal Voice" should be authorized to draft a constitution that would be
subject to "the Inspection and Perusal of the Inhabitants."[78]

The house's action was striking in several respects. In making a special
request, it acknowledged that constitution writing was unlike drafting
statutes.[79] Furthermore, when the house sought authority for the general
court to draft a constitution, it planned to have the house and council act
as one body to write a constitution, and it proposed a constitution to the
towns for popular ratification.

Historians have ignored the significance of the house's proposal, and
dismissed it as a legislature's offer to write a constitution—little different
from the writing of ordinary laws.[80] But if the general court acted in its capacity as an ordinary legislature, then it would have enacted the constitution as the work of a bicameral legislature, with the council empowered
to reject the work of the house, with its much broader popular base.
Clearly, the general court did not have this in mind. The combination of
the two houses transformed the drafting process; the bicameral legislature
would have to adjourn and assemble as a separate entity—a constitutional
convention.

The general court went further when it enfranchised all free adult male
town inhabitants for the duration of the constitution-making process. In
so doing, it created the broadest electorate (albeit temporarily) of any state
(the Pennsylvania conference had enfranchised taxpaying associators). By
broadening the electorate, the court revealed how the people of Massa-

chusetts imagined themselves creating government for the first time, as if revolution had cast them back into a state of nature wherein they would reestablish government based upon the consent of all.[81] Moreover, the promise of popular consideration of a draft of the constitution (a practice carried out in Maryland and Pennsylvania) reinforced the idea that they were engaged in something far more consequential than the passage of a new statute.

Although the vast majority of the towns approved the house's proposal, many towns criticized the vague promise to allow the people to review a draft of the constitution. They demanded popular ratification. Other towns denounced the proposal for insufficiently distinguishing the drafting of fundamental and statutory law. The most famous objection came from Concord, which called for a special constitutional convention instead of the legislature because a constitution set up principles to secure rights and privileges of individuals "against any Encroachments of the Governing Part."[82]

After receiving approval from the towns, the general court made good on its proposal. After the house rejected a committee proposal to hold a second, independently elected, convention, the general court responded to two criticisms. First, it called for new elections to the general court, so that the electorate could choose delegates and vest them "in one body with the Council with full powers to form . . . a Constitution of Government." Second, instead of the vague commitment to allow the inhabitants "perusal" of the draft, legislators promised popular ratification (a two-thirds majority was required) by the same expanded electorate that authorized the general court to write the constitution.[83]

Once the general court determined to write a constitution in 1777, members carefully separated their work as a legislature and a constitutional convention. When the new delegates arrived, they reviewed their instructions to ensure popular support for drafting a constitution and determined that voters in the towns had empowered their representatives to write a constitution. On June 15, the general court resolved itself into a constitutional convention. The convention then established a drafting committee composed of one member chosen by the delegates of each county and five others chosen by the convention, a committee much larger and more representative than ordinary legislative committees.[84] The committee proposed a draft on December 11, 1777. The phrasing of the draft is telling for the distinction that it made between the general court in itself and the general court sitting as a convention. The committee addressed its draft to "The Members of the General Assembly impowered in Convention to 'form such Constitution of Government as they shall judge best calculated to promote the Happiness of this State.'" The convention accepted the report on February 28, 1778. On March 4, it submitted the proposed constitution to an electorate once again composed of all free adult men, who in turn rejected it by an overwhelming margin.[85]

Several towns attacked the general court for writing the constitution. Boston had protested the house's proposal in 1776. During the ratification struggle in 1778, a town meeting of nearly one thousand Bostonians unanimously denounced the constitution. Following Pennsylvania's radicals of 1776, Bostonians insisted that a constitution be drafted by a specially elected convention whose sole purpose was to write a constitution and "whose Existence is known No Longer than the Constitution is forming." Members of such a temporary body could "have no Prepossessions in their own Favor," unlike members of the general court, whose self-interest influenced their deliberations.

The house responded in February by asking the towns to allow "their Representatives" to call a convention "for the sole Purpose of forming a new Constitution."[86] When the towns answered positively, the house called in June for the election of delegates by the state's freemen, the same broad electorate as in 1778. It also announced that ratification would require the support of two-thirds of the voters.[87] The convention assembled on September 1, 1779, completed its work on March 2, 1780, and submitted its draft to the people. The towns responded more favorably than in 1778. Although the convention later twisted some equivocal responses into positive ones in order to find the necessary two-thirds majority for ratification, the method of ratification ensured remarkable popular participation in the constitution-making process.

The apotheosis of the Massachusetts constitution of 1780 has led historians to conclude that preceding efforts revealed neither a clear understanding of the distinction between fundamental and statutory law, nor a modern conception of a constitution as written *by the people*, in convention, to empower and restrain their government. But there is a huge difference between knowing that a constitution is fundamental, not statutory, law, and agreeing about what instruments or institutions might be used to make constitutions fundamental law. At the beginning of the Revolution, citizens distinguished readily between constitutional and statutory law and believed that the people themselves created and restricted government. A meeting called to defend the Pennsylvania constitution declared: "The Constitution has ever been understood to be the charter or compact of the whole people, and the limitation of all Legislative and Executive powers."[88] Although that had not always been true, the idea was widely shared by constitution makers in revolutionary America.

How was a constitution to be established, especially during wartime? The answer differed according to the kind of government in place during the revolutionary crisis. Those colonies—like Massachusetts, Delaware, and Pennsylvania—that maintained legislative authority *before* the writing of the constitutions turned to the constitutional convention, an extralegal mode for creating a form of government. In those provinces with such temporary, extralegal political bodies already in place and governing, political leaders used provincial congresses to devise constitutions.

Virtually all agreed that constitution making required special popular sanction. Most of the constitution-writing provinces sought popular approval for drafting a constitution. Maryland and Pennsylvania, writing constitutions in 1776, offered constitutional drafts for popular review. But only Massachusetts in 1780 and New Hampshire from 1779 to 1784 required popular ratification, by a two-thirds majority. The people of New Hampshire rejected three drafts of a constitution before accepting the fourth in 1784. The seemingly endless constitution-making process in New Hampshire may have discredited popular ratification of state constitutions for many years, for it did not become a common practice until the 1830s.[89]

Therefore, the history of constitution making in revolutionary America needs to be reconsidered. Revolutionary leaders did not have to learn about the dangers of legislative power before they could distinguish between fundamental and statutory law. Nor did they need to see the legislatures exercise enormous power before they recognized that it was dangerous for such bodies to draft constitutions. Rather, English constitutional tradition and their experience with Parliament's exercise of legislative power convinced Americans from the beginning that a constitution was a document designed to restrain government and that only an extraordinary, temporary political body could be safely entrusted to write fundamental law.

★ ★ ★ ★ ★ ★ ★ ★ ★ ★ The Compact of the

Whole People and

the Limitation of

All Legislative and

Executive Power

Declarations of Rights

and Constitutions

3

Delegates to provincial congresses drafted constitutions to create and restrain governments. They expressed their purposes in the declarations of rights with which most of the states prefaced their plans of government, in the constitutions, and in the constitutional amendment process. When delegates wrote these declarations and constitutions or drafted restrictive amendment procedures, they intended to contain not only the executive, but all of government—including the legislature.

Historians often contend that the framers of revolutionary state constitutions primarily sought to render the executive impotent and to augment the powers of the legislature. In Gordon Wood's view, Americans feared that an executive might use vast patronage powers to corrupt the legislature, just as the ministry in England had corrupted and manipulated the House of Commons. For that reason, they stripped or substantially

reduced gubernatorial patronage powers and generally prohibited legislators from holding other public offices. They also eliminated the governors'
legislative vetoes. As a consequence, governorships became little more
than prestigious ceremonial offices.[1]

Power slipped increasingly into the hands of legislators. The constitutions authorized them to appoint officials and, by ending the governors'
veto power, gave them untrammeled legislative control. But legislators
went further. Historians often have observed the supremacy of the legislatures, especially the lower houses, in the early state governments and
identified numerous times when legislators usurped powers belonging to
other officeholders, in violation of state constitutions.[2] The great power
exercised by state legislatures has encouraged some historians to contend
that the legislatures were "omnipotent."[3] In this view, revolutionaries
should have expected legislatures to mutilate the constitutions and govern
arbitrarily. After all, legislators themselves had written their own constitutions and had no clear idea of a constitution as an extragovernmental, limiting frame of government.

But, as we have seen, legislators generally did not write state constitutions, and the framers clearly believed that organic law both created and
checked government. Further, to say that a constitution failed to restrict
government is not to say that its authors never sought to bridle government in the first place. We cannot assume that, because a legislature
stretched or breached a constitution, the framers did not associate the constitution with governmental limitation. For example, in the late 1770s the
Georgia House of Assembly altered several sections of the constitution by
reinterpreting them instead of pursuing the cumbersome constitutional
amendment process. Those actions do not prove that the constitution's
authors possessed an indistinct understanding of fundamental law. Even
acts of reinterpretation reveal legislators who believed that the constitution circumscribed statutory law. If, instead, they had perceived the legislature as sovereign, then they could have ignored the amendment process
and blithely altered the constitution.

In developing theories of rights and governmental restraint, the authors
of the first state constitutions retained the traditional belief that declarations of rights protected the people from their rulers, but they perceived
danger in different parts of government. Whereas English constitutionalists located the threat of tyranny in the monarch, revolutionary constitution makers identified both legislators and executives as potential oppressors. They did not embrace James Madison's modern theory of rights,

which posited that the greatest threat to liberty came from unchecked popular majorities expressing their will through legislatures. In 1776, constitutional framers believed that government, not the people, posed the greatest threat to freedom.[4]

Declarations of Rights

Most of the state constitutional congresses adopted declarations of rights; others specified inviolable rights in the texts of their constitutions. Drawing upon Magna Carta, the English Bill of Rights of 1689, and colonial statutes and traditions, seven states (Virginia, Pennsylvania, Maryland, Delaware, North Carolina, Vermont, and Massachusetts) prefaced their constitutions with declarations of rights.[5] All of the other constitutions, excepting the temporary ones of New Hampshire and South Carolina in 1776, listed some rights considered to be inalienable and beyond the reach of any governmental power. South Carolina's first permanent constitution (1778) listed several rights near the end of the document, and New Hampshire's (1784) began with a declaration of rights.

In other states, framers embedded bills of rights in the state constitutions. At the end of the preamble, the New Jersey provincial congress declared that it had "agreed upon a set of charter rights and the form of a Constitution." The congress integrated a list of rights and a plan of government into one document; delegates lumped the listed rights together into a "bill" and located it near the end of the constitution.[6] This practice—adopted in spirit by congressmen in Georgia,[7] New York,[8] and South Carolina in 1778[9]—effectively incorporated "declarations of rights" into the constitutions. Incorporation lent greater verbal and legal force to assertions of rights; they often used the peremptory "shall" to limit government activity, unlike the separate declarations of rights, which generally relied upon the word "ought."[10]

Most historians have interpreted state declarations of rights as traditional English statements of principle aimed at limiting the royal prerogative, similar to Magna Carta or the Declaration of Rights of 1689. In this view, the bills faintly resembled the prohibitions found in the first ten amendments to the United States Constitution of 1787–89.[11] According to Gordon Wood, framers worried little about bills of rights because the constitutions already limited executive power, and the framers' fear of power was "narrowly focused on the magistracy."[12] Donald Lutz, noting that "bills of rights were not generally incorporated into constitutions" and employed prescriptive language, contends that they "did not effectively prohibit or limit legislative action."[13]

Constitution makers surely drew upon English constitutional sources, expressed general principles, and restricted magistrates. But they also aspired to write declarations that were much more broadly conceived, internally coherent, and intimately interwoven with the plans of government than historians have allowed. By incorporating the declarations into the constitutions, framers infused their plans of government with the idea of limitation. Declarations explained the fundamental principles of government, identified inviolable and violable rights originating in those principles, and furnished the theoretical underpinnings for the rule of law. Their authors then fashioned systems of government compatible with principles so established. As Baptist minister Isaac Backus advised a delegate to the Massachusetts constitutional convention of 1779: "it is Esensually nesasary that in the first place thare should be a bill of Rights assertaining what are the natural sivel and Religious Rights of the peopple and a forme of government predicated upon said bill of rights perfectly agreabel thare to and Never know laws afterwards made Repugnant unto said Bill of Rights."[14]

Delegates revealed the intended unity of the declarations and plans of government during their planning and adoption proceedings.[15] Delegates usually entrusted the task of drafting both the declaration and the form of government to a single committee or created separate committees with virtually the same memberships. They approved the declaration and form of government separately, but invariably adopted the bill of rights before the plan of government because they viewed the bill as the foundation for the rest of the constitution.

Virginia's convention appointed more than one-fourth of the delegates to the committee to draft a declaration and plan of government. The committee began work on May 15, 1776. Twelve days later, it reported a declaration of rights, which its primary author, George Mason, called "the Basis and Foundation of Government." The convention adopted it on June 12. Only then did framers turn to Mason's other handiwork, the constitution, which they approved on June 29. Although convention members published the declaration and the constitution separately, a recent historian of the convention surmises that they "intended the declaration as a foreword to the constitution."[16]

On September 2, 1776, members of the Delaware constitutional convention appointed ten men to a committee to draft a "Declaration of Rights and Fundamental Rules of this State." Five days later, they added an eleventh member, and simultaneously appointed the same eleven men and two others to a committee to frame "a Constitution or System of Government for this State." The first committee reported a draft of the declaration early on September 17. After the convention amended and adopted the declaration that same day, it received a draft of the constitution. The convention debated the proposed text, amended it, and adopted it on September 20.[17]

Some weeks earlier, on August 17, Maryland delegates had elected a committee of seven to draft "a declaration and charter of rights, and a plan of government." On August 30, they added two members to the committee, which reported on September 10. Meeting as a committee of the whole, delegates initiated discussion of the declaration and plan of government on October 4. At month's end, the convention began to debate and amend the declaration, adopting it on November 3. Only then did the delegates consider "the constitution and form of government," which they discussed and amended until adoption on November 8.[18]

Delegates to the North Carolina provincial congress waited until November 13 to appoint a committee "to form, and lay before this House a Bill of Rights, and Form of a Constitution for the Government of this State." Unlike similar committees in other provinces, North Carolina's submitted the plan of government first, on December 6, and the bill of rights eight days later. But, significantly, the congress adopted the bill of rights on December 17 and the constitution the next day.[19]

The final documents revealed how the framers treated a declaration and a plan of government as one document. The preamble to the Pennsylvania constitution, echoed in the Vermont and Massachusetts constitutions, proclaimed "the following *Declaration of Rights* and *Frame of Government*, to be the CONSTITUTION of this commonwealth."[20] In case readers missed that statement, the Pennsylvania constitution included a separate section asserting that "the declaration of rights is hereby declared to be a part of the constitution . . . and ought never to be violated on any pretence whatever."[21] The North Carolina constitution similarly made the declaration of rights "part of the Constitution"; framers in Maryland and Delaware required the general assemblies to follow extraordinary procedures to alter either the form of government or the declaration of rights.[22] The Delaware constitution adopted only so much of English common and statute law as was not "repugnant to the Rights and Privileges contained in the Constitution and Declaration of Rights."[23] Both the New Hampshire constitution of 1784 and the Massachusetts constitution made the bill of rights "Part I" and the form of government "Part II."[24]

Constitution makers wove the declarations and plans together because they believed that the declarations structured and moralized the plans of government. Maryland delegates asserted that they wrote a declaration "for the sure foundation and more permanent security" of the constitution.[25] Virginia's declaration established "which rights do pertain to them [the good people of Virginia] and their posterity, as the basis and foundation of government."[26] Both declarations explained the purpose of government and the limits placed on governmental power.

The declarations, though sometimes treated as hodgepodges of principles and rights, represented strikingly coherent statements of principle.[27] They differed from one another in particulars but not in their general design and goal. All of the declarations avowed that the people created government by compact, that only the people could regulate their government, and that rulers possessed no part of sovereign authority. They then delineated rights that could not be infringed upon by magistrates but could be altered or abrogated by legislatures, and described others that could not be violated by any branch of government, including the legislature.

Drawing upon John Locke, other political writers, and English constitutional tradition, the declarations began with sketches of either the origins of society or the origins of government. Several followed Virginia's lead, with the assertion that "all men are by nature equally free and independent," possessing "inherent rights" that they cannot alienate when they enter society, among them "the enjoyment of life and liberty, with the means of acquiring and possessing property, and pursuing and obtaining happiness and safety." It followed "that all power is vested in, and consequently derived from the people."[28] In Maryland, delegates preferred to say, "All government of right originates from the people, is founded in compact only, and instituted solely for the good of the whole."[29] Hence, the people had "the sole and exclusive right of regulating the internal government and police thereof."[30] New Yorkers ruled out all powers to "be exercised over the people or members of this State but such as shall be derived from and granted by them."[31] Persons in power—whether magistrates or legislators—were not parties to an agreement with the people about the powers of government, but instead were, as the Maryland declaration stated, "the trustees of the public, and, as such, accountable for their conduct."[32]

If future magistrates and legislators paid no heed to their responsibilities, "perverted the ends of government," and threatened civil liberty, the people retained the right to change or abolish the government. The Virginia declaration asserted that if government, which was "instituted for the common benefit, protection, and security of the people, nation, or community," should be found "inadequate or contrary to these purposes, a majority of the community hath an indubitable, inalienable, and indefeasible right to reform, alter, or abolish it."[33] The authors of Pennsylvania's declaration agreed that, because government aimed to promote the public good, "the community" retained the "right to reform, alter, or abolish" it.[34]

When framers expressed these fears of government, they meant all of government, including the legislature. Delaware's declaration of rights defended the people's obligation to alter government "whenever the Ends of Government are perverted, and public Liberty manifestly endangered by the Legislative singly, or a treacherous Combination of both" the legislature and the executive.[35] Because "all persons invested with the legislative or executive power of government are the trustees of the public," maintained the Maryland declaration, "whenever the ends of government are perverted, and public liberty manifestly endangered, . . . the people may, and of right ought, to reform the old or establish a new government." The framers reminded Maryland citizens that "the doctrine of non-resistance, against arbitrary power and oppression, is absurd, slavish, and destructive of the good and happiness of mankind."[36]

The fear that government might escape the control of its creators, the people, prompted the authors of the declarations to pursue other means of seeking redress short of revolution. So that the "legislative and executive powers of the State . . . may be restrained from oppression, by feeling and participating the burdens of the people," asserted Virginia's declaration, "they should, at fixed periods, be reduced to a private station."[37] Similarly, the Pennsylvania declaration demanded frequent elections so that "those who are employed in the legislative and executive business of the State, may be restrained from oppression."[38] The authors of the declarations considered all men in power, whether seated in a governor's chair or in a house of assembly, to be potential oppressors.

Because of the importance of election, the declarations all demanded frequent and "free" elections and broad electorates. All but one adopted some variation of the Virginia declaration's insistence "that all men, having sufficient evidence of permanent common interest with, and attachment to, the community, have the right of suffrage."[39]

In order to ensure that government officials remained faithful trustees of the people and that they not wield unlimited power, the authors of the declarations sought to distribute and divide, or otherwise limit, power. Several averred, for example, "that the legislative, executive, and supreme judicial powers of government, ought to be forever separate and distinct from each other."[40] The Virginia convention inserted its demand for a separation of powers into the state's form of government and, in the same paragraph, denounced plural officeholding. Similarly, the Maryland declaration insisted that "no person ought to hold . . . more than one office of profit."[41]

After delineating the fundamental principles upon which government was based, each declaration considered the rights people possessed. The bills asserted that some rights could be alienated by the people's own representatives, but not by any other part of government. Other rights could not be touched even by the legislatures. To be sure, English constitutional tradition and their own colonial experience had imbued the framers with considerable faith in legislatures and deep fear of powerful magistrates. But the men who wrote the constitutions trusted no man or group of men with limitless power.

To some extent, constitution makers designed the declarations of rights to inhibit the power of magistrates and enhance the authority of legislatures, which they viewed as bulwarks of popular liberty against executive prerogative. Insofar as the declarations expressed confidence in the legislatures as defenders of the people's liberties against the encroachments of the executive, they typified past English declarations of rights, such as the Bill of Rights of 1689. The Maryland and Delaware declarations expressed the English Whig understanding of the legislature's role when they asserted that the people's right "to participate in the Legislature is the best security of liberty." Further, either in declarations or plans of government, most states explicitly protected free debate in the legislatures, granted the assemblies control over their own memberships, and required legislatures to assemble frequently in fixed locations.[42]

The framers also expressed this traditional understanding of a declaration of rights as a curb on the magistrate by permitting legislatures to limit key procedural rights. All of the declarations prescribed that only "by the judgment of peers, or by the law of the land" could a person be imprisoned or deprived of property, liberty, or life.[43] All prohibited taxation "without consent of the Legislature."[44] Maryland maintained that "no man ought to be compelled to give evidence against himself, in a common court of law," unless the legislature determined otherwise.[45] The Massachusetts declaration called general warrants intolerable because they subjected citizens to "unreasonable searches," but it allowed them "in cases . . . prescribed by the laws."[46] Delaware's declaration, like those of Maryland and Massachusetts, denounced peacetime "standing Armies" as "dangerous to Liberty" but permitted them with "the Consent of the Legislature."[47]

Although they criticized the quartering of soldiers in private houses, the same declarations permitted the legislatures to authorize the practice during wartime.[48] And, finally, Massachusetts ruled out martial law "but by the authority of the legislature."[49]

All of the declarations acknowledged that legislators could tamper with two kinds of rights. Legislative consent could supplant direct popular consent when the government levied taxes or otherwise took an individual's property for public purposes. Also, through the passage of laws, the legislature could jeopardize an individual's security in liberty.

Given the revolutionary context, it is difficult to imagine more restrictive stipulations. The articles protecting individuals from arbitrary arrest, drawn from Magna Carta, were aimed primarily at magistrates. While citizens risked arrest based upon arbitrary legislation, the framers expected other parts of the declarations and the structure of government to mitigate the danger. Similarly, delegates never considered lodging the taxation power in any other part of government. But they rendered lawmakers less threatening by dictating the process by which they could enact tax bills.[50] In general, the states either followed or slightly modified British parliamentary procedures—practices that colonial assemblies either had struggled for or had obtained by the time of the Revolution. The idea that only the lower house could introduce tax legislation expressed the traditional English idea that the House of Commons, as the people's representative, granted taxes to the Crown. By the late seventeenth century, the House of Commons had secured the authority to originate all money bills; the House of Lords consented to or rejected money bills but could not amend them. Some colonial assemblies established similar procedures. Virginia, New Jersey, and South Carolina in 1776 and 1778 prohibited amendment of money bills by the upper house.[51] New Hampshire (in 1776), Delaware, and Massachusetts required that all money bills originate in the lower house but, implicitly or explicitly, permitted amendments by the upper house.[52]

Maryland, Pennsylvania, Vermont, Massachusetts, and New Hampshire (in 1784) further restricted legislative taxing powers. In its declaration of rights and in the frame of government, Maryland substantially narrowed the legislature's power over taxation. Marylanders recently had quarreled about use of a poll tax to finance the provincial government and, especially, to support the colony's Anglican clergy.[53] Some 885 citizens of Anne Arundel County instructed their delegates to the provincial convention to abolish the poll tax, which they called "unjust," and establish a system of taxation "by a fair and equal assessment" of property.[54] In response, the convention outlined the state's tax policy in the declaration of rights. It abolished the poll tax, denouncing it as "grievous and oppressive," forbade taxation of paupers, and ordered the legislature to lay taxes on every other Marylander "according to his actual worth, in real or personal property."[55]

Then, the plan of government carefully delineated the process by which the general assembly would enact tax legislation. Like most of the other state constitutions, it allowed only the lower house to originate money bills and disallowed senate amendments. But it also prohibited the House of Delegates from adding unrelated riders to the money bills.[56]

As did Maryland, Massachusetts and New Hampshire (in 1784) dictated the contours of future state tax policy, but with different consequences. Whereas Maryland's declaration abolished regressive poll taxes, the New England states enshrined them. Massachusetts, as did New Hampshire, endorsed continued reliance "on polls and estates, in the manner that has hitherto been practised." So that property assessments "be made with equality," Massachusetts required revaluations of estates every ten years. The New Hampshire constitution contained the same stipulation but prescribed new property valuations every five years.[57]

Pennsylvania and Vermont also established constitutional procedures outlining the legislatures' taxing power. Both admonished legislators to be sure that, as described in Pennsylvania, "the purpose for which any tax is to be raised ought to appear clearly . . . to be of more service to the community than the money would be, if not collected."[58] But both also subjected legislative tax policies to external review. They established councils of censors, which would meet septennially to ensure that "the constitution has been preserved inviolate in every part." With other specific tasks, the councils were "to enquire whether the public taxes have been justly laid and collected in all parts of this commonwealth."[59]

As with legislative control of taxation, constitution makers also indirectly permitted legislative abrogation of an individual's right to be free of arbitrary arrest. The various articles, drawn directly from Magna Carta, aimed to control potentially despotic magistrates, allowing legislative sanctions for arbitrary arrests, and, by implication, legislative approval of other arrests. But the framers restrained legislatures and magistrates by protecting rights related to common-law and parliamentary procedures. They stipulated the rights of a criminal defendant: "to be informed of the accusation"; to have sufficient time to prepare a defense; to have counsel; to confront and examine all witnesses; "and to a speedy trial by an impartial jury, without whose unanimous consent he ought not to be found guilty."[60] They also forbade ex post facto legislation, "excessive" bail and fines and "cruel and unusual punishments . . . by the courts of law," and declared "illegal" general warrants that failed to specify the person or place to be searched.[61] Maryland's declaration prohibited bills of attainder, and the New York constitution banished them at war's end.[62] The declarations also insisted that, in "controversies at law" over property, trial by jury "ought to remain sacred and inviolable."[63]

Most efforts to protect procedural rights guarded individual rights against executive and legislative power. Some, like the prohibitions of ex post facto legislation and bills of attainder, targeted the legislature exclusively. But other parts of the declarations prohibited legislators from violating enumerated rights. Not only did the declarations forbid magisterial issuance of general warrants, but they also stopped future lawmakers from granting such authority to a magistrate. In New Jersey, for instance, the constitution asserted "that the inestimable right of trial by jury shall remain confirmed as a part of the law of this Colony, without repeal, forever." Then it required every member of the state's legislative council and House of Assembly to take an oath promising to oppose any attempt to "annul or repeal" the constitutional provision "respecting the trial by jury."[64]

Declarations of rights also restricted assemblymen in numerous other ways. Several prohibited legislatures from establishing monopolies, because—according to the Maryland declaration—"monopolies are odious, contrary to the spirit of a free government, and the principles of commerce."[65] Others forbade legislators or executives to grant "title[s] of nobility, or hereditary honours," for (as the Massachusetts declaration put it) "the idea of a man born a magistrate, lawgiver, or judge, is absurd and unnatural."[66] The declarations usually asserted that freedom of the press should remain inviolable.[67] They also guaranteed freedom of assembly, and asserted the right to instruct and petition legislators.[68] They denied assemblies the authority to establish standing armies in peacetime[69] and required that, at all times, military power would remain subordinate to civil.[70]

Of all the rights enumerated in the declarations and constitutions, the one that appeared in all and received the most extended treatment was freedom of religion. The religion clauses disclose both the boundaries surrounding governmental power in religious affairs and the constitution makers' vision of Protestant or Christian commonwealths.[71]

Every declaration of rights asserted a commitment to freedom of religion. Virginians insisted that "religion . . . can be directed only by reason and conviction, not by force or violence . . . therefore all men are equally entitled to the free exercise of religion, according to the dictates of conscience."[72] Neighboring North Carolinians put it more succinctly: "All men have a natural and unalienable right to worship Almighty God according to the dictates of their own consciences."[73] In the New Jersey constitution, delegates asserted "that no person shall ever . . . be deprived of the inestimable privilege of worshipping Almighty God in a manner agreeable to the dictates of his own conscience; nor, under any pretence whatever, be compelled to attend any place of worship."[74] Similarly, framers of Pennsylvania's declaration, like those in Delaware and Vermont, defended the "natural and unalienable right to worship Almighty God according to the dictates of their own consciences and understanding" and forbade state compulsion of attendance at "any religious worship." They concluded that "no authority . . . shall . . . interfere with . . . the right of conscience in the free exercise of religious worship."[75] In Georgia, the constitution maintained that "All persons whatever shall have the free exercise of their religion; provided it be not repugnant to the peace and safety of the State."[76] New York's founding text contended that the need "to guard against that spiritual oppression and intolerance wherewith the bigotry and ambition of weak and wicked priests and princes have scourged mankind"[77] required protection of religious freedom. The Massachusetts declaration insisted that "no subject shall be hurt, molested, or restrained . . . for worshipping GOD in the manner and season most agreeable to the dictates of his own conscience."[78] In keeping with these convictions, several states exempted from military service any man "conscientiously scrupulous of bearing arms," who paid an equivalent in fees.[79] Most permitted individuals, in accordance with their religious scruples, to make affirmations instead of swearing oaths.

Other states were less tolerant. South Carolina's constitution of 1778 limited freedom of religion to "persons and religious societies who acknowledge that there is one God, and a future state of rewards and punishments, and that God is publicly to be worshipped."[80] As elsewhere, Maryland's article on religious freedom began with the assertion that it was "the duty of every man to worship God in such manner as he thinks most acceptable to him," but concluded that only "persons, professing the Christian religion, are equally entitled to protection in their religious liberty."[81]

Having established, to varying degrees, toleration for personal religious beliefs, many states disestablished all particular sects. New Jersey prohibited the "establishment of any one religious sect in this Province, in preference to another."[82] Pennsylvania's and Delaware's declarations banned compulsory religious worship and efforts to force citizens to "erect or support any place of worship, or maintain any ministry."[83] The North Carolina constitution forbade the legislature to establish "any one religious church or denomination in this State, in preference to any other."[84] New York voided all laws sustaining the establishment or maintenance of "any particular denomination of Christians or their ministers."[85]

The constitutions further barred formal church influence in state affairs by excluding clergymen from legislatures. Virginia, North Carolina, Delaware, Georgia, New York, and South Carolina (in 1778) prohibited clergymen of all faiths from serving in the legislature.[86] South Carolina's constitution not only denied a minister a seat "while he continues in the exercise of his pastoral function," but extended the ban for two years after the end of his ministry. Whenever framers specified the reasons for clerical exclusion, they invariably insisted that ministers "by their profession" were "dedicated to the service of God and the cure of souls," and so "ought not to be diverted from the great duties of their function."[87] That explanation captured the traditional idea that officeholding was an obligation to be borne, not a right to be exercised, but it obscured a broader effort to limit clerical influence in the legislature. One goal of clerical exclusion was to eliminate the church's role in the legislature; it also compromised the legislature's control over its own membership because representatives could admit no clergyman to their ranks.

Even those states that embraced toleration effectively created Protestant, or simply Christian, establishments, by guaranteeing the civil rights of Protestants (or all Christians), creating religious requirements for officeholding, and permitting legislatures to levy general assessments to support all churches. They began by securing the civil rights of named religious groups—usually Protestants, but sometimes all Christians or, as in Pennsylvania, all believers in God. The New Jersey constitution, in language similar to that adopted in Vermont and in South Carolina in 1778, directed "that no Protestant inhabitant of this Colony shall be denied the enjoyment of any civil right, merely on account of his religious principles."[88] Acknowledging Maryland's substantial Catholic minority, that state's declaration forbade the legislature to adopt "any law . . . molest[ing]" a Christian's "person or estate on account of his religious persuasion or profession."[89] Pennsylvania's declaration reflected that state's liberal religious heritage, but still excluded godless citizens from full citizenship. No man, wrote Pennsylvanians, "who acknowledges the being of a God, [can] be justly deprived or abridged of any civil right as a citizen, on account of his religious sentiments or peculiar mode of religious worship."[90]

The authors of constitutions expressed their commitment to these principles by establishing religious qualifications for officeholders. New Jersey, in the article disestablishing particular churches and protecting the civil rights of Protestants, permitted all "professing a belief in the faith of any Protestant sect" to hold public office.[91] North Carolina, Georgia, Delaware, and Vermont also limited officeholding to Protestants.[92] Maryland, Pennsylvania, and Massachusetts required that officeholders be Christians; Massachusetts also demanded a special test oath designed to limit Roman Catholic officeholding.[93] Only Virginia's constitution and the temporary documents adopted in South Carolina and New Hampshire established no religious criteria for officeholding. But this apparently was an oversight: the first permanent constitutions of South Carolina and New Hampshire required all officeholders to be Protestants.[94]

State constitutions also left open the possibility of the tax-supported establishment of Protestant or, more generally, Christian churches.[95] The Maryland declaration forbade the legislature from forcing anyone to support any particular sect but permitted it to levy a tax "for the support of the Christian religion" or secular charities. It then specified precisely that each individual taxpayer could choose whether the funds would go to a minister or church, "the poor of his own denomination," or to the county's poor fund. The declaration protected the existing properties of the Church of England "forever." It also regulated the donation of property to a minister, church, or denomination by requiring legislative approval. But the declaration exempted from this demand, and hence from legislative control, tracts of less than two acres donated to build a "house of worship" or cemetery.[96]

South Carolinians chose a different route: the constitution of 1778 established "the Christian Protestant religion." Obsessed with the religious question, legislators devoted an extraordinary one-fifth of the constitution's text to religion in article 28. After establishing Protestantism, the constitution explained how Christian Protestants could become "incorporated." Fifteen male adults would agree "to unite themselves in a society for the purposes of religious worship." They would become "a church," then petition the legislature for incorporation. So long as the church met certain doctrinal requirements, it would "be entitled to be incorporated and to enjoy equal privileges." The article then guaranteed that a majority of church members could appoint the church's ministers, who in turn had to subscribe to certain basic doctrinal requirements and to a declaration about their future personal behavior and church leadership. In addition, the article prohibited interference with "any religious assembly." Finally,

South Carolina opened the door to a tax-supported Protestant establishment: "No person shall, by law, be obliged to pay towards the maintenance and support of a religious worship that he does not freely join in, or has not voluntarily engaged to support." The state *could*, however, compel an individual to pay taxes for a church that he did support.[97]

In Massachusetts, as in New Hampshire, the state constitution stipulated that because the "preservation of civil government, . . . depend upon piety, religion and morality," assemblymen must ensure local "support and maintenance of public protestant teachers of piety, religion and morality."[98] Citizens might pay the tax to a teacher in their own sect; otherwise the tax revenue went to the town's minister or ministers, almost invariably of the local Congregational church.[99]

Framers in other states also permitted or required some form of general assessment. In New Jersey and North Carolina, they disallowed compulsory payments to support a church or minister "contrary to what he believes right" unless he "has voluntarily and personally" agreed to do so.[100] Georgians required that "all persons . . . shall not, except by consent, support any teacher or teachers except those of their own profession."[101]

The careful constitutional delineation of religious rights, obligations, and exclusions reveals a great deal about how the framers viewed declarations of rights, the constitution-making process, and the restraint of governmental power. On a subject of great moment to the framers, the declarations of rights could be remarkably specific. Moreover, the framers clearly sought to identify and circumscribe the powers of government, including the legislature, in matters of religion. The declarations or constitutions prohibited legislatures and magistrates from infringing upon an individual's freedom of worship, from establishing any particular churches, and from permitting clergymen and non-Protestants (or non-Christians) to hold public office. Maryland's declaration also protected from legislative interference the Anglican church's property and the transfer of small plots of land for the construction of churches or cemeteries. On the other hand, the declarations permitted, and sometimes required, the legislatures to provide financial support for (usually Protestant) ministers. In sum, when framers dealt with what they regarded as the most important of rights, they defined carefully the limits of government authority.

Constitutions of Restraint

Revolutionary republicans designed their plans of government to fulfill the promise of, and guard against the dangers identified in, declarations of rights. For instance, the state bills required frequent elections and enfranchised men who proved their permanent interest in and attachment to the community; the plans of government defined "frequent" as "annual" and established property-owning or tax-paying suffrage qualifications. A review of constitutional provisions reveals the extent to which the framers aimed to use constitutions to thwart arbitrary government. The frames, forms, or plans of government created the structure of state governments, which in turn limited governmental powers in numerous ways. Many of these constitutional restrictions will be discussed more particularly in subsequent chapters. Here they will be considered generally to establish the extent of constitutional restraint.

The very structure of the assemblies themselves constrained the legislatures. By determining whether legislative authority was to be lodged in one or two houses, the constitutions shaped and restricted legislative power. This decision implicitly and sometimes explicitly prohibited legislators from altering their own department. According to the second article of the Delaware constitution, the legislature would "be formed of two distinct branches." But delegates to the constitutional convention worried enough about the fate of the bicameral general assembly to specifically prohibit the representatives from changing it.[102] Likewise, the creation of Pennsylvania's unicameral legislature infuriated many citizens. But after encouraging the first legislature to abolish itself through constitutional amendment, they resigned themselves to unicameralism until they could eliminate it by the amendment procedures outlined in the constitution.

The constitutions then established suffrage and officeholding qualifications, all of which constrained the government. Whether a constitution required real estate ownership (New York), or real or personal property ownership (Massachusetts), or taxpaying (New Hampshire and Pennsylvania), it placed suffrage requirements beyond the purview of ordinary legislation. Similarly, constitutions imposed age and residency, and sometimes racial, religious, occupational, and gender qualifications as well. For example, New Jersey, the only state to enfranchise property-owning women, granted the right to vote to inhabitants at least twenty-one years old, "worth fifty pounds proclamation money" free of debt, and with one year's residence in the county where they voted.[103] Georgia limited the suffrage to adult "male white inhabitants" who owned property worth ten pounds and were "liable to pay tax," or who pursued "any mechanic trade."[104] Except in Delaware, potential voters had to meet constitutional requirements, not statutory ones.[105]

The same was true for officeholders. Some constitutions established property requirements, others did not. Maryland set extremely high qualifications. It required senators to own at least £1,000 worth of real and personal property, twice as much as required for representatives.[106] Virginia, by contrast, omitted all mention of property. Furthermore, as we have seen, the constitutions also imposed religious qualifications for officeholders. Finally, the constitutions all demanded that legislators meet residency requirements in the districts they represented. The standards ranged from two years in Pennsylvania to seven years for New Hampshire senators.[107]

In all of the state constitutions, the framers hemmed in legislators and executives by stipulating terms of office and capping the number of terms an officeholder could serve. Every state but South Carolina ordered annual elections for representatives and governors. The Georgia constitution included in the oath of the annually elected governor a promise to "peaceably and quietly resign the government to which I have been elected at the period to which my continuance in the said office is limited by the constitution."[108] Of the nine states with bicameral legislatures, four restricted the terms of senators to one year. In the remaining states, senators served from two years in South Carolina to five in Maryland.[109]

Requirements for rotation in office limited executive power, but they also restricted legislative control of the executive branch. The exclusion in Virginia, Delaware, and North Carolina of any man from holding the governorship more than three years in any six thwarted the governor's acquisition of perpetual power, but it also prevented legislative extension of the governor's term. Maryland's governor and Pennsylvania's "supreme executive council" could serve three one-year terms, followed by a four-year hiatus. The governor of Georgia could hold the position for only one year in every three.[110]

The states also required the rotation of other offices. Pennsylvania and New Jersey limited sheriffs and coroners to three one-year terms; Pennsylvania made them ineligible for four years thereafter, and New Jersey for three.[111] New York's sheriffs and coroners could serve no more than four successive one-year terms.[112] South Carolina permitted sheriffs one two-year term in every six years and allowed state officials two two-year terms in every eight.[113] Maryland and North Carolina restricted the terms of their delegates to the Continental Congress; the former to three one-year terms in six years, the latter to three one-year terms in four. Pennsylvania's constitution took the idea of restriction to its logical extreme and revealed the extent to which fear of legislative tyranny might be carried: it limited representatives to four one-year terms in any seven.[114]

When the constitutions specified the method of election, again they restricted the autonomy of the legislatures. Virginia and Maryland required oral voting, while Pennsylvania, Georgia, and North Carolina demanded voting by ballot.[115] Only the New York constitution, which authorized an experiment in ballot voting, explicitly left the final determination to the general assembly.[116]

Constitutions also regulated the ways in which legislatures conducted their business. In one of its great victories in the seventeenth century, England's House of Commons gained the right to judge the qualifications of its members. Every state constitution enshrined this important statement of institutional independence. But framers restricted that power by excluding clergymen and men who did not meet special property, religious, or residency requirements. Responding to the plight of radical English politician John Wilkes, who repeatedly was denied a seat in the House of Commons, Americans permitted legislators to expel members only once for the same offense. If reelected, the ousted member had to be seated.[117] Furthermore, the constitutions demanded quorums for legislative business, usually a majority, but two-thirds in Pennsylvania and only one-fourth in South Carolina. New Hampshire's constitution (1784) permitted the legislature to conduct business with a majority of the elected legislators present, but if less than two-thirds attended, then majorities of two-thirds in the house and five-sevenths in the senate were required to pass legislation.[118]

The constitutions also required legislatures to meet and dissolve themselves at regular, predictable intervals. The Massachusetts General Court, for one, met the last Wednesday in May and concluded business a year later.[119] Such stipulations reflected both the House of Commons' attainment in the 1690s of regular sessions and a reaction to the colonial governor's control of when the colonial legislature assembled and adjourned. Those requirements ensured legislative independence, but they also prevented legislatures from making themselves perpetual.

The plans of government also intruded upon legislative authority in other ways. They established specific requirements for naturalization.[120] They often prohibited or compelled legislatures to regulate entails. Georgia's constitution simply stated: "Estates shall not be entailed."[121] The constitutions also restricted legislatures when they determined the method of succession if a governor vacated his position, when they prohibited legislators from holding other public offices, and when they dictated the method of apportionment of representation in the assembly.[122] Pennsylvania's constitution required the assembly to keep its doors open, print a weekly account of votes and proceedings, and record roll call votes when two members demanded it.

Finally, several constitutions curbed legislatures by proscribing measures that violated fundamental law. Georgia's empowered the House of Assembly "to make . . . laws and regulations . . . not repugnant to the true intent and meaning of any rule or regulation contained in this constitution."[123] The Massachusetts constitution granted authority to the general court to establish "orders, laws, statutes, and ordinances, directions and instructions . . . not repugnant or contrary to this constitution."[124] Similarly, New Jersey's framers required that the founding document "remain firm and inviolable."[125]

Constitutional Amendment

The idea that a sovereign people might wish to revise a constitution sometime in the future grew out of the Machiavellian and Lockean beliefs of the founding generation, though neither Machiavelli nor Locke had any modern conception of constitutional revision. Nevertheless, implicit in both their philosophies was the prospect of changes in organic law. Locke articulated the widely held view that the people constituted government. But he broke new ground when he argued that power devolved back to the people when the existing government became oppressive. Locke situated the people's right to reform government at the moment of dissolution. The people individually and collectively retained the right of withdrawal and reformation, and hence the right to change government against despotic rulers. Only then did the people directly resume their original political authority.[126] Therefore, Locke provided Americans with the intellectual rationale for popular authority to change government.

Machiavelli provided them with the reason for exercising that authority. Following classical writers, he believed that, in order for a society to forestall inevitable decay and corruption, it needed to recur to the fundamental principles upon which it was based. Political bodies were, like all living things, subject to degeneration. If deterioration had proceeded far, then only the absolute power of one man could restore government to its original principles. But in a republic where degeneration had not advanced greatly and where there was considerable equality, "a prudent man who was familiar with the civic institutions . . . of antiquity could easily introduce a constitutional government."[127]

Both Locke and Machiavelli imagined the possibility of reformed governments; Locke in the time of government dissolution, Machiavelli in the effort to restore the original principles of a decaying society. Radical Whig writers of eighteenth-century England echoed Machiavelli as they persistently bemoaned the corruption of the ancient English constitution and demanded a return to its original Saxon purity. Imbibing that tradition, Thomas Jefferson urged Virginians to replicate the ancient Saxon constitution. "Has not every restitution of the antient [sic] Saxon laws had happy effects?" he asked. "Is it not better now that we return at once into that happy system of our ancestors, the wisest and most perfect ever yet devised by the wit of man, as it stood before the 8th century?"[128]

What were the fundamental principles to which future generations must frequently recur? As we have seen, they were rooted in the ideas enunciated especially in the declarations of rights, but also in the plans of government. Jefferson called his second draft of a Virginia state constitution "A Bill for new modelling the form of government and for establishing the Fundamental principles of our future Constitution."[129] The Virginia provincial congress referred to its declaration as "the Basis and Foundation of Government."[130] Similarly, the Delaware constitutional convention adopted a "Declaration of Rights and Fundamental Rules of this State."[131]

Virtually all of the declarations acknowledged the people's "right to reform, alter, or abolish government,"[132] but the commitment to the idea of constitutional change was both reactionary and progressive. It was progressive in the sense that the framers assumed that their handiwork was imperfect and that citizens, as they identified those imperfections, would alter the constitution. The Massachusetts convention's 1780 address to the state's citizens urged them to put aside disagreements over particular parts of the proposed constitution because in fifteen years they would have an opportunity to amend it "as Experience, that best Instructor, shall then point out to be expedient or necessary."[133] The Philadelphia author of *Four Letters on Interesting Subjects* argued that "it will probably be of benefit to have some little difference in the forms of government[;] . . . by trying different experiments, the best form will the sooner be found out."[134] Another Philadelphian, the radical George Bryan, reassured Philadelphians in the spring of 1776 that "whatever inconveniences may be found unprovided for [in a constitution], may be candidly advertised to the public" and revised by a future constitutional convention.[135]

But amendment was also reactionary in the sense that future alterations would be aimed at restoring the purity of the original constitution and be part of that "frequent recurrence to fundamental principles," which was "absolutely necessary, to preserve the blessings of liberty" and prevent revolutions.[136] Thus, Bryan urged that a decennial constitutional convention in Pennsylvania would keep "the constitution in health and vigor" by ensuring "that it did not depart from its first principles."[137]

The two constitutions that explained the rationale for an amending process exemplify both the progressive and reactionary natures of constitutional revision. The Pennsylvania constitution provided for the septennial election of a council of censors as a means of protecting the constitution's original purity. It emphasized preservation, not alteration. The council would meet so "that the freedom of the commonwealth may be preserved inviolate forever." Its primary obligation was to discover if "the constitution has been preserved inviolate in every part." But the council also could propose constitutional revisions "if there appear to them an absolute necessity of amending any article . . . which may be defective" and add provisions "necessary for the preservation of the rights and happiness of the people."[138] The Massachusetts constitution of 1780 called for a referendum on a new convention in 1795 "the more effectually to adhere to the principles of the Constitution, and to correct those violations." A convention also would make any necessary alterations in light of experience with the present constitution.[139]

Although many framers assumed that some revision of their work would be necessary, they also believed that constitutions were immune to ordinary legislation. Precisely the same objections to legislatures writing constitutions applied to amending them. A legislature that could amend a constitution through ordinary statutes could claim tyrannical power. "As the constitution limits the authority of the legislature," one writer observed, "if the legislature can alter the constitution, they can give themselves what bounds they please."[140] Most states rejected such an amendment process.

Framers in three states—Virginia, North Carolina, and New York—provided no way to alter their constitutions. Although Jefferson accused subsequent Virginia legislatures of repeatedly violating the state constitution, it appears that few constitution writers in Virginia, North Carolina, or New York believed that their constitutions were subject to legislative emendation.[141]

At another extreme were South Carolina and New Jersey. In 1776, the South Carolina provincial congress omitted amendment procedures, but, its constitution was explicitly temporary. The intentions of congressional delegates became a matter of dispute when state legislators drafted a new constitution. Governor John Rutledge vetoed the constitution on the grounds that legislators had no constitutional authority to destroy the original document. "A Legislature has no lawful Power, to establish a different one," he wrote in Lockean fashion, "but that, such Power is, only, in the People, on a Dissolution of Government, or Subversion of the Constitution." Furthermore, the constitution imposed an oath on all legislators to maintain the government; by altering the constitution, legislators perjured themselves and nullified the very purpose of a constitution. Rutledge was not alone. After he resigned, the legislature's new choice, Arthur Middleton, refused the governorship on the grounds that the legislature had no power to alter the constitution.[142] The legislators who drafted the new constitution evidently had some misgivings about the amending process. The new constitution distinguished between fundamental and statutory law by requiring ninety days public notice before the legislature could amend the constitution. It also demanded a majority vote of all the members of the senate and house, a more stringent standard than the quorum of one-fourth of the members needed to pass statutory law.[143] Constitutional revision required 102 votes in the house, but ordinary legislation might be passed with 26 or fewer votes.

The New Jersey constitution included a special article prohibiting legislative amendment of several articles. Article 23 compelled legislators to swear that they would not repeal the provisions for annual elections, the articles opposing church establishment and conferring equal civil rights on all Protestants, and trial by jury.[144] It is unclear whether delegates to the provincial congress intended that all other parts of the constitution be susceptible to revision by simple legislative enactment; they did, after all, say that the document was to "remain firm and inviolable." But subsequent legislatures so interpreted it and amended the constitution by ordinary statute.[145]

Delawareans also enumerated a list of unamendable articles, and they required extraordinary majorities to alter other parts of the constitution as well. By article 30, legislators could not alter the declaration of rights or the articles establishing the state's name, the bicameral legislature, and the legislature's power over its own officers and members. Nor could lawmakers repeal the ban on slave importation, "the Establishment of any one Religious Sect," and clerical officeholding. All other parts of the constitution could be amended, but only with five-sevenths of the entire assembly and seven of the nine-member legislative council in agreement.[146]

Like South Carolina, Maryland provided for constitutional revision by a legislative majority, but not with a statute. It required that two successive assemblies—separated in time by the election of a new assembly—pass a bill to amend the constitution in order to ratify it. But for amendments affecting the Eastern Shore (and therefore the state's delicate balance of power), the plan of government specified a two-thirds majority of all the members of two successive legislatures. The constitution also provided for indirect popular ratification. After senators and representatives endorsed an amendment for the first time, they had to publicize the proposed amendment for three months before the next election. Finally, the next legislature had to ratify the bill during its first session.[147]

The constitutions of Pennsylvania, Vermont, Georgia, Massachusetts, and New Hampshire (in 1784) explicitly prohibited legislative amendment. Instead, Pennsylvania and Vermont created councils of censors, which would be popularly elected every seven years. Each city and county would elect two councillors. The censors were to ensure that "the constitution had been preserved inviolate." In particular, they were to find out if "the legislative and executive branches of government" fulfilled their constitutional obligations or if they had "assumed to themselves or exercised other or greater powers than they are intitled to by the constitution." The constitution also required the council to review government fiscal policies and to evaluate the execution of the laws.

If the council of censors discovered problems, it had several means of obtaining redress—some more drastic than others. It could "pass public censures," "order impeachments," and recommend the repeal of unconstitutional laws. But if the problem lay not in the laws or the government but in the founding document itself, then the council (with a two-thirds majority) could call a convention to alter the constitution. The council would publish its recommendations at least six months before the election of convention delegates so that voters could instruct their delegates.[148]

By establishing councils of censors, the Pennsylvania and Vermont plans of government divorced constitutional revision from ordinary government processes. Unlike a legislature, which had permanent institutional interests, the council was a temporary body composed of non-officeholders. The councillors' powers expired one year after the date of their election.

The establishment of the council also regularized a difficult revision process. Pennsylvanians could modify their constitution once every seven years. To do so, they had to elect the council of censors; two-thirds of the councillors needed to call a convention and recommend constitutional changes; and, finally, the popularly elected and instructed convention could alter the constitution. But unlike any of the other constitutions drafted in 1776, Pennsylvania's provided for regular review and amendment of the constitution.

The opportunity to change or replace the document in 1783 did not pacify opponents of the constitution. They viewed the amendment process as an intolerable barrier to immediate amendment. Nevertheless, they ultimately conceded that constitutions confined legislatures and therefore could not be altered by them. The anti-Constitutionalists or Republicans, as they soon came to call themselves, initially insisted that the people, through their legally elected representatives, should be able to amend their constitution whenever they wished. Arguing that the people's representatives expressed the will of the people, they contended that delegates to the first assembly should take an oath to support independence, refuse the oath to sustain the constitution, and, after popular consultation, amend the constitution.[149] In one writer's view, "the *fundamental principles* of a government should never be altered by a legislature; but these fundamental principles are contained in the *Bill of Rights*." Because the "constitution is only the executive part of a bill of rights," it could be amended by ordinary legislation "provided *no infringement* is made upon the bill of rights." If the people had no power to change the form of government for seven years, then they were "as much enslaved as the subjects of the British Parliament."[150] As a group of Philadelphia anti-Constitutionalists declared: "A SEVEN YEARS familiarity with slavery, may render us ever afterwards unfit to assert and maintain the privileges of freemen."[151]

The constitution's defenders immediately denounced "the consequences of suffering the Legislature to amend constitutions." One writer reminded Philadelphians that "the Constitution has ever been understood to be the charter or compact of the whole people, and the limitation of all Legislative and Executive powers." Only "the community at large" could change it. Legislative amendment would send the commonwealth hurtling toward disaster: "The slavery and misery of every State that ever lost its liberty, was the consequence of people's negligence in this very point."[152] Convention delegates knew, said another supporter, that if they allowed the legislature to alter the constitution they would "have made the legislature their own carvers, and in a convenient time had them as independent, nay indeed as absolute master of the lives and fortunes of their constituents in Pennsylvania as they now are in Great-Britain."[153]

Opponents of the constitution began to retreat. They had not meant exactly to recommend legislative amendment, they declared, but to suggest either that the legislature act as a constitutional convention—by writing a new constitution and then dissolving itself and authorizing elections for a new legislature—or call a special convention.[154] This new position reaffirmed the idea that a document meant to circumscribe government could not be amended by ordinary legislative means, that the constitution stood apart from and restrained the legislature and its acts. In the end, Republicans waited until 1790 to revise organic law at another constitutional convention.

The Georgia constitution also excluded the legislature from the amendment process with a provision for amendment by popular initiative. When a majority of the citizens in a majority of the counties petitioned for a constitutional convention, the assembly would call one. The content of the petitions would also determine the convention's agenda; the assembly was to specify "the alterations to be made, according to the petitions."[155]

Massachusetts and New Hampshire (in 1784), like Pennsylvania and Vermont, called for regular opportunities to review the constitution. New Hampshire went further, requiring the general court to call a convention in seven years. Its handiwork had to be approved by two-thirds of the qualified electors who voted.[156] The Massachusetts constitution mandated a popular referendum on constitutional revision in 1795. If two-thirds of the voters supported revision, then the general court would call for a new constitutional convention.[157]

In all of the states, with the partial exception of New Jersey and the possible exception of South Carolina in 1776, constitution makers recognized both the significance and fundamental nature of their productions and expressed considerable distrust of all governmental bodies (including the legislature) by making it difficult, or impossible, for assemblymen to revise their state's constitutions.

The authors of the first state constitutions believed that they were writing documents that would influence future generations. They might trust themselves to shun arbitrary power, but given the seductions of power and the inevitable decay of polities, they necessarily distrusted their contemporaries and their successors. Viewing the constitutions as fundamental law, they wrote declarations of rights and plans of government that defined and restrained rulers, in legislatures and elsewhere; they also protected the constitutions by restricting the amending process.[158]

★ ★ ★ ★ ★ ★ ★ ★ ★ Represented According
to the True Intent
and Meaning Thereof

Political Representation

4

Americans assumed they would protect their rights not only through declarations of rights and constitutional limitation but also through full, fair, and equal representation in state legislatures. Following English constitutional tradition, the founding generation saw the primary function of representation as the restraint of government. But unlike their English counterparts, who believed that the representative House of Commons curbed arbitrary exercises of royal prerogative, American revolutionaries perceived representation as protection against tyrannical behavior by all parts of government, including the legislature.[1] For that reason, they decided to elect their representatives annually, tether them with instructions on enacting laws, and require them to live in the districts they represented. Demanding "equal representation," they ensured that all regions of a state were represented, and, in most states, they also provided for apportionment of representation by population. As we shall see in the next chapter, their understanding of representation also transformed how they thought about the suffrage.

In 1763, as Great Britain emerged triumphant from the Seven Years' War, it confronted a national debt doubled by wartime expenses, costly maintenance of troops in North America to protect the spoils of victory, and concerns about North American colonists drifting toward independence. The king's ministers, led by First Minister George Grenville, responded by toughening enforcement of the existing Navigation Acts and proposing to Parliament (which quickly endorsed them): a Sugar Act (which reduced duties on molasses and tightened the mechanism for collecting duties), a Currency Act (which extended a ban on paper emissions to all colonial legislatures), and a Quartering Act to help defray the cost of British troops on North American soil. Grenville also proposed a colonial stamp tax on all legal documents, newspapers, playing cards, and the like, but asked Parliament to delay enactment for a year to allow for a colonial response. The stamp tax triggered a heated and lengthy debate over Parliament's authority to tax, the relationship between taxation and consent, and the nature of political representation.[2]

The Meaning of Representation

As early as 1765, British policymakers and outraged colonists agreed that taxes could be levied only with the consent of taxpayers. They concurred with Pennsylvanian John Dickinson's declaration: "Men cannot be happy, without Freedom; nor free, without Security of Property; nor so secure, unless the sole Power to dispose of it be lodged in themselves; *therefore* no People can be *free*, but where Taxes are imposed on them *with their own Consent*, given personally, or by their Representatives."[3]

But agreement about the necessity of representation masked a violent quarrel over the meaning of consent. The English position was best articulated by Thomas Whately, an officer in Grenville's treasury department, a member of Parliament, and the primary author of the Stamp Act. Whately acknowledged and endorsed the American insistence on "the Privilege, which is common to all *British* Subjects, of being taxed only with their own Consent, given by their Representatives." Not only taxes, but all legislation, he said, required "the Concurrence of our Representatives."

Whately then cited precedents to prove that colonists had never challenged Parliament's right to legislate for or tax the colonists. But, he argued, even without precedents, Parliament possessed the authority to tax Americans because they were represented in the House of Commons. To be sure, the colonists did not "chuse the Members of that Assembly"; then again, neither did "Nine Tenths of the People of *Britain*." In England, the right to vote was "annexed to certain Species of property, to peculiar Franchises, and to Inhabitancy in some particular Places." Most people, even most property holders, were disfranchised. Moreover, residents of major cities like Birmingham, Leeds, and Manchester enjoyed no special borough representation in the Commons. Colonists, Whately contended, were "in exactly the same Situation: All *British* Subjects are really in the same; none are actually, all are virtually represented in parliament." Because members of Parliament represented the entire British empire, not particular constituencies, "the Colonies and all *British* Subjects whatever, have an equal Share in the general Representation of the Commons of *Great Britain*, and are bound by the Consent of the Majority of that House."[4]

Americans vigorously disputed the assumptions supporting Whately's argument. The validity of virtual representation rested upon the belief that Englishmen, whether they lived in England or in a remote colony, were, in Gordon Wood's words, "a unitary homogeneous order with a fundamental common interest. What affected nonelectors eventually affected electors; what affected the whole affected the parts; and what affected the empire ultimately affected every Englishman in it."[5] Resistance leaders denied the colonies' commonality of interest with England and insisted that true representation required direct election by freemen in all communities.

Taken together, two colonial pamphlets—one by Daniel Dulany, the other by "A Plain Yeoman"—summarized the American response. In the most widely disseminated colonial rejoinder, Maryland's Dulany conceded the possibility of virtual representation under certain conditions, none of which prevailed in relations between the House of Commons and the American colonists. He accepted Whately's argument that most British subjects, as nonelectors, were virtually represented in Parliament, but he denied that colonists were similarly situated. "A Plain Yeoman," who argued that representation depended upon election, agreed that colonists were unrepresented in Parliament but mocked the idea of virtual representation and contended that all Englishmen were directly represented in Parliament.

In Dulany's view, legitimate representation required that a lawmaker share the same interests and burdens as his constituents. In England, Dulany concluded, the interests of "the nonelectors, the electors, and the representatives are individually the same, to say nothing of the connection among neighbors, friends, and relations." Nonelectors were protected "against oppression" because it would "fall also upon the electors and the representatives. The one can't be injured and the other indemnified." At least theoretically, all nonelectors could become electors; and because many electors owned nonfreehold and monied property, they represented the interests of property-owning nonelectors.

Whether the members of Parliament represented all English property owners virtually or directly, Dulany argued, they did not represent North Americans. He could find no "intimate and inseparable relation between the *electors* of Great Britain and the *inhabitants of the colonies* which must inevitably involve both in the same taxation." Indeed, British electors and members of Parliament could reduce their own taxes by heaping ever greater burdens on the colonists. A "total *dissimilarity*" in the situation of colonists and British electors, Dulany concluded, rendered those electors incapable of representing the colonists.[6]

"A Plain Yeoman" denounced as absurd the idea that Americans were represented in Parliament, arguing that election necessarily preceded representation, and "not one *American* ever gave, or can give, his suffrage for the choice of any of these pretended representatives." He thought it almost "magic, that such a vast extent of an inhabited country as this, should be represented in parliament, and . . . should never have found it out."

Turning to Whately's comparison of Americans and British nonelectors, "Yeoman" agreed that, although many English subjects were nonelectors, the House of Commons represented all Englishmen. How did he know this? A "right of election," he noted, "is annexed to a certain species of property, franchises, &c. and every man in *England*, who falls under these descriptions, hath a right to vote, either for knights, citizens, or burgesses." But in America, even the many who could meet England's suffrage qualifications could not vote for members of Parliament. The crucial difference between Englishmen and Americans was "a privilege to choose 558 members to represent them in parliament, though in unequal proportions to the several districts, . . . and not having liberty to choose any."[7]

In "Yeoman"'s widely shared view, the idea of direct representation did not affect how individuals were represented within communities but expressed the belief that all political communities be represented. When he insisted upon direct representation, he was not considering the relationship of nonelectors and electors, but rather arguing that all who met suffrage requirements, however defined, were entitled to representation. Direct representation did not necessarily mean that everyone had to vote in order to be represented. White male Georgians, for example, might readily accept the disfranchisement of women, minors, Catholics, Jews, free blacks, paupers, and others within a community, but they insisted upon the community's representation. They would guarantee representation to unrepresented communities but not extend it to the disfranchised within those communities.

Taken together, Dulany and "Yeoman," though they disagreed about the possibility of virtual representation, captured colonial thinking about representation. Dulany's pamphlet expressed the traditional view, shared by the British, that legitimate representation required a representative to share his constituents' interests and the consequences of government behavior. "A Plain Yeoman" demanded enfranchisement of all who met the legal requirements for voting, which in turn dictated the election of representatives by freemen in all settled communities.

From the early days of settlement to 1767, representation expanded haltingly and often incompletely to accommodate a growing and expanding population. Depending upon the colony, legislators and/or governors responded by granting some representation to newly settled areas. And representatives usually resided, and in some cases were required to reside, in the districts they represented, so as to represent better the interests and share the burdens of their constituents.

Equal Representation and Apportionment

In 1767, new imperial policies halting further expansion of the provincial assemblies impelled colonists to apply the lessons of the Stamp Act crisis to their own legislatures. After the Seven Years' War and the suppression of Pontiac's Rebellion in 1763, colonists flooded into frontier areas. Colonial legislatures quickly granted representation to the new communities. The Board of Trade then disallowed such legislation from five provinces and instructed governors to disapprove similar bills. British policymakers rejected the colonists' contention that their assemblies were coordinate legislative bodies; instead, they assumed, in Leonard Labaree's words, "that the assemblies were inferior bodies, limited in powers, and constituted by royal grace and favor."[8]

The instructions of 1767, coming on the heels of the Stamp Act crisis, forced colonists to articulate their understanding of representation. During much of the succeeding decade, they regularly demanded "equal representation." Everywhere, equal representation meant *at least* the guarantee of representation for every settled community. In 1776, the South Carolina General Assembly rejoiced that the state's "most remote Districts" were "now immediately represented in the legislative Body of this State, a Privilege hitherto cruelly witheld by the unrelenting Tyranny of Kingly Government." Now, all South Carolinians could present "local and particular Grievances" through their representatives and obtain redress.[9]

Constitution makers generally agreed that equal representation meant that all communities should be "immediately" or "particularly" represented, but they disagreed about how far to carry the idea of equal representation. In the Chesapeake region, where county representation had long been the norm, constitution writers were primarily concerned with admitting all constituted communities to representation. They continued the practice of county representation, albeit with some significant modifications. In New England, where all incorporated towns were entitled to representation regardless of population, they adopted a modified version of corporate representation with substantial accommodations made for population. The Middle Atlantic and Deep South states retained the traditional geographical frameworks of counties or parishes but often apportioned representation to reflect the number of voters or inhabitants, or taxes paid. Even more significantly, they provided for future reapportionment, usually at regular intervals.[10]

All four Chesapeake states maintained or fulfilled the tradition of equal county representation. In North Carolina, the constitution's apportionment of two representatives for every county resembled the county representation of the colonial era. The constitution treated all counties (and several towns) as equal political entities, regardless of their population. Equal county representation allowed the east to control the legislature by limiting the creation of western counties. It also realized the provincial congress's aim of equal representation for the state's communities.

When North Carolina became a royal colony in 1729, it maintained the apportionment of representation of the proprietary years. The northeastern counties surrounding the Albemarle Sound each sent five delegates to the colonial assembly, while the newer counties of the south and west elected two each. During the 1740s, in concert with the governor, the southern counties dominated a rump assembly, which equalized representation among the counties at two each. When the Albemarle counties boycotted subsequent assemblies, the southern-led commons granted representation to numerous counties and some towns. In 1754, the privy council finally voided the laws and restored five-member delegations to the northeastern counties. It also prohibited the assembly from increasing its membership (or altering methods of distributing representation). As amity between north and south returned, the assembly reestablished the counties and created new ones into the late 1760s.[11]

The new statutes passed muster with the privy council, apparently because they contained no provisions for representation. But once the counties were established, the assembly asked the governor to issue writs of election in those counties. Following tradition, he invariably acceded. In this way, the North Carolina assembly successfully extended representation to the newly settled areas of the west. Measured by population, the west was woefully underrepresented and the Albemarle region remarkably overrepresented. Yet, the assembly ensured representation for all settled parts of the colony.[12]

During the Revolution, constitution makers provided equal representation for all counties. The North Carolina council of safety asked each county to send five representatives to the provincial congress charged with drafting the state's constitution. That request eliminated the disproportionate power held by the Albemarle region in the colonial House of Commons. The congress then wrote a constitution that similarly granted two representatives and one senator to each county.[13]

Virginia and Delaware essentially retained colonial systems of representation. In Virginia, each county sent one representative, and the district of West Augusta elected two. During the 1760s, when British authorities clamped down on the claims of colonial assemblies to enlarge their own bodies and grant representation, Virginia (like North Carolina) successfully extended the body politic into recently settled regions simply by creating counties without positively asserting their right to representation. But custom dictated that all Virginia counties have a representative in the House of Burgesses, and tradition prevailed. As in North Carolina, Virginians thus associated county representation with "equal representation." In Delaware, where all parts of the colony had been represented in the assembly since the colony's inception, constitution makers simply increased each county's delegation from six to seven.[14]

Neighboring Maryland, like Virginia, apparently duplicated its colonial House of Delegates. Under both the proprietary government and the constitution of 1776, each county elected four delegates. But continuity obscured important changes. The convention, for instance, recognized Baltimore's special commercial significance and its rapidly growing population by giving Baltimore, like Annapolis, two representatives. In addition, the fourth convention divided Frederick into three districts for purposes of representation at the fifth convention, which wrote the state constitution.

And the constitutional convention split Frederick County, with nearly one-eighth of the state's population, into three counties, thereby trebling representation from the same geographic area.[15]

As in the Chesapeake, the New England provinces of New Hampshire and Massachusetts distributed representation by corporate units (but by towns rather than counties). State constitution makers continued the practice, but crucially modified it to accommodate towns of varying size. In New Hampshire, the governor's power to grant representation to new towns, secured by Governor Benning Wentworth by 1750, effectively disfranchised numerous towns. Wentworth and his nephew and successor, John Wentworth, worried that a larger legislature would undermine their authority, extended representation to new towns infrequently. As a consequence, 101 of 147 towns were unrepresented in the assembly in 1773, although they paid more than a third of the province's taxes.[16]

After the Tea Act controversy, New Hampshire rebels focused on the representation issue. Newspaper writers demanded "this inherent right of representation" for "many of His Majesty's subjects."[17] Unrepresented towns petitioned the house for representation. Early in 1775, as the assembly contested his authority, Wentworth offered representation to several small towns whose leaders sympathized with him. Outraged inhabitants denounced him for granting representation to small towns when many larger ones remained unrepresented. In June, the assembly denied seats to the new delegates.[18]

During the assembly's meeting, as Wentworth fled the colony and New Hampshire's provincial congress assumed authority, resistance leaders moved quickly to enfranchise unrepresented towns. Even before the end of British rule, when the committee of correspondence called for a provincial congress to elect delegates to a Continental Congress, the committee invited every town to send a delegate—an invitation it would repeat for each of the next three congresses. One hundred thirty-three towns sent delegates to the fourth provincial congress, which established representation roughly proportional to population for the fifth congress. Delegates to the fourth congress permitted small towns to combine with others of like size to attain the 100 voters required for representation. The congress allotted two delegates each to the five largest towns, save the largest, Portsmouth, which received three. New Hampshire retained this distribution scheme in its constitution of 1776.[19]

The constitution faced criticism both from small western towns and the state's largest town, Portsmouth. At one extreme, Portsmouth citizens resented the cap on their delegation, no matter how many people lived in the town. At the other, residents of Grafton County, which had no representatives during the Wentworth regime, insisted that each town, as an autonomous political body, merited separate representation. Often portrayed as reactionaries for defending representation of corporate bodies rather than people, they nevertheless conceded greater weight in legislation to greater populations. They demanded representation for each town but acknowledged that larger towns should have additional members.[20]

The constitution of 1784 made assemblies more responsive to changes in population and conceded some ground to western demands for corporate representation. It allotted a delegate to every town with 150 male poll-tax payers and added one representative for every additional 300. Residents of towns with fewer than 150 male poll-tax payers could join with other small towns to send a delegate, but if distant from other small towns, then they could petition the general court for their own delegates.[21] The constitution, which ensured representation for all eligible voters, blended corporate representation of "every town, parish or place intitled to town privileges" with a sliding scale based upon population.

Unlike New Hampshire, provincial Massachusetts had little difficulty extending representation because the charter of 1691 and subsequent legislation required each incorporated town with forty qualified voters to send a delegate to the House of Representatives. Towns with fewer eligible voters were entitled, but not obliged, to send representatives, and towns with 120 or more could elect two. Bostonians could elect four.

For many small towns, the problem was too much representation, not too little. Regardless of size, each town paid the transportation and lodging costs of its deputy, a prohibitive expense for smaller towns. In 1726 the general court, responding to pleas from smaller towns, required only towns with sixty voters to send deputies.[22] All towns *could* choose delegates, but many refused.

Inhabitants of the province's largest towns also felt aggrieved, and, in response, the general court redistributed the size of delegations in March 1776. All towns could still send two assemblymen, but towns populated with 220 freeholders could send three. For every additional 100 freeholders, a town could elect an additional deputy. Boston, the primary beneficiary, tripled its delegation to twelve. But the house became unwieldy. Eastern towns rebelled against the cost of so many delegates and elected only a fraction of the number to which they were entitled.[23]

In 1777, the constitutional convention (a joint assembly of the council and house) adopted a plan of representation that preserved for every incorporated town both the right to send a delegate to the house and the obligation to pay his expenses. It also increased a town's delegation based upon the number of that community's eligible voters (white male taxpayers), but at a decreasing rate. A town with 300 voters could send two deputies, one with 520 voters three, one with 760 voters four, and so on. A town wishing to share the burden of representation could join another town to send a delegate to the legislature.

Popular defeat of the proposed constitution compelled Massachusetts to try again. Delegates to the constitutional convention of 1779–80 attempted to determine representation in the lower house "upon the principle of equality." By equality, they meant representation roughly apportioned by population. The constitution provided one lawmaker for every town with at least 150 tax-paying heads of households and an additional representative for every additional 225 taxpayers. Bowing to tradition, the convention allowed towns already incorporated to retain the right of representation and thereby made it possible for Massachusetts to recreate large numbers of Britain's easily manipulated, and often maligned, "rotten boroughs." In another provision unique among the constitutions, it denied representation to some settled communities by excluding new, unincorporated towns until they obtained the minimum 150 ratable polls.[24]

In their address to constituents, delegates explained that equal representation did not and could not mean exact apportionment according to a "just proportion" of a town's "Numbers and property." Such a system would be "unpracticable" even if Massachusetts inhabitants hoped to create a government "from the State of Nature"; the state already was "divided into nearly three hundred Corporations."[25] In the end, the constitution erected numerical representation on a foundation of town representation.[26]

At the other end of the country, in the Deep South, the struggle to gain representation for newly settled communities shaped revolutionary understandings of representation. Constitution makers in Georgia and South Carolina ensured that all parts of their states were represented in their state legislatures and made some accommodation for changes in population, although South Carolina broke more fully with the corporate past.

In 1769, the Georgia assembly pressured Governor James Wright to award representation to four newly settled parishes south of the Altamaha River that had become part of the province in 1763. Although sympathetic, Wright refused. In 1770, the four parishes petitioned for representation and the commons endorsed the petitions, but the governor rejected them. Because the parishes were not "*Particularly* represented," (that is, "not being represented according to the true Intent and meaning thereof") the commons relieved them of their provincial tax obligation. A year later, the commons reaffirmed its position by passing no tax legislation until the parishes gained representation. Wright, with permission from England, exercised the royal prerogative and granted the parishes representation in the assembly.[27]

The 1777 Georgia constitution reflected the decade-long preoccupation with "particular representation." The constitution gave five counties ten representatives, Liberty (composed of three parishes) fourteen, and Glynn and Camden one joint representative. All parts of Georgia sent at least one representative to the unicameral legislature. Georgia's framers also fulfilled their commitment to representation for all communities and their interests by making special provision for the towns of Sunbury and Savannah, allowing Sunbury two and Savannah four members "to represent their trade."

Then, Georgia's founders ensured an apportionment of representatives responsive to population growth. They made no provision for population decline, perhaps because a decreasing population was unimaginable in half-settled and rapidly growing Georgia. Counties that sent ten delegates would continue to elect the same number of delegates regardless of future demographic changes. But the framers held out the possibility of in-creased representation for sparsely settled areas. The constitution pro-vided that Glynn, Camden, "and any new country which the Assembly might lay out" would obtain "representation based upon the size of their electorate, progressing from one representative for ten electors to ten rep-resentatives for one hundred electors." Here was particular representation with a vengeance. A community required only ten electors (and property requirements for electors were minimal) to secure representation. The limit of ten representatives for a county indicates that the ultimate object of constitution makers was equal county representation.

South Carolina also blended corporate and numerical representation, but emphasized the numerical. Until 1765, the South Carolina commons responded slowly to demands for representation from newly settled areas. In that year, the large number of widely dispersed inhabitants living be-yond South Carolina's lowcountry, lumped into one parish, elected two representatives.[28] The house finally responded by creating new parishes in 1765 and 1767.[29] Because every new parish gained representation in the assembly, the council vetoed the bills. The council permitted the establish-ment of new parishes in 1768, but only after the assembly reduced delega-tions from two existing parishes.[30] The assembly's willingness to reappor-tion representation reflected its members' sense of urgency in response to the Regulator insurgency in the backcountry and to the imperial crisis.[31]

English limitations on assembly size restricted the house's ability to assign greater legislative power to the backcountry. In 1771, the commons again attempted to enlarge itself; expansion was "absolutely necessary to the equal representations of the Province." But the colonial council, heeding royal instructions, rejected the bill.[32]

As South Carolina's royal government crumbled, resistance leaders quickly rectified the imbalance. In 1774, when the general committee announced elections for delegates to a provincial congress, it gave backcountry parishes and hitherto unrepresented districts 55 of 187 delegates.[33] The constitutions of 1776 and 1778 further increased backcountry participation, respectively to 76 and 96 of the assembly's 202 seats. Although not proportional to population, the backcountry presence had increased enormously, from about 6 percent of the seats under royal authority to about 30 percent in the provincial congresses to nearly 40 percent under the first state constitution, and to 48 percent under the second.[34]

The decade-long struggle for more equitable representation left South Carolina's political leaders anxious to ensure that representation might always reflect the distribution of wealth and population in the state. The provincial congress followed no formal guidelines when it apportioned representatives among the parishes. But its plans for the future broke new ground. The constitution continued to use parishes as the basic unit of legislative apportionment, but it required the legislature to reapportion in seven years and every fourteen years thereafter so that representation would reflect "the number of white inhabitants and . . . taxable property."[35] The inclusion of white population *and* taxable property reflected political realities in a state where wealth from slaveholdings was concentrated in the lowcountry and white population in the upcountry. It also indicated that the members embraced no pure modern concept of representation of individuals. Yet by mandating representation for white inhabitants, constitution writers ensured that white inhabitants, as individuals, should and would be represented in the legislature.

As in the Deep South, the Middle Atlantic states moved substantially in the direction of apportioning representation according to numbers of individuals. New Jersey's apportionment of representation, for example, though it apparently resembled that of the Chesapeake states, pointed in this new direction. On the eve of the Revolution, few New Jersey residents complained about the legislative apportionment. Since 1702, the two former proprietary colonies, East Jersey and West Jersey, held equal power in the legislature. The towns of Perth Amboy and Burlington received two representatives each and the ten counties (five in the East and five in the West) secured two each.[36]

In 1768, new rules made representation more equal. Despite the instructions of 1767 prohibiting the enlargement of legislatures, the privy council approved a bill providing representation for three New Jersey counties formed over the previous several decades. The act increased the legislature's size from twenty-four to thirty and shifted the balance of power to West Jersey. The new law, historian Richard P. McCormick concludes, created a system of representation "that left no area underrepresented and that was fairly well proportioned to population."[37] The constitution of 1776 eliminated borough representation and allowed each of the state's thirteen counties three delegates in the general assembly and one in the legislative council. In addition, it permitted the legislature to increase or decrease a county's delegation in both houses "on the principles of more equal representation."[38] Although the provincial congress retained the system of equal county representation, it also laid the groundwork for a plan rooted in population.

Colonial New York's small assembly similarly approximated the distribution of the colony's inhabitants. Regardless of population, every county had two representatives, as had been the case in English counties. But special representation for New York County and borough representation, though designed simply to represent urban communities, made apportionment roughly commensurate with population. Thus, the colony's most populous counties enjoyed greater representation than others. New York County received an additional two representatives; Albany (which contained Schenectady, Livingston Manor, and Rensselaerwyck) held five seats; and Westchester (which surrounded Cortland Manor and the borough of Westchester) claimed four.[39]

The constitutional framers of 1777 created procedures for allocating representation based primarily upon individuals, not communities. Constitution makers continued the colonial tradition of roughly approximating population, giving some counties only two representatives and others up to ten. More important, it provided for future apportionment of representatives by the number of electors (not the number of inhabitants) in each county. So that the legislature would be sensitive even to rapid shifts in population, it required a septennial census and subsequent reapportionment. The constitution also abolished borough representation.[40]

Neighboring Pennsylvania's colonial assembly responded sluggishly to westward migration. It created new counties slowly and granted them reduced representation. The original three counties of Chester, Philadelphia, and Bucks each had eight delegates, and the city of Philadelphia two. The assembly allotted two each to Lancaster in 1728 and to York and Cumberland in 1749 and 1750, but only one each to Berks and Northampton in 1752.[41] Until the eve of the Revolution, the original counties maintained their power, which became increasingly disproportionate as new settlers swelled the western population.[42]

In 1776, Pennsylvania's radicals hoped that an expanded assembly, more fully representative of western settlers, would respond favorably to demands for independence. On February 28, residents of five counties appealed simultaneously for greater representation. Two weeks later, the assembly assigned more representatives to all but the original counties.[43] Radicals had calculated correctly. By preventing a quorum several times in early June, an enlarged pro-independence delegation compelled the assembly, on June 8, to permit its congressional delegates to vote for independence. After June 13, pro-independence representatives destroyed the assembly by frustrating efforts to gather a quorum.

Meanwhile, radicals planned a new government with a new system of apportionment. When the colony's June provincial conference organized a constitutional convention, it diminished eastern power by granting eight delegates to each county.[44] Convention delegates temporarily resolved the apportionment problem by assigning six seats to each county and to Philadelphia for two years. They also provided a permanent solution, structuring representation to reflect the distribution of the new state's population. The framers declared that "representation in proportion to the number of taxable inhabitants is the only principle which can at all times secure liberty, and make the voice of a majority of the people the law of the land." They required the state assembly, in 1778 and every seven years thereafter, to take a census of taxable inhabitants and apportion legislators accordingly.[45] The method of apportionment revealed both the constitution makers' definition of the people as the taxpaying inhabitants and their belief that representation ought to reflect a county's proportion of the state's population—"the voice of a majority of the people"—and not its wealth.

In sum, of the twelve states writing constitutions, eleven provided representation for all communities. They sometimes did not distribute representation equitably (if population is taken as a measure of fairness), but, except for Massachusetts, they guaranteed representation for all settled communities. In so doing, they ensured, in Edmund S. Morgan's words, "the local character of representation." Furthermore, despite differing methods, all states retained some form of what Willi Paul Adams calls "the territorial principle": counties in the Chesapeake, the Middle Atlantic states, and Georgia; towns in New England; and parishes in South Carolina.[46] Although the constitutions retained the forms of corporate representation, only four (the Chesapeake states) preserved equal representation for geographical areas regardless of population. A substantial majority of eight states provided for present or future representational systems that accommodated population growth. Seven also promised adjustment for population decline. In most of the states, constitution makers carried the idea of "equal representation" beyond "particular representation" toward representation apportioned by population.

When constitution makers considered population in allocating representatives, they excluded boroughs from their theory of representation. Urban centers once had required special representation of their interests. But now that numbers ruled, the interests of more heavily populated urban centers benefited from enlarged representation, and borough representation became redundant. New York, which apportioned (and reapportioned septennially) representation among counties by numbers of voters, abolished borough representation. In so doing, New York's provincial congress expressed a new way of thinking about political representation.

In Maryland, Virginia, and North Carolina, where the English county system persisted, so did borough representation. But even then, constitution makers sought to prevent American replication of England's infamous decayed and depopulated "rotten boroughs" by setting minimum population requirements. The Virginia constitution eliminated several special constituencies from the colonial era, like the College of William and Mary, but confirmed Norfolk and Williamsburg's practice of sending a representative, and permitted the legislature to create other boroughs. It required all boroughs to maintain a population with at least half of the voters "in some one county in Virginia."[47] The Maryland provincial convention expressed no concern about Annapolis's demographic future, granting it two representatives "forever thereafter," but Baltimore faced minimum population requirements similar to those of the Virginia boroughs.[48] Minimum populations, the convention hoped, would prevent the emergence of Englishlike rotten boroughs.[49] Only the North Carolina constitution maintained traditional borough representation, giving one representative each to Edenton, New Bern, Wilmington, Salisbury, Hillsborough, and Halifax.[50]

Georgia seems to have been an exception to the rule. It provided a sliding scale of representation based upon numbers of electors, yet it also retained traditional borough representation. Constitution makers granted new borough representation to Savannah (four members) and Sunbury (two members) "to represent their trade."[51] But in this case, the exception proved the rule. The Georgia constitution, reflecting the state's frontier conditions, had provided some representation for newly settled areas and allowed for increased representation as a county's population grew. Nevertheless, by their distribution of ten members to virtually all counties and their cap of any county's representation at ten, state constitution makers expressed their vision of a state legislature eventually composed of equally represented counties.

Instructions

However they apportioned representation in the state legislatures, framers expected representatives to express the views of their constituents. They assumed that the representative was not an independent actor pursuing the common good. Rather, he was a *dependent* actor pursuing the common good, a servant of the people he represented. The revolutionary generation expressed this view most forcefully in its recreation of the people's traditional right to instruct their representatives.[52]

The doctrine of instruction originated in the ancient Saxon constitution, under which all freeholders belonged to the governing assembly. As the population grew and all freeholders could no longer gather, explained Virginia's Richard Bland, "every Freeholder, had a Right to vote at the Election of Members of Parliament." Each was "present in that Assembly, either in his own Person or by Representation." Although all freeholders could not always participate directly in parliamentary deliberations, they could maintain their presence through the right of instruction.

Instruction of representatives dated back to the early days of Parliament, when the monarch gathered the people's deputies together to gain their consent to taxation and to consult with them about other matters. Those who sent knights of the shires often instructed them about how to behave in matters relating to their particular shire or county. Over the centuries, constituents retained the power and right to instruct their representatives how to vote in matters relating to the parochial interests of the constituencies (e.g., roads). On matters of more general import to the kingdom, members of Parliament thought of themselves as trustees of the kingdom and generally acted on their own.

Although the right of instruction remained part of English political culture, the idea that the representative expressed the will of his constituents faded. The House of Commons in the eighteenth century eventually recognized the growing separation of commoner and constituents and the fact that members of Parliament increasingly did not reside in the districts they represented. In 1774, Parliament finally eliminated the requirement that a member of Parliament reside in the district from which he was elected.[53] This alteration expressed the changed relationship between the House of Commons and the electors. By the mid–eighteenth century, members of the House of Commons generally asserted that they represented the entire British empire, not particular constituencies. In order to fulfill that responsibility, members had to be independent of their constituents. That was the import of Edmund Burke's famous refusal to obey the instructions of his constituents after his election by Bristol's voters.[54]

During the revolutionary crisis, Americans rejected Burke and embraced the doctrine of instruction. Political elites may have instigated instructions, but their reliance upon them suggests broad acceptance of the idea of actual direct representation of free men.[55] While making the decision for independence, the Continental Congress called upon the people to instruct their representatives about that decisive step. Similarly, the New York provincial congress also sought instructions from the province's electorate about whether the next congress should adopt a state constitution. In the end, instructions expressed a relationship in which constituents could not trust their representatives to express their will without an explicit list of expectations.

Furthermore, interpretations of the doctrine of instruction changed during the revolutionary crisis. In the past, both in the colonies and in England, constituents occasionally utilized instructions for matters of special concern to them. But from the beginning of the imperial crisis, popular meetings throughout the various states asserted the need for the people to instruct their representatives especially on matters of greatest moment— like independence and the formation of new state governments. They explicitly left smaller matters to the judgment of their representatives.[56]

The turmoil surrounding instructions in Maryland illustrates the changing relationship between representatives and their constituents. In June 1776, Maryland Whigs frantically tried to compel their hesitant convention to embrace independence. Upon his return to Maryland after acting as the Continental Congress's delegate to the failed Canadian campaign, Samuel Chase encouraged Whig leaders around the colony to organize county meetings, which in turn would instruct convention delegates to allow the province's delegates to the Continental Congress to vote for independence.[57] The counties responded quickly. Virginia's Richard Henry

Lee reported that Marylanders were overcoming the convention's hesitancy on independence: "The people were up, and instructions sending from all parts to their Convention" to rescind its instructions to Maryland's Continental Congress delegates to oppose independence.[58] Residents of Chase's home county, Anne Arundel, asserted that they "have determined to exercise our unquestionable right of instructing our Delegates in Convention. No apology is necessary; neither is any, we presume, expected from us. From the very nature of the trust, and the relation subsisting between constituent and representative, the former is entitled to express his sentiments, and to instruct the latter upon all points that may come under his consideration as representative."[59] On June 28, the convention unanimously declared for independence. "See the glorious Effects of County Instructions," an exhilarated Chase declared.[60]

Several weeks later, county instructions seemed less glorious to Chase. A remarkable 885 freemen in Anne Arundel County (which contained within its borders the capital of Annapolis, with separate borough representation) offered to their representatives detailed instructions about the kind of constitution they expected the convention to approve. Three of the county's representatives were among the most powerful and able leaders in revolutionary Maryland—Chase, Charles Carroll of Carrollton, and Brice T. B. Worthington. They were infuriated by the instructions, especially those portions calling for popular election of local officials and suffrage rights for all adult men "well-affected to the present glorious cause," who met a one-year residency qualification.[61] "This county's instructions have made their appearance," seethed Carroll of Carrollton, "they are weak, impudent & destructive of all government."[62]

Although angry, the representatives accepted their constituents' right to instruct them. Addressing themselves "to the electors" of Anne Arundel, they requested a meeting with the county's freeholders to explain their position. They warned voters that they "conceive several of your last instructions, if carried into execution, destructive of a free Government." Yet, "As your Delegates, we esteem ourselves bound by your instructions, though ever so contrary to our opinions."[63] The instructions left them with only two choices: "either endeavour to establish a Government without a proper security for liberty or property," or resign.

Carroll and his colleagues feared democracy; they were certain that ordinary people were gullible and easily manipulated. In Carroll's view, "selfish men . . . are busy every where striving to throw all power into the hands of the very lowest of the People in order that *they* may be their masters from the abused confidence *wh*[ich] the People has [*sic*] place in them. . . . Men of desperate fortunes or of desperate & wicked designs," he warned, "are endeavouring under the cloak of procuring great privileges for the People to introduce a levelling scheme, by *wh*[ich] . . . evil men are sure to profit."[64]

Carroll moved quickly to marshal popular opposition to the instructions. "If two or 3 hundred of the Substantial freeholders were to mee[t]," they might "check" those men "who are endeavouring to involve their country in the utmost confusion in this time of danger & distress." He implored his father to rouse the heads of the prominent Howard family "to prevail on them to get the People to attend at Annapolis," warning that "Unless the Howards and gentlemen of Character [&?] property will bestir themselves, and counteract the malicious falsehoods that are propogated about this county, & other counties, it will be impossible to have a good govern[ment]."[65]

At the meeting, the chagrined representatives did not get their way, so they resigned. Even those powerful men did not feel they could ignore the instructions. They protested that the instructions endangered liberty, but as representatives they could only obey or resign. Ignoring the will of their constituents was simply unthinkable. In the replacement election, only Carroll and Worthington were reelected; in Chase's place, electors chose John Hall, a vigorous proponent of a more democratic Maryland.[66]

Whereas the right of instruction traditionally was generally acknowledged as valid in matters of local concern, during the revolutionary crisis matters of the greatest moment occupied the instructions of towns and counties in the colonies. Sometimes, constituents instructed their delegates about matters both large and small, as when one town commanded its delegate to support independence and obtain a probate of wills and register of deeds in the town.[67] The town of Scituate, Massachusetts, instructed its delegate to support independence, but "touching other matters, we trust in your discretion, fidelity, and zeal, for the publick welfare."[68] The freeholders of James City County, Virginia, required Robert Carter Nicholas and William Norvell "to exert your utmost ability" to gain American independence.[69]

Although some voters timidly advanced instructions, most vigorously asserted their power over their representatives. The unassertive citizens of Buckingham County, Virginia, gave to their representatives "some instructions concerning the discharge of your great trust[,] . . . but would not tie you down in a manner too strict and positive. Though a general confidence in your honesty and wisdom may be required, yet, in some great and leading questions, it may not be unnecessary to take the sense of your constituents."[70] Staunton, Massachusetts, was more typical. The town told its representative that its instructions "must be agreeable to you (if you consider yourself the servant of the town, and accountable to them as you really are) to know the minds of your constituents respecting the important duties of your station, who have chosen you to act for their safety and happiness as connected with the whole, and not for your own private emolument or separate interest."[71]

The very act of instruction expressed constituents' distrust of representatives. If the people in the towns and counties expected delegates to reflect automatically the will of their constituents, then instructions would have been unnecessary. But some matters were too important for electors to entrust to legislators. The freemen of Augusta County, Virginia, reminded lawmakers that their election signified "great confidence in you." Yet just in case that confidence was misplaced, "gentlemen, as our representatives, [we] most solemnly require you, and positively command you, that, in the General Assembly of this commonwealth, you declare it the ardent desire and unanimous opinion of your constituents, should such a declaration become necessary, that all religious denominations within this dominion be forthwith put in the full possession of equal liberty." On all "other things, how material soever they may be," the freemen left their representatives to exercise their own discretion, "to be managed conformable to the declaration of rights."[72] Such mistrust was evident, too, when one Virginia planter advised his fellow citizens that he hoped all representatives would be men of "wisdom and integrity. . . . But, relying on their virtue as much as it deserves, it will be a useful expedient to keep alive the flame of liberty and public spirit among the people at large, never to neglect the exercise of the undoubted prerogative of freemen to instruct their representatives."[73]

The triumph of the idea of instruction was captured well in Delaware in the spring of 1776, as Whigs attempted to nudge the assembly to act on the Continental Congress's proclamation of May 15, which required provincial governments to sever all ties to royal or proprietary governments. The Whigs in Kent County initially planned to petition the assembly to assume the reins of government, "but as there seems some impropriety in a petition—we have changed the mode into Instructions to the Members for this County to Comply with the recommendation of Congress," reported Thomas Rodney to his brother Caesar.

To be sure, these instructions were initiated and manipulated by Whig leaders. But two points should be made. Delaware Whigs chose instructions over petitions, suggesting that the relationship between constituent and representative changed dramatically during the revolutionary crisis. Moreover, Rodney and his cohorts still needed to persuade men to sign the instructions. "It was offered to my Company yesterday," he informed his brother, "& twenty six of them signed it, the rest Chose to have it under Consideration Till next muster day but many of them say they are now ready to sign." Several days later, he happily reported that "all the officers & principle persons in my Company signed our instructions yesterday, a few of the inconsiderable ignorant ones declined it."[74]

Four of the seven states that adopted declarations of rights explicitly affirmed the right of instruction. The declarations of rights of Pennsylvania, North Carolina, Vermont, and Massachusetts all asserted (in the words of the Pennsylvania declaration) "that the people have a right to assemble together, to consult for their common good, to instruct their representatives."[75]

If people could instruct their representatives as to the policies they ought to pursue and hold representatives accountable, then it seemed necessary for constituents to know how their delegates voted. Historian J. R. Pole has described how colonial assemblies, in the name of legislative independence, generally deliberated in private. The imperial crisis undermined their privacy, and assemblies began regularly to record and publish their votes and proceedings. The assembly of Virginia in 1764, followed by Massachusetts two years later, became the first colonial legislature to admit the public to its deliberations. Among the state constitutions, five required the legislature to record and publish proceedings. North Carolina and New Hampshire (1784) insisted on publication "immediately after adjournment," Pennsylvania and Vermont weekly, and New York daily. Although Pennsylvania, New York, and Vermont were the only three states whose constitutions opened the legislatures' doors, the Virginia and Massachusetts assemblies continued to admit the public, and the open door soon became common practice. Furthermore, to provide the fullest information about the behavior of representatives and to allow dissenters a public voice, the constitutions of Pennsylvania and North Carolina required a record of divisions at the request of only two members, and New Hampshire of only one.[76]

Annual Elections

Popular exercise of instructions revealed a view of the representative as both the mouthpiece of his constituents and a fallible human being sure to pursue selfish interests if not curbed. "To be under the government of a legislative body that is independent of us, over whom we have no controul, is the essence of slavery," warned one writer.[77] Fearful of legislative independence and suspicious of the motives of all men who wielded power, constitutional framers established residency requirements and annual elections for members of the lower houses.

Residency requirements supposedly ensured the representatives' familiarity with the communities they represented. Delegates who lived among their constituents and therefore shared interests and burdens, the revolutionaries thought, were most likely to be faithful representatives. The constitutions of New Jersey, Maryland, North Carolina, Vermont, and Massachusetts required of each lawmaker a one-year residency in his county or town. Perhaps because of the state's relatively unsettled character, Georgia insisted on one year in the state but only three months in the county. Virginia required residence but did not stipulate a minimum duration. Pennsylvania and New Hampshire demanded two years. South Carolina called for three years' residence in the state, plus ownership of 500 acres and ten slaves. But South Carolinians, in a unique provision, also permitted a nonresident to act as a representative if he possessed a freehold worth £3,500 in the parish or district.[78]

Constitution makers assumed that residency requirements alone were insufficient. Representatives otherwise independent of their constituents might exempt themselves from burdens they imposed upon the citizenry. "Our safety," concluded one writer, "doth not consist so much in having our legislative body chosen from among ourselves, as it doth in reserving a power in the good people to correct and detect misdemeanors in government."[79] By electing legislators frequently, the people could protect their liberty.

The revolutionaries' commitment to annually elected houses of representatives developed in response to the English and colonial experience. Few colonies had regular terms of office. Governors, outside of the annually elected men in Rhode Island and Connecticut and royally appointed judges, had served at the pleasure of the Crown or proprietor. In most colonies, governors determined when and whether to hold legislative elections and when legislative sessions began and ended. Governors in all of the royal colonies retained the authority to adjourn legislative sessions whenever and for as long as they wished.[80]

In 1694, Parliament passed the Triennial Act, a part of the constitutional settlement reached by William of Orange and Parliament, which dictated new elections for members of the House of Commons every three years. Members of the Commons hoped the act would create greater institutional independence. The king, following the traditional practice of the Crown summoning Parliament for advice and revenues, customarily had determined the frequency of parliamentary elections and sessions. That practice rendered the Commons wholly dependent upon the Crown. Frequent elections and regular sessions would establish the Commons's institutional autonomy from the Crown, for it would meet every three years regardless of the Crown's desires. The act, however, also made commoners vulnerable to electoral pressures.[81]

In 1716, Parliament resolved the problem of legislators' dependence upon the electorate, however modestly, when it adopted the Septennial Act, which lengthened the maximum time between parliamentary elections to seven years. The act raised the specter of tyranny by extending the life of the sitting House of Commons for four years. By making commoners vastly more independent of English voters, the Septennial Act further solidified the oligarchic character of the Commons and made it a political body freed from the constraints of the king, the House of Lords, and the electorate. As a consequence, the act greatly enhanced the powers of sitting members of the House of Commons, permitted them to act imperiously, and left them more susceptible to ministerial influence.[82] If Parliament could extend the life of the Commons by four years, could not Parliament make itself omnipotent and perpetual? During succeeding decades, the Radical Whig opposition denounced the Septennial Act as a betrayal of the Glorious Revolution and insisted upon a restoration of the Triennial Act or the establishment of annual elections.

In the colonies, royal governors often maintained the Crown's traditional powers to assemble the lower house and retain it in session for as long as desired, dissolve the lower house, and call or suspend new elections. In response, colonial assemblymen, who viewed their legislatures as the American equivalents of the House of Commons, attempted to pass triennial acts of their own. South Carolina and New Hampshire succeeded, but Crown resistance thwarted repeated efforts to establish frequent elections and regular meetings elsewhere.[83] The colonial assemblies' quest for institutional independence culminated in constitutional provisions for periodic elections and sessions.

But the establishment of legislative independence, in turn, aroused fears of the consequences of that independence. What would prevent independent legislators from becoming independent not only of the magistrate but of the electorate? The framers of the revolutionary state constitutions worried that legislators, just as the House of Commons did in 1716, might attempt to extend their terms of office in order to insulate themselves from their constituents and assume tyrannical power. When Maryland's convention ordered local committees of observation to continue beyond the one year for which they had been elected, the Harford County committee refused. Chairman Benjamin Rumsey, militia colonel and future delegate to the Continental Congress, reported to the council of safety that the committee had dissolved itself, declining to continue "without a new election." The committee's members "universally looked upon the Convention's continuing them beyond the time for which they were elected by the people to be unconstitutional, and laying a foundation and precedent for one of the most alarming stretches of power—the continuation of some future Convention or publick body for many years." [84]

Harford's committee of observation was not alone. William Gordon of Massachusetts denounced the Septennial Act as one of the great evils in English political life and worried that American legislators might seek greater power through extended terms. "Suppose . . . an American Parliament met," fretted another writer. "Suppose when thus met, a motion is made, shewing the inconvenience and difficulties of frequent elections, and proposing the making a law extending their political existence for seven years; precedents may be pleaded for it?" [85] North Carolina's Samuel Johnston probably had the Septennial Act in mind when he worried about "representatives of the people . . . assuming more power than would be consistent with the Liberties of the People, such as increasing the time of their duration." [86] James Madison, in *The Federalist Papers*, number 53, explained the American obsession with the Septennial Act. The "dangerous practices" endorsed by the act, he wrote, created "a very natural alarm in the votaries of free government, of which frequency of elections is the cornerstone." [87]

Constitution makers expected voters to scrutinize their representatives' behavior through regular and frequent elections. If legislative elections were infrequent and legislators were not held continually accountable, then representatives would develop interests different from those of their constituents. Only by keeping them dependent upon their constituents for continuance in office could their interests be made consonant and corruption of the legislature prevented. [88] Corruption could be spotted quickly and excised before it could fester and grow. Thus, as the declarations of rights repeatedly affirmed, by often threatening to return rulers to the commonality, frequent elections remedied the tendency of rulers to become corrupt and accumulate dangerous power.[89]

When members of the revolutionary generation thought of frequent elections, they contemplated annual ones. Annual balloting, concluded one group of Pennsylvanians, was "essentially necessary to the liberty of freemen."[90] The militia of Anne Arundel County, Maryland, demanded that the legislature and executive be elected every year, "as annual elections are most friendly to liberty, and the oftener power reverts to the people the greater will be the security for a faithful discharge of it."[91] Philadelphia's "Demophilus" applied the principle more generally: "While all kinds of governmental power reverts annually to the people, there can be little danger of their liberty."[92] In 1778, Plymouth, Massachusetts, approved heartily of annual elections as "Fundementual in Every free Government, and the best barrier against Corruption, and the restless passions of Mankind."[93]

Fear of unchecked representatives and support for annual elections cut across the political spectrum. One conservative southern revolutionary asserted that "there can be no check on the Representatives of the People in a Democracy but the people themselves, and in order that the check may be more effectual I would have Annual elections."[94] More radical contemporaries, who preferred direct democracy and viewed representation as "a species of aristocracy," agreed: "To check the aristocratick principle, which always inclines to tyranny, it will be necessary to keep the Representatives dependant on the people by annual elections."[95]

John Adams, in his influential *Thoughts on Government*, summarized the early revolutionary view of annual elections. Endorsing the ideas of England's Radical Whigs, he declared that "where annual elections end, there slavery begins." If officials experienced insecurity in office, they would learn "the great political virtues of humility, patience, and moderation, without which every man in power becomes a ravenous beast of prey."[96]

In response to such widespread sentiments, the authors of every state constitution but South Carolina's specified annual legislative elections.[97] The Georgia constitution of 1777, for instance, prescribed yearly balloting for members of the unicameral legislature. In case there was any doubt, a separate article established the "unalterable rule that the house of assembly shall expire and be at an end, yearly and every year."[98]

For the most part, annual elections, instructions, open assembly doors, equal representation, and residency requirements for representatives revealed the revolutionaries' commitment to direct representation of all freemen and their fear of faithless representatives. With other men who exercised power, representatives could not be trusted. Only by requiring them to face reelection every year could citizens compel politicians to follow the will of their constituents. If that were insufficient, then they would command them through instructions. To make sure that representatives obeyed those instructions, some states opened the doors of the legislatures, built public galleries, and required legislatures to publish their proceedings, including divisive roll-call votes.

★ ★ ★ ★ ★ ★ ★ ★ ★ The Greatest

Right of Freemen

The Suffrage

5

When Americans denounced the idea of taxation without representation, they placed at the center of the revolutionary crisis the rights of election and of consent. They reconsidered time-honored English understandings of the suffrage and the composition of the political nation. State constitution makers dramatically altered suffrage qualifications within a male electorate. The conflict over taxation led many states to abolish property qualifications in favor of a taxpayer qualification and to enfranchise Catholics and Jews. In a more restricted fashion, it encouraged the enfranchisement of propertied women in New Jersey and the preservation of the suffrage for free black men in Massachusetts. Moreover, the act of revolution itself spurred Americans to think about loyalty and military service, not property, as the primary qualifications for admission to the political community. The War of Independence thus began another kind of revolution, in which political rights became rooted in people—not property. As one Massachusetts town declared in 1778, "It is Our Fundamental Principle that taxation and Representation Cannot be Seperated,—that the Great Secret of Government is Governing all By all."[1]

In recent years, historians generally have contended that revolutionary leaders perpetuated traditional beliefs in "political inequality," and as a consequence, either thought little about voting rights or insisted upon preserving unequal political rights among free men.[2] Gordon Wood, for one, contends that the revolutionary republican belief in a homogeneous people virtuously committed to the common good precluded widespread interest in the issue of voting rights. In the newly formed states, the interests of the representative and his constituency were presumably the same. What benefited or injured one benefited or injured the other. Because the interests of all were the same, the disfranchised were as well represented as the electors. Therefore, the decision to limit the suffrage to propertied, adult males required no justification. To the framers of the state constitutions, Wood and others argue, the acts of election and voting were not nearly as significant as they would come to be. Only after revolutionary beliefs in the homogeneity and virtue of the American populace broke down and conflict drowned out cries for consensus did Americans finally replace virtual representation with voting and direct representation.[3]

Yet, as numerous writers, petitioners, and crowds attested, the right of election lay at the very heart of the Revolution. Members of one New York militia company protested bitterly to the provincial congress about the arbitrary appointment of their officers and demanded that the congress order an election as required by that body's resolutions. The company complained that the present officers "determined [to] get into office without the vote of the people, depriving us of the privileges that we are now contending for."[4] As one Pennsylvanian put it in 1776: "Where there is no election there can be no liberty."[5] Another declared that "the first right of Freemen [was] . . . choosing their Legislators."[6] In the same year, a Connecticut town called voting the "one privilege which we deem essential to the preservation of all the rest";[7] another writer asserted that the election of legislators was "the greatest right of freemen," and their "birth-right."[8]

Concern about elections and, more abstractly, about the significance of voting in a republic led constitution makers to reconsider, and sometimes reaffirm, traditional notions of political capacity. Belief in the importance of voting in American political society did not require framers to embrace political equality. Because "all other rights absolutely depend on this great right of election," wrote one Pennsylvanian, voting was too important to be entrusted to the propertyless. "The most flourishing commonwealths that ever existed, *Athens* and *Rome* were RUINED by allowing this right to people without property." [9]

John Adams understood that the logic of the revolutionary argument encouraged Americans to reinvent their political community, but he feared an egalitarian polity and disruption of the war effort. Changes in existing suffrage regulations, including any reductions in property qualifications, he warned, might open a Pandora's box of political dangers: "New Claims will arise. Women will demand a Vote. Lads from 12 to 21 will think their Rights not enough attended to, and every Man, who has not a Farthing, will demand an equal Voice with any other in all Acts of State. It tends to confound and destroy all Distinctions, and prostrate all Ranks, to one common Levell." [10]

Men like Adams held fast to the English belief that economic independence earned a man membership in the political nation. In England, political privileges were impersonal, attaching to particular kinds of land or places, rather than to individuals. Men who possessed income-producing land were presumed to be independent and therefore could be trusted to make disinterested political decisions. They would act in the public's interest out of self-interest. [11]

On the other hand, England and its colonies excluded from the polity dependents presumed incapable of making independent or rational political decisions and those who lacked attachment to the community's interests. Women, tenants, journeymen, apprentices, the propertyless, and paupers were assumed to be susceptible to the demands of those upon whom they depended for their livelihood, and hence were excluded. Married women voted through their husbands, and unmarried women living at home through their fathers, who had property rights in their labor; only widows with property posed a serious challenge to an all-male electorate. [12] Catholics were disfranchised both because of their dependence upon the church and because, like Jews and aliens, they supposedly lacked the necessary attachment to the community. [13] Slaves, as property, had no civic identity.

The disfranchisement of tenants, journeymen, apprentices, the propertyless, and paupers sprang from two notions. The primary one was that their political independence would be compromised by those upon whom they were dependent. Maryland's Charles Carroll of Carrollton denounced efforts to enfranchise all loyal men. He blamed "the designs of selfish men, who are busy every where striving to throw all power into the hands of the very lowest of the People in order that *they* may be their masters from the abused confidence *wh*[ich] the People has [*sic*] place in them." [14] John

Adams asked rhetorically: "Is it not equally true, that Men in general in every Society, who are wholly destitute of Property, are also too little acquainted with public Affairs to form a Right Judgment, and too dependent upon other Men to have a Will of their own?" As a consequence, "If you give to every Man, who has no Property, a Vote, will you not make a fine encouraging Provision for Corruption by your fundamental Law? Such is the Frailty of the human Heart, that very few Men, who have no Property, have any Judgment of their own. They talk and vote as they are directed by Some Man of property, who has attached their Minds to his Interest."[15]

The propertyless, Adams and others believed, were not only corruptible, but their self-interest made them a threat to property rights. During the years of resistance to English policies, the political elite had discovered to their dismay that they often could not control the crowds of persons drawn from society's lower ranks. At different times, such people threatened not only English or pro-English targets, but also economic targets unrelated to those initially planned. They easily might turn against propertied patriots.[16] A concerned Elbridge Gerry observed in 1775: "The people are fully possessed of their dignity from the frequent delineation of their rights, which have been published to defeat the ministerial party." As a consequence, "they now feel rather too much their own importance, and it requires great skill to produce such a subordination as is necessary."[17]

Such fears persisted. In 1780, delegates to the Massachusetts constitutional convention argued that a small property requirement for voting was needed to secure property rights. Some of those excluded, the convention acknowledged, were young men living in their fathers' home and others were "those whose Idleness of Lif and profligacy of manners will forever bar them from acquiring and possesing Property." It then asked children of the propertied to forgo voting for a few years so they would not "forever hereafter to have their Privileges liable to the control of Men, who will pay less regard to the Rights of Property because they have nothing to lose."[18]

Thus, some framers never reconsidered the fundamental issues that underlay suffrage qualifications—notably, the expectation of personal economic independence and attachment to the community's interests. In Virginia and Delaware, the constitutions retained existing voting qualifications.[19]

Even revolutionary leaders who wished to preserve traditional suffrage qualifications hoped to maintain and expand large electorates through widespread land ownership. Building upon James Harrington's precept that "Power always follows Property," John Adams asserted "that the Ballance of Power in a Society, accompanies the Ballance of Property in Land." In order to ensure that "the Ballance of Power" sided with "equal liberty and public Virtue," it should be easy for "every Member of Society" to acquire land. Land, Adams urged, should be divided "into Small Quantities, So that the Multitude may be possessed of landed Estates." If "the Multitude" owned the land, they would hold the "Ballance of Power" and "take Care of the Liberty, Virtue, and Interest of the Multitude in all Acts of Government."[20] This was what Thomas Jefferson had in mind when he proposed that the Virginia constitution require the government to grant fifty acres of land to every adult man.[21] Furthermore, it partially explains the revolutionaries' hatred of primogeniture and entail and embrace of partible inheritance.[22]

Framers also enfranchised more men by lowering property qualifications. New York halved its requirement from a freehold worth forty pounds to one valued at twenty pounds. And in a state where many men rented land, it also enfranchised tenants on land with "the yearly value of forty shillings" who paid taxes during the previous year.[23]

Elsewhere, delegates either replaced their freehold requirements or permitted voters to meet property qualifications if they owned sufficient personal property. Maryland's constitution maintained a fifty-acre freehold requirement but lowered the standard for total estate from forty pounds sterling to thirty pounds "current money," a 50 percent reduction.[24] New Jersey eliminated its colonial freehold requirement of 100 acres and reduced its estate qualification, including personal and real, from fifty pounds sterling to fifty pounds "proclamation money"—a decrease in value of about one-third. It also erased the freehold restriction, as did Georgia, which stipulated that electors own property valued at only ten pounds.[25]

The shift in New Jersey and Georgia from freehold to personal property requirements detached voting from ownership of real estate and undermined Whig suffrage theory. In the traditional view, the permanence of land ownership proved a man's *permanent* attachment to his community. The vote, wrote Virginia's Edmund Pendleton, "should be confined to those of fixed Permanent property or Substituting another proprietor, and whom alone I consider as having Political Attachment." Men who owned transportable personal property could not be entrusted with the vote. "When they have produced burthens on the State, [they] may move away and leave them to be born by others." Such men should be considered merely as "Sojourners."[26] Pendleton's views were reflected in Virginia's and Delaware's retention of a freehold requirement, but nowhere else.

The significance of personal property qualifications paled beside the changes wrought by the four states—Pennsylvania, North Carolina, South Carolina, and New Hampshire—that adopted taxpayer qualifications for the suffrage and by Vermont's enfranchisement of all free men. Three more—Massachusetts, Maryland, and New York—very nearly adopted taxpayer suffrage. Massachusetts had included it in the defeated constitution of 1778. New York's constitutional committee had recommended a taxpayer qualification in the draft presented to the provincial congress. And Maryland's provincial convention defeated a proposal for taxpayer suffrage by the narrow margin of twenty-nine to twenty-four.[27] Even the Virginia convention had considered, but rejected, Thomas Jefferson's call for the enfranchisement of men "who shall have paid *scot* and *lot* to government the last [two] years."[28]

To a certain extent, the taxpayer qualification, which permitted all male adult taxpayers to vote for all or some popularly elected offices, represented important continuities with the past. At least in some states, the qualification was linked to more traditional notions that contribution to society was a prerequisite for participation in government. According to J. R. Pole, the taxpayer qualification in the Pennsylvania constitution of 1776 expressed older Whig notions of political competence. According to Pole, "The constitution-makers . . . stated that all ought to contribute, and . . . the right to vote was earned by contribution." The declaration of rights did assert "that every member of society hath a right to be protected in the enjoyment of life, liberty and property, and therefore is bound to contribute his proportion towards the expence of that protection." In this way, framers linked taxpayer suffrage to the concept of contribution.

But the taxpayer qualification also expressed a very different understanding of that relationship, one that undermined traditional Whig thinking about the right to vote. Historians often treat the taxpayer requirement as an attenuated property qualification. But, as Pole observes, the taxpayer qualification erased "the basic economic presupposition that the ownership of a specified amount of property was an essential guarantee of political competence."[29] It also potentially eliminated property as *any* kind of measure of political competence and enfranchised unpropertied men. This dramatic expansion of the political community occurred ironically because of the regressive poll tax. Many colonies had relied upon poll taxes as major sources of revenue. Although Maryland's declaration of rights denounced the poll tax as "grievous and oppressive" and abolished it, other states—like New Hampshire, Massachusetts, Pennsylvania, and North Carolina—retained the tax.[30]

Parliament and the colonial legislatures—and some of the revolutionary state constitutions—had based requirements for voting upon proof of sufficient independence to act uncoerced by others and a demonstration of investment in the community's well-being. But whatever economic basis for voting was provided by the taxpaying qualification, it could no longer be argued plausibly that paying taxes rendered a man economically independent. No one argued that a North Carolina man's payment of his poll tax established his economic attachment to the community.[31]

Instead, the taxpayer qualification expressed a new American understanding of representation, the absorption of radical Whig ideas, and the logical conclusion of the conflict over English taxation of the colonies. In the taxation dispute, American patriots argued that, because they were unrepresented in Parliament, they could not consent to taxation by Parliament and therefore could not be taxed by it. This argument repudiated English constitutional understandings about consent and the theory of virtual representation. Americans had inherited the English theory that governmental authority rested upon popular consent. But "consent" entailed participation in the original social contract, continued residence in the country, and custom, not voting at regular elections.[32] The theory of virtual representation assumed that each member of Parliament represented the entire population and whole empire, not merely the interests of men at the polls. Because America's concerns differed from England's, Americans claimed, they were unrepresented in Parliament. Their argument assumed that representatives directly expressed the views of their constituents and that voters consented to government by participation in regular elections.

However, the assault on parliamentary taxation of the colonies took the revolutionary political elite further than most intended to go. In making that argument, they assumed that voters represented the disfranchised and that local assemblies represented the entire colony, though only a fraction of the colony's inhabitants elected legislators.[33] They based their assumption upon the plausible argument that the voter and legislator lived in the community and that whatever helped or hurt the community also helped or hurt them. But the antitaxation argument encouraged citizens in the new states to argue that consent to taxation required direct consent, demonstrated at the polls.[34]

These ideas powerfully shaped the debate over suffrage qualifications. Throughout the colonies, citizens demanded the enfranchisement of all taxpayers. In general, many Americans believed, but rarely said explicitly, that it should be restricted to adult, male taxpayers. Underlying the plea for a taxpayer franchise was the conviction that all who paid taxes needed to consent directly to taxes laid by local assemblies. The suffrage became a defensive device capable of protecting popular liberty against potentially rapacious legislators.

Here was a revolutionary conception of the right to vote. Instead of property serving as a measure of one's personal independence and attachment to the community, the taxpayer qualification signified that the elector voted to protect himself and the community against oppression by the assembly. "An Elector," writing in Philadelphia in April 1776, contended that the restricted suffrage in England enabled "the opulent" to shift much of the financial burden of the state on to "Excises on the indispensable necessaries of life," which weighed most heavily on the poor. His solution "to such a *pernicious* partiality" was to extend suffrage rights to "*every man who pays his shot and bears his lot.*"[35] Dorchester, Massachusetts, made precisely the same point when it denounced the property qualifications for voters in the Massachusetts constitution of 1780. The town argued that landlessness was becoming more prevalent and that soon more than half the men in the state would be disfranchised. Yet they remained "liable . . . to pay such a proportion of the Publick Taxes as they [the general court] shall Judge reasonable." Because legislators would be "men of Considerable Property," self-interest would lead them "to lay too great a proportion on the Polls, and by that means ease their Estates, and bring a heavy burden on those who have no power to remove it."[36]

Taxpayer suffrage, which assumed an adversarial relationship between voter and legislator, undermined the classical ideal of the independent citizen participating actively in the polity for the common good, but it expressed well the fear of power embedded in English Radical Whig and American revolutionary ideology. The pseudonymous "Essex" of Morris County, New Jersey, writing in September 1775, pointed out that the earliest New Jersey provincial congresses had permitted all taxpayers to vote, but that the latest one had reverted to the colonial property restrictions. "Essex" complained that "many true friends of their country, who are obliged to pay taxes, are excluded from the privilege of a vote in the choice of those by whom they are taxed, or even call out to sacrifice their lives." And when the Massachusetts constitutional convention of 1779–80 limited the vote to property owners, it set off howls of protest from numerous towns. Lee declared its opposition to the property qualifications for house electors on the grounds that "we think it unreasnabul that any shud be taxed With ou[t] a vorse in Electing."[37] The town of Colrain tersely insisted that all male inhabitants twenty-one years and older and approved by a town's selectmen should have the right to vote: "Taxation without Representation we Consider unreasonable."[38]

Taxpayer suffrage ought not to be confused with modern democracy. Although it enfranchised most adult males, especially in poll-tax states, the taxpayer suffrage was fragile. A legislature could disfranchise thousands by altering methods of taxation.[39] But if they chose, generous legislators could shift power to previously powerless classes.

The logic of the taxpayer suffrage was spelled out most clearly in an essay by a Marylander who identified himself as "A Watchman." Writing in August 1776, in the hopes of influencing the provincial convention's deliberations over the state constitution, he reminded delegates that "every poor man has a life, a personal liberty, and a right to his earnings; and is in danger of being injured by government in a variety of ways." Therefore, those men "should enjoy the right of voting for representatives, to be protectors of their lives, personal liberty, and their little property, which, though small, is yet, upon the whole, a very great object to them." The disfranchisement of those who were poor would also "be unjust and oppressive in the extreme" because they paid "a very heavy share in the support of government." It was, he declared, "an established maxim in free states, that whoever contributes to the expences of government ought to be satisfied concerning the application of the money contributed by them."

"A Watchman" understood the vote as both an instrument for the protection of the elector's life, liberty, and property, and a recognition of a man's contribution to government. But he went further to claim the suffrage as a natural right, "the antecedent right which the people possess in their aggregate or legislative state." As a natural right, it "cannot be destroyed or abridged by their representatives; and are inseparable by any power on earth. Every member of this state, who lends his aid to the support of it, has an equal claim to all the privileges, liberties and immunities with every of his fellow countrymen." Maryland's property qualifications deprived half of the state's freemen of "their inherent right of free suffrage . . . the grandest right of a freeman." "The ultimate end of all freedom," he declared, "is the enjoyment of a right of free suffrage," a right "inseparable from the exercise and operation of a free people."[40]

The idea that voting might be a natural right prompted citizens of Orange County to protest a disputed election of delegates to the North Carolina provincial congress, which would write the state constitution. At Hillsborough, site of the county courthouse and of the county's only polling place, crowds of potential voters had overwhelmed election officials. Several times during the day, officials adjourned and then attempted to restart the election. But continued disorderly conduct caused them to close the polls early, thereby excluding many of the county's eligible electors from the polls. Hundreds of potential voters "found it impossible to go into the Courthouse . . . without great danger of bodily hurt, by reason of the Riot and Tumult which prevailed in and about the . . . Courthouse." In response, more than five hundred of the disfranchised petitioned the congress for a new election because "the right of Electing . . . such persons as we think fit to represent us is a right Essential to and inseperable from freedom."[41] The congress, after initially rejecting the petitions, reconsidered and ordered several of its members to supervise a new election.[42]

The beliefs that suffrage was a natural right more than a privilege and that assemblies could oppress the colonists, through legislation as well as taxation, carried some beyond even taxpayer suffrage. Implicit in "Watchman"'s essay was the recognition that government potentially endangered the life and liberty of all citizens. But he did not extend his analysis beyond taxpayer suffrage. James Sullivan, a member of the Massachusetts House of Representatives, went further. Sullivan began with the common understanding that "Laws and Government are founded on the Consent of the people." But then he leaped to direct consent by all: "Every member of Society has a Right to give his Consent to the Laws of the Community or he owes no Obedience to them." He assumed that this statement was self-evident and "will never be denied by him who has the least acquaintance with true republican principles." Nevertheless, "a very great number of the people of this Colony have at all times been bound by Laws to which they never were in a Capacity to Consent not having estate worth 40/ per annum." Their disfranchisement made consent into a "Fiction of Law." It was impossible for Sullivan to understand "why a man is supposed to consent to the acts of a Society of which in this respect he is absolutely an Excommunicate." Sullivan's argument, which represented the logical conclusion of the idea of direct consent, ultimately led in the direction of voting rights for all free adults—male and female, black and white. He was unwilling to go that far, and most of his contemporaries were unwilling to go as far as he, but they did take those ideas up to taxpayer suffrage and beyond.[43]

This changing understanding of the suffrage as protection against potential governmental tyranny explains the enfranchisement of Catholics and Jews and the persistence of religious restrictions for officeholders.

Most colonies had excluded both groups from participation in politics and government. During the Revolution, devout Protestant citizens of the states vociferously demanded that only Protestants be allowed to hold office, but they ignored Jewish and Catholic enfranchisement.

Many citizens apparently distinguished between voting and officeholding. They paid little attention to Jewish or Catholic voting (for even Jews and Catholics needed to protect themselves from potential tyrants), but they worried deeply about the prospect of having Jews and Catholics as *rulers* and potential tyrants. The Massachusetts constitution's provision requiring officeholders to be Christians provoked an enormous outcry, even though the constitution also included an officeholder's oath designed to limit Catholic officeholders. "We think it Dangerous Even to leave any the least opening for a Roman Catholick to fill the first Seat in the Government," declared the town of Norton.[44] When the citizens of Orange and Mecklenburg counties instructed their delegates to the North Carolina provincial congress, they insisted that all officials be Protestants.[45] Orange County residents wanted all freeholders and householders to vote for representatives and all freeholders for senators, but they demanded a religious qualification for officeholders. Catholics as rulers might destroy the Protestant character of American society; but they posed no such threat as voters. The South Carolina constitution, the only one to establish a religious qualification for voting, reinforced this point. The constitution limited the vote to white men who believed in God and "in a future state of rewards and punishments," thereby enfranchising Catholics and Jews but not nonbelievers. It also restricted officeholding to Protestants.[46]

The virtual end of religious restrictions on voting and the growing reliance upon tax-paying or personal-property qualifications expressed the growing sentiment that the vote was an instrument for protecting all other rights, individual and communal, and that ownership of real estate was not the only measure of permanent attachment to the community. How would the citizenry determine a person's ties to the community? The solution lay in residency requirements. By living in a state for a specified period of time, one could prove fidelity to the state and its interests.

South Carolinians, in particular, wrestled with the question of residency requirements. The constitution of 1778 required two years residence; an election law passed in 1784 allowed men to become citizens after one year, voters after two. Two years later, the legislature continued the one-year requirement for citizenship, but, in order to obtain the vote, a man had to be naturalized by a special legislative act. The constitution of 1790 simplified matters by granting the suffrage once again to white adult males who lived for two years in the state.[47] South Carolina's efforts were more tortured than those in other states, but they exemplified the problem of gauging individual attachment to the community in the absence of real estate ownership. Virtually all states required state residence for one to two years as evidence of permanent attachment. Such a requirement could prove meaningless; residence hardly demonstrated permanent attachment, but without a substantial real estate qualification, it provided the best evidence potential voters could offer. In 1778, the town of Boothbay, Massachusetts, sought a broader suffrage in the state, but at the same time urged the extension of the residence requirement so that an enemy of the country would find it more difficult to qualify for the vote.[48] "Time alone," historian James Kettner concludes, "could insure that those imbued with 'foreign principles' had the opportunity to assimilate the habits, values, and modes of thought necessary for responsible participation in a virtuous, self-governing, republican community."[49]

Loyalty and the Suffrage

If residency requirements and the taxpayer qualification partially detached political rights from their propertied foundations, the act of revolution itself and subsequent turmoil in the states threatened to wrench those rights completely free of their economic moorings. During a revolution, commitment to the cause itself becomes a measure of one's faithfulness to the community's interests. In that sense, the American Revolution was typical, as a portion of the populace began to conceive of the political community as composed of those men who supported the Revolution, no matter how little property they owned, and to exclude from it Tories and neutrals, no matter how much property they possessed. Both the inclusion of the unpropertied associator and the exclusion of the propertied Tory revealed much about the Revolution's influence on measures of political competence.

The radical critique of the Whiggish connection between voting and property began in the military, among associators. Military service, not property ownership, they declared, offered the firmest proof of fidelity to the community. As the privates of the Military Association of the City and Liberties of Philadelphia pointed out to the general assembly in February 1776: "It has been the practice of all countries, and is highly reasonable, that all persons (not being mercenaries) who expose their lives in defence of a country, should be admitted to the enjoyment of all the rights and privileges of a citizen of that country which they have defended and protected."[50] Such a petition was radical indeed, for it promised extension of the suffrage to dependent apprentices and minors, because any male over sixteen could associate. The provincial conference that organized the election of delegates to the constitutional convention enfranchised all tax-paying associators. The Pennsylvania constitution broadened the suffrage further. It ignored association as a measure of political attachment but enfranchised most men by establishing a tax-paying requirement and required voters to swear allegiance to the state and the constitution. Moreover, on the eve of independence, the Pennsylvania assembly resolved that German and other foreign associators hitherto "not entitled to the privileges of freemen of this Province" should "be entitled to the same rights and privileges, as natural-born subjects."[51]

In Maryland, legally unqualified militiamen seized the vote. When the provincial convention called an election of delegates to a new convention that would draft a state constitution, it retained the colonial-era requirements of ownership of fifty acres of land or a personal estate worth forty pounds sterling.[52] Soldiers from Prince George's County ignored the resolution. "The inhabitants of the county agreed, that every taxable bearing arms, being an inhabitant of the county, had an undoubted right to vote for representatives at this time of public calamity." Judges appointed by the convention resigned, so the inhabitants "appointed the judges." The rebellion took a slightly different turn in the lower district of Frederick County. The committee of safety appointed election judges in place of those chosen by the convention. The new judges then accepted the ballots of "a majority of voters, resident of the district, and who had armed in defence of the country." Similarly, in Worcester County, "The election . . . was held contrary to the resolves of the last convention, ascertaining and declaring the qualifications of voters." Queen Anne's County "freemen" selected their own judges and voted in the election. In Kent County, the election judges "were prevented from carrying on the election . . . by a number of people not qualified to vote by the resolves of the last convention." Nevertheless, enough associators were kept from the polls to elicit a petition from Kent County "freeholders and freemen" for a new election in which "every associator resident of the county one year, and 21 years of age, might be enabled to vote."[53]

The convention responded quickly to suppress the suffrage rebellion. It voided the elections, reappointed the original judges, and set aside August 22 and August 27 for new elections held under the old rules. It even passed resolutions requiring "all friends to America" to aid the election judges.[54]

What did suffrage rebels seek? There is no evidence to suggest that the rebels were acting in concert. The counties affected were geographically dispersed; lower Frederick and Prince George's were on the western shore, and Kent, Worcester, and Queen Anne's on the eastern. Nor does the rebellion seem to have been about the men elected to the convention. In Queen Anne's and the lower district of Frederick, in both the irregular and the legal elections, voters elected the same four men to the convention.[55] The legally qualified electors of Worcester and Prince George's reelected three of the four original delegates from each county.[56]

Instead, the conflict seems to have been directly about the right to vote. In Anne Arundel County, one of the election officials, James Disney, reported that just after the judges opened the polls, they "were interrupted by a number of the people present, which insisted on every man's having a vote that bore arms."[57] The judges immediately closed the polls and ordered Disney to read the election regulations. But that only infuriated "the By-standers, who cryed pull him down, he shall not read, we will not hear it, and if you do not stop and let every Freeman Vote, that carry's Arms, we will pull the House down from under the Judges." Nevertheless, the judges reopened the polls, and one voter was challenged by a militia captain. In response, "a number of the people present threatened to take his life . . . if he offered to object to any persons voting." The judges adjourned the election again.

The frustrated militiamen left the polling place and reassembled outside of town. There someone urged the men "to lay down their Arms and go Home" if they could not vote. According to several deponents, one of the candidates for a seat in the convention, Rezin Hammond, "address[ed] the people from the Hustings and in his address he advised the people to lay down their arms if they were Denied the privilege of Voting for it was their Right and they ought not to be deprived of it."[58] Nevertheless, unlike in the other counties, the suffrage rebellion dissipated. Thomas Harwood, one of Hammond's leading supporters, spoke to the crowd of militiamen, whom he addressed significantly as "Gentlmen." He reviewed the convention's suffrage regulations, agreed they were "a great Hardship," but urged the crowd to obey. He was sure that "by Instructing your Representatives in the next Convention . . . no doubt but you'l[l] get relief." Harwood then asked the judges to reopen the polls, which they did, and the election proceeded without incident.[59]

Congresses rejected all proposals for soldier suffrage, and the Maryland convention disallowed the unauthorized votes. Nevertheless, loyalty became a precondition for participation in public life. Disfranchisement of Loyalists may have been an obvious necessity, but it compelled political leaders to reconsider the boundaries of the political community.[60] The North Carolina provincial congress, in its explanation of the removal of Tory prisoners from their homes to the interior, exposed the ways in which the Revolution unhinged customary conceptions of the political community. Because the Loyalists were "Members of the same political body with ourselves," the congress felt "the convulsion which such a sever-ance occasions; and shall bless the day which shall restore them to us friends to liberty, to the cause of America, the cause of God and mankind."[61]

Provincial congresses and, subsequently, state legislatures disfranchised Loyalists, many of whom met all traditional conditions for participation in political life, by requiring electors to take an oath or affirmation of al-legiance.[62] As the colonists prepared to write state constitutions and consider independence, they took special care to ensure the loyalty of all voters. The Maryland provincial convention disfranchised any man "pub-lished" by any committee of observation or by the Maryland council of safety, "as an enemy to the liberties of America" and not "restored to the favour of his country."[63] The Delaware assembly required "every Elector" for delegates to the constitutional convention to swear his support for in-dependence.[64] New Jersey's provincial congress insisted that voters had "signed the General Association."[65] Several days after the Continental Congress declared the colonies independent, the New Jersey congress de-clared that, because it was "highly unreasonable that the enemies of *Amer-ica* should be admitted to take an active part in our publick measures," it required all voters to swear or affirm their allegiance.[66]

Pennsylvania went further in its use of loyalty to measure political com-petence. The provincial conference of local committees of safety, which established the rules to govern the election of delegates to the constitu-tional convention, created two categories of voters—members of which would have to prove their allegiance to the revolutionary cause. The con-ference first enfranchised all adult associators who had paid public taxes during the previous year and took an oath of loyalty. Those who did not serve as soldiers fit into a second category with more stringent require-ments. Such men had to meet the existing property qualifications and, by oath or affirmation, repudiate their allegiance to the king and promise they would not "directly or indirectly oppose the establishment of a free government in this province," or the measures of the Continental Con-gress. The conference also explicitly disfranchised any person "published by any committee of inspection, or the committee of safety, in this province, as an enemy to the liberties of America, and has not been re-stored to the favor of his country."[67]

By passing such resolutions and acts, the congressional delegates and state legislators followed the reasoning of North Carolina governor Thomas Burke, who contended that Loyalists never could be citizens because all civil governments had to be "Composed entirely of Citizens who own allegiance."[68] When the provincial congresses disfranchised neutrals and Tories, they recast the political community by using loyalty to the Revolution as the requirement for membership. It was not that the revolutionary constitutions admitted all men who supported the revolutionary cause into the political community, for even Pennsylvania's provincial conference required associators to be taxpayers.[69] But the exclusion of propertied men of doubtful loyalty from the community reoriented the understanding Americans had of the requirements for entrance into a political community. At the end of the war, the assumption of permanent residence signified an elector's allegiance to an independent America.[70]

The congresses not only used loyalty to define political competence; they also used the suffrage to secure men's loyalty. In so doing, they again modified American thinking about voting rights. At the beginning of the war, only a minority of the colonists ardently supported independence. The revolutionaries desperately needed to broaden their base of popular support. Some believed that expansion of the political community by reduced suffrage requirements would cement the allegiance of those formerly excluded, for now they would have a political and personal stake in the Revolution's success.[71] As the privates of the military association of Philadelphia declared when they petitioned the legislature for the enfranchisement of German associators: "Good policy, as well as gratitude, suggest the propriety of granting every indulgence which can attach them to this country, and animate them in its defence."[72] The constitutional convention responded by enfranchising taxpaying foreigners who resided in the state for one year, like natives.[73] Similarly, in an apparent effort to attract the support of former Regulators living on Lord Granville's massive land holdings,[74] the North Carolina provincial congress enfranchised householders living on his land, "who have improved Lands in possession, except such as hold land by lease for years or at Will."[75]

Historians have recognized that the constitution makers expanded the electorate to gain adherents, but they have ignored the impact on suffrage theory.[76] Expanding the suffrage for this purpose inverted the traditional relationship between personal attachment and political competence. Traditional suffrage theory dictated that a man prove his attachment to the community by owning substantial property. Even the most radical pleas for enfranchisement, like those demanding the vote for all soldiers, were based upon one earning or proving one's political competence. Attachment preceded political rights. But by altering property requirements for the purpose of expanding popular support—by extending political rights to encourage political attachment—constitution makers inverted the process. Whereas attachment to the community once legitimized a citizen's claim to political rights, now framers granted political rights to legitimize the state's claim to govern.[77] Although few revolutionaries would have acknowledged this policy as a proper means for determining a person's right to vote, it became an increasingly important function of the suffrage in the nineteenth century.

The Disfranchised

For all the alterations in political rights wrought by the Revolution, more than half the adult population remained disfranchised. Among them were many propertyless men, women, slaves, some free black men, apprentices, indentured laborers, felons, and persons considered *non compos mentis.* Slaves and indentured servants, because of their legal subordination to others, were by definition excluded from the political community, and statutes barred felons and the insane, one for showing no attachment to the community's best interests, the other for incompetence.

Women posed something of a different problem, both for contemporaries and for historians. Even historians who have carefully examined the relationship of women and citizenship in revolutionary America contend that the revolutionaries assumed that women ought not to vote. The striking aspect of the woman suffrage question is not that they did not generally become voters, but that some did, and, perhaps even more, that citizens discussed it publicly and privately. Given the rigid exclusion of women from the public sphere in the preceding decades, any discussion of woman suffrage, for or against, testified to the transformative impact of the American Revolution.

The logic of rebellion and of the taxation argument led straight to direct consent. Just as the attack on Parliament's power compelled a reconsideration of voting rights for men, it also spurred some men and women to consider whether women ought to possess what the revolutionaries considered to be the most important of rights, the right to vote.

By addressing the issue of woman suffrage, opponents confronted the problem of defining the contours of the political community in a revolutionary society. According to these writers, men disfranchised women on two grounds: the first, a reading of women's natural attributes and sphere, the second, the "fact" of the lawful erasure of female will during coverture.

Theophilus Parsons, author of the *Essex Result*, a critique of the proposed Massachusetts constitution of 1778, defended female disfranchisement as a consequence of biological necessity, social circumstances, and law. He argued that "all the members of the state" should able to vote, "unless they have not sufficient discretion, or are so situated as to have no wills of their own." Women possessed insufficient discretion. They were disfranchised "not from a deficiency in their mental powers, but from the natural tenderness and delicacy of their minds, their retired mode of life, and various domestic duties." Together, these factors "prevent that promiscuous intercourse with the world, which is necessary to qualify them for electors."[78]

John Adams also defended disfranchisement of women because of their supposed physical incapacity and social role. "Whence arises," he asked, "the Right of the Men to govern Women, without their Consent?" "Their Delicacy," he answered, "renders them unfit for Practice and Experience, in the great Business of Life, and the hardy Enterprizes of War, as well as the arduous Cares of State. Besides, their attention is So much engaged with the necessary Nurture of their Children, that Nature has made them fittest for domestic Cares."[79]

But male revolutionaries' primary reason for excluding married women from the polling place was that, under coverture, women had no legal will of their own. Women's disfranchisement rested thus on their dependent state. During coverture, married women could not own property, and propertyless women, in Linda Kerber's words, had neither "the political or economic self-interest that attached men to the state" nor the economic independence to act as responsible citizens.[80] Furthermore, such dependent women had other duties—obligations to husbands, not to the state. Husbands, in turn, represented their wives in public affairs.

However, coverture failed to justify the disfranchisement of propertied unmarried women, *feme sole*, or widows, and it was with regard to those women that the revolutionary argument ran its course. Some men and women endorsed their enfranchisement and one state actually enfranchised them. In light of the customary exclusion of most women from public life, it is remarkable that at least some men and women argued in favor of suffrage for propertied women. They simply carried the American position on representation to its logical conclusion. Hannah Corbin, the sister of Virginia's Richard Henry Lee, complained "that widows are not represented, and that being temporary possessors of their estates ought not to be liable to the tax."

Lee's response was equally significant. Unlike Adams and Parsons, Lee endorsed woman suffrage. He first explained why woman suffrage had "never been the practice either here or in England." Like Parsons, he suggested that "'twas thought rather out of character for women to press into those tumultuous assemblages of men where the business of choosing representatives is conducted." Then he described how the doctrine of virtual representation had applied to women. Suffrage for widows and other unmarried women had seemed unnecessary because representatives shared the burden of taxation with their constituents. Although Lee found this argument generally persuasive, he "would at any time give my consent to establish their right of voting." Indeed, he continued, "the doctrine of representation . . . ought to be extended as far as wisdom and policy can allow; nor do I see that either of these forbid widows having property from voting." Lee even claimed that Corbin already had "as legal a right to vote as any other person" in the election of county tax commissioners (who reviewed appeals from those aggrieved by their tax assessment).[81]

Woman suffrage also received public support. In one of the many newspaper articles urging model constitutions on the states in 1776, New Jersey's "Essex" urged that "widows paying taxes to have an equal right to a vote, as men of the same property." He reached this conclusion by applying revolutionary political theory to the case of unmarried women. "Every person excluded by the above rules from a share in the choice of representatives, to be exempted from paying taxes raised for the support of legislation."[82] In regard to woman suffrage, "Essex"'s result differed markedly from the *Essex Result*.

But constitution writers went beyond discussion by enfranchising women in New Jersey, thereby fulfilling John Adams's prophecy that revision of suffrage requirements would open the door to claims for woman suffrage. "Essex" may have been one of New Jersey's leading politicians and a member of the provincial congress that authored the state's constitution.[83] If so, that would suggest that the congress was fully aware that its remarkable suffrage provision enfranchised some women. Furthermore, New Jersey's provincial congresses had been debating suffrage qualifications for more than a year before the third congress drafted the state constitution. The third congress also substantially revised the suffrage clause offered by the drafting committee. There may be insufficient evidence to prove definitively that the congress intended to enfranchise any women, but the failure to include a gender-defined electorate certainly was not a result of pressure for instant action. The suffrage article granted the vote to "all inhabitants" who were "worth" fifty pounds and resided in the place of voting for one year.[84] In subsequent years, election officials interpreted the provision literally and permitted propertied single women to vote.[85]

The continued disfranchisement of women in every other state should not obscure the significance of New Jersey's enfranchisement of propertied women. During the colonial era, election officials in several provinces occasionally had permitted propertied women to vote in elections because of their weight in the community. But because female voting in colonial America depended upon the sufferance of public officials, it reinforced the belief that women had no place in public life. The New Jersey provincial congress enfranchised any (probably unmarried) woman who owned the same constitutionally specified amount of property as any man. Constitutional rules gave women claims to political rights and accepted implicitly women's political capacity.

Retreat from this revolutionary stance came quickly. In the 1790s, when substantial numbers of women acted like men and voted, many New Jersey politicians were appalled by the full implications of female suffrage. They disfranchised women in 1807.[86]

Free blacks posed yet another problem that revealed ways in which the Revolution unhinged traditional notions of the American polity. Slaves, of course, were excluded from political society because they were property. With few exceptions, however, the colonies drew no distinctions between whites and free blacks. Early in the eighteenth century, only Virginia, North Carolina, and South Carolina barred free blacks from the polls. North Carolina had reenfranchised them in 1737, but Georgia joined the disfranchisers in 1761.[87] All other colonies permitted free blacks to vote.

In the revolutionary constitutions, constitution makers continued colonial practices without question, except in Massachusetts, where they considered but ultimately rejected black disfranchisement. The proposal in the Massachusetts constitution of 1778 to disfranchise blacks and Indians sparked such a storm of protest that the provision was eventually dropped from the successful constitution of 1780. Most of the towns objecting to the provision did so on the grounds that it deprived men of the "natural" right to direct representation and to consent to their own taxation. They assumed that all free adult taxpayers had to give their actual consent to laws (via their representatives) before they could be expected to obey them. Spencer, for example, denounced disfranchisement of "any men or

Set of men for the Sole Cause of Colour" as "an Infringement upon the Rights of Mankind." At the very least, they should be exempted from taxation, because "it is Our Fundamental Principle that taxation and Representation Cannot be Seperated,—that the Great Secret of Government is Governing all By all."[88] Sutton warned that black and Indian male disfranchisement wore "a very gross complextion of slavery." It was "diametrically repugnant" to the "Fundamental maxim of Humane Rights; viz. *'That Law to boind all must be assented to be all.'*"[89] Westminster objected to any provision "which Deprives a part of the humane Race of their Natural Rights, mearly on account of their Couler—Which in our opinion no power on Earth has a Just Right to Doe."[90] One writer mocked the disfranchisement provision. "Would it not be ridiculous, inconsistent and unjust," he asked, "to exclude *freemen* from voting for representatives and senators, though otherwise qualified, because their skins are black, tawney or reddish? Why not disqualify for being long-nosed, short-faced, or higher or lower than five feet size?" Then, the writer identified the Revolution's impact on the political nation. "A black, tawny or reddish skin is not so unfavourable an hue to the genuine son of liberty as a tory complexion."[91] It would be unwise to overstate the significance of the opposition to disfranchisement because only a small minority of the towns objected to the provision. Nevertheless, their objections contained sufficient force that the constitutional convention of 1779–80 established color-blind suffrage requirements.

It is apparent that revolutionary Americans thought carefully and deeply about the suffrage issue. To them, the act of voting was critically important from the onset of the Revolution. The changes they made were sometimes tentative, and sometimes they did not recognize the implications of what they were doing. They had unhinged relationships between property and voting, but they had by no means demolished them.

Of greatest significance were not the changing rules for admission to the political nation—in the nineteenth century, New Jersey's women would lose the vote, as would most free black men; the taxpayer requirement would be ignored when it was not repealed; and white manhood suffrage would sweep the land—but the way in which the debates over admission to the political nation moved the suffrage to the center of American political thought and redefined the act of voting. The right to vote, not necessarily the exercise of that right, became the standard of full citizenship. Citizens needed the vote to protect themselves and their communities from the potentially rapacious and tyrannical actions of men in power. This understanding of voting fostered the emergence of a mechanical political culture, as Americans increasingly equated participation in the mechanics of governance, by casting a ballot, with political participation. Men acted politically by voting. Maryland's suffrage rebels implicitly rejected this view when they seized the polling places, but they accepted it by demanding inclusion in the formal political process. The equation of voting and political participation, detached as it was from the traditional organic polity, did not triumph entirely during the Revolution—Shays's Rebellion, the Whiskey Rebellion, and the riots of the Jacksonian era attest to that—but the suffrage debates fostered by the revolutionary crisis pointed American political culture in that direction.

By Their United
Influence Become
Dangerous

*The Separation
of Powers*

Constitution makers brought to their task an obsession with governmental power. They believed that men in power invariably lusted after more power and would attempt in myriad ways to obtain it. In this view, because power was always aggressive and bent upon expansion, liberty was perpetually endangered. When republicans framed state constitutions, they erected barriers against arbitrary exercise of power. By separating the functions of government among different branches and men, they hoped to prevent this headlong rush toward tyranny and slavery.

The idea of the separation of powers came to the revolutionary generation partly from Baron Montesquieu's *The Spirit of the Laws*. His chapter "On the constitution of England" concluded that, if all governmental powers resided in the same hands, tyranny would result. Montesquieu succinctly explained the rationale for a separation of powers. "Political liberty in a citizen," he wrote, "is that tranquillity of spirit which comes from the opinion each one has of his security, and in order for him to have this liberty the government must be such that one citizen cannot fear another citizen." Political liberty so defined could not exist when the powers of government were united in the hands of one man or a body of men. Montesquieu identified "three sorts of powers": legislative, executive, and judicial.[1] Freedom required scrupulous separation of these departments: "When legislative power is united with executive power in a single person or in a single body of the magistracy, there is no liberty, because one can fear that the same monarch or senate that makes tyrannical laws will execute them tyrannically. Nor is there liberty if the power of judging is not separate from legislative power and from executive power. If it were joined to legislative power, the power over the life and liberty of the citizens would be arbitrary, for the judge would be the legislator. If it were joined to executive power, the judge could have the force of an oppressor."[2]

What did the idea of a constitutional separation of powers signify to the revolutionary generation? What exactly did Virginia's provincial convention delegates mean when they boldly declared: "The legislative, executive and judiciary departments shall be separate and distinct, so that neither exercise the powers properly belonging to the other: nor shall any person exercise the powers of more than one of them at the same time"?[3]

Historians generally consider the separation of powers as part of the revolutionary effort to enfeeble the magistrate. As Gordon Wood has argued, separation of powers meant "insulating the judiciary and particularly the legislature from executive manipulation."[4] That required elimination of the governor's patronage powers. During the imperial crisis, American patriots accused the king's ministers in England of corrupting Parliament by appointing members and their friends and family members to lucrative government positions. In return, Parliament, and especially the House of Commons, did the ministry's bidding.

To address this problem, according to this interpretation, constitution writers generally stripped governors of their patronage powers and excluded officeholders from the legislature. After protecting the disinterestedness of the legislature, framers granted most of the state's power to it. Given the general belief that the legislature embodied the people, in this view, most citizens accepted the legislature's virtual omnipotence. Only as people became discontented with their assemblies' behavior and concluded that their legislators could not truly represent them did they embrace a modern understanding of the separation of powers.[5]

This description of the doctrine's evolution, although sustained by substantial evidence, tells only part of the story. The broad and deep support that Americans gave to the idea of a separation of powers rested upon their fear that one man *or* body of men, not only the executive, might gain unrestrained power. When the framers of the state constitutions severely weakened state executives, they treated what they considered only one symptom of a disease, not the disease itself. The disease was the concentration of government power. When the state constitutions stripped governors or presidents of many powers previously associated with colonial governors, they inevitably transferred greater power to the state assemblies. But such decisions did not signal confidence in the fidelity of representatives; constitution makers trusted no man or group of men with all governmental powers.

From the first, constitution makers aimed to divide governmental powers among distinct branches of government as a means of preventing arbitrary government and preserving liberty. The separation of powers was not a doctrine limited to protecting the legislature from executive corruption.[6] American patriots embraced the doctrine partially in reaction to colonial practice and the imperial crisis but also in response to their experience with all-powerful provincial congresses, which consolidated executive, legislative, and judicial powers. As a consequence, they attempted to separate powers by barring any member of one branch of government from assuming the powers of another (sometimes slighted by historians as a mere prohibition of plural officeholding), by stripping governors of the veto, and by dividing the functions of the colonial council between an executive council and, usually, a senate.

The Provincial Congresses

Government by provincial congresses in 1774 and 1775 spurred broad popular support for separating government powers and isolating the branches of government from one another. As royal and proprietary governments crumbled in response to the Coercive Acts and the outbreak of war, local committees and provincial congresses challenged and then replaced the colonial governments. The congresses assumed control of all aspects of provincial government—legislative, executive, and judicial.

Befitting their status as revolutionary institutions, the provincial congresses wielded extraordinary powers. New Jersey's second provincial congress levied taxes, appointed a treasurer to collect them, and organized the state's military forces. Such actions suggest that the congress had taken over the legislative functions of the provincial assembly, council, and governor. But the congress went further. It performed in both judicial and executive capacities when it demanded that local committees provide it with a list of non-associators. Furthermore, it created and appointed a committee of safety to serve as the provincial executive between sessions of the provincial congress. This decision revealed the executive character of the congress, for it remained both the source of the committee's authority and superseded the committee when it was in session.[7]

Similarly, the Virginia convention performed various functions that ignored distinctions between executive, legislative, and judicial powers. Acting in a judicial capacity, it functioned as a prize court. It also served as an appellate court for men accused of loyalism by local committees. In those cases, it frequently softened the prescribed punishments ordered by the local committees and required accused Loyalists to join the army or leave the colony. In addition, the convention assumed the governor's executive functions in the appointment of county sheriffs. Whereas before the Revolution the governor chose sheriffs from lists submitted by the county courts, now the convention authorized county committees to appoint sheriffs. The convention thus consolidated all of the colony's legislative power, once shared by the burgesses, council, and governor.[8]

Even in those colonies in which regular assemblies continued to sit, they held vastly greater powers than did pre-crisis assemblies. After May 1775, the Delaware and Pennsylvania assemblies assumed the executive powers of their helpless common governor, John Penn.[9] In Massachusetts, the House of Representatives reconstituted the general court under the charter of 1691 by electing the members of a council that served both as the upper house of the legislature and as a collective executive.

Although patriots recognized that those legislatures and the provincial congresses needed extensive powers during the revolutionary crisis, they worried about the consolidation of so much power in the hands of a relatively few men. The experience left an indelible impression on members of the congresses that framed the state constitutions. It also lent irresistible force to the argument for a functional separation of powers in the new state governments.

The attack on the provincial congresses for absorbing all government powers emerged most fully in Maryland, as revolutionaries pressured the reluctant provincial convention to support independence. As late as May 21, 1776, convention members had reaffirmed their earlier instructions to Maryland's congressional delegates to seek reconciliation with England.[10]

Pro-independence congressional delegate Samuel Chase returned to Maryland in mid-June after serving as an envoy to American forces in Quebec and turned up the pressure on the convention. He sparked a barrage of county instructions to convention delegates demanding that Maryland join the movement for independence.[11]

The county instructions drew upon popular fears of the convention's accumulation of power. One district committee of Frederick County asserted "that the Legislative, Judicative, Executive, and Military powers, ought to be separate, and that in all countries where the power to make laws and the power to enforce such laws is vested in one man, or in one body of men, a tyranny is established." A meeting of the militia battalion of Anne Arundel County declared it "essential to liberty that the Legislative, Judicial, and Executive powers of Government be separate from each other." Whenever "they are united in the same person, or number of persons, there would be wanting that mutual check which is the principal security against their making of arbitrary laws, and a wanton exercise of power in the execution of them."[12]

Marylanders then criticized the convention for violating those principles. One Marylander argued that the convention endangered the people's liberties by engrossing all governmental power. "What is it that constitutes despotism," he asked, "but the assemblage and union of the legislative, executive, and judicial functions in the same person, or persons? When they are united in one person, a monarchy is established; when in many, an aristocracy, or oligarchy, both equally inconsistent with the liberties of the people." The convention's far-reaching powers made it dangerous and undermined its authority, just like the infamous Long Parliament of the English Civil War.[13]

Because Maryland needed a lawful government that properly separated governmental powers, the authors of county instructions demanded that their delegates support independence and the drafting of a state constitution. The citizens of Talbot denounced the "present mode of Government by Conventions and Committees, as . . . dangerous, so far as it unites the Legislative and Executive power in nearly the same persons, which is the true definition of tyranny." They did not question the motives of convention delegates but warned that "it is proper to guard against probable evil, where the liberties of mankind are concerned."[14] Therefore, they concluded, their delegates should endorse independence and compel the convention (or a new convention) to draft a state constitution. Similarly, the citizens of the upper district of Frederick County denounced the convention's accumulation of executive, legislative, and judicial powers. Because "the present mode of Government in this Province is incompetent to the exigencies thereof, and dangerous to our liberties," they called for a new convention to establish a state government under the guidelines of the Continental Congress's resolution of May 15.[15]

The attack on the convention for absorbing all governmental power persisted even after delegates endorsed independence and called for a new convention to write a state constitution. As Marylanders prepared to elect delegates to the convention, "An American" reminded them that government by convention endangered their liberties because it consolidated the different powers of government into a few men's hands. "All men, by nature fond of power, are unwilling to part with the possession of it," he explained. "The desire to command increases every day." If unchecked, tyranny inevitably followed. "The exercise creates affection; and what was granted as a trust, is soon claimed as a right. The affable, courteous, patriotick citizen out of power, frequently degenerates into the haughty, insolent tyrant, when vested with supreme command." Therefore, "no man, or body of men, ought to be intrusted with the united powers of Government, or more command than is absolutely necessary to discharge the particular office committed to him." Just look at the convention, he urged: "A complete tyranny is established by such a combination of powers."[16]

The new convention assembled on August 14 and spent most of the next three months drafting the state constitution. Delegates evidently heeded the demands of the Anne Arundel battalion, the county instructions of June, and other pleas for the separation of powers. The record of the proceedings reveals that delegates carefully drafted the constitution and debated numerous provisions, but none disagreed with the sixth article of the declaration of rights: "The legislative, executive and judicial powers of government, ought to be forever separate and distinct from each other."[17]

It is tempting to dismiss the Marylanders' concern about the separation of powers because their motives were often partisan: they sought independence and not simply the fulfillment of abstract political principles. But the political motives underlying the appeal indicate that the various authors assumed an assault on the convention's accumulation of wide-ranging powers would be well received. Critics might have assailed the convention on other grounds, but their decision to emphasize the separation of powers suggests the currency and broad acceptance of those ideas.

Marylanders were not alone. After the North Carolina provincial convention and committee of safety created a provincial council of thirteen in

December 1775, one inhabitant worried because "the Legislative, Judicial, and Executive powers of Government, are now entirely in the hands" of the council.[18] In Pennsylvania the next June, "A Watchman" complained that, although the Pennsylvania assembly still sat, it had become just like the extralegal congresses of other colonies. "ALL power," he wrote, "legislative, executive and judicial is lodged in one body, by which means we live under a species of government which has always been reprobated by good men as the worst in the world."[19] In its place, Pennsylvanians wanted "the legislative, executive and judicial powers separated and lodged in different hands," a "Protestor" insisted.[20] Writing generally about extralegal governments throughout the colonies, another author observed: "The Provincial Conventions, or Congresses have inadvertently pursued the very conduct they so justly condemn in the British Parliament, which has exceeded the limits prescribed by the constitution to its operations."[21]

Even delegates to provincial congresses fretted about their own extensive powers. In a remarkable statement, members of the New York provincial congress worried about attaining too much power for the people's good. In its response to the Continental Congress's May 15 resolution, the congress supported the call for organization of a new government. New Yorkers had instituted government by convention, a committee declared, to fight usurpation until reconciliation, but that prospect was now "remote and uncertain." The current government could not continue to act because it united "Legislative, Judicial and Executive powers"; the committee therefore recommended that a new convention write a state constitution.[22]

The consolidation of power in the provincial congresses and Thomas Paine's support for unicameral government also troubled John Adams as he considered the separation of powers in his influential *Thoughts on Government*.[23] Historians stress those aspects of the pamphlet advocating balanced government, a "mixed state," and bicameralism, but they largely ignore his opposition to the concentration of all power in "a single assembly."[24] Adams denounced the idea of entrusting all governmental powers (not only legislative power) to a unicameral assembly—just the kind of powers held by the provincial congresses. After explaining the importance of a representative assembly, he urged the functional division of governmental powers. Adams asked whether "all the powers of government, legislative, executive, and judicial, shall be left in this body" and answered in the negative. "A SINGLE Assembly" would possess "all the vices, follies and frailties of an individual." As in Holland, it would "exempt itself from burthens which it will lay," would be "apt to grow ambitious," and ultimately would "not hesitate to vote itself perpetual."[25]

There were other problems, too. An assembly was unfit to hold executive power because it could not act with "secrecy and dispatch"; nor could it hold judicial power, for it would be "too little skilled in the laws." But most important and most frightening, "a single Assembly, possessed of all the powers of government, would make arbitrary laws for their own interest, execute all laws arbitrarily for their own interest, and adjudge all controversies in their own favour."[26] Thus, the experience with the provincial congresses shaped Adams's influential pamphlet and, through it, the revolutionary generation's conception of the separation of powers.

The Separation of Powers, Patronage, and Officeholding

Advocates of a constitutional separation of powers carefully addressed the problems of patronage and officeholding. They were concerned not only about the magistrate's manipulation of a representative assembly but also about the concentration of all power in the legislature.

Perceptions of English governance and their own colonial experience shaped Americans' thinking about patronage. The stability of the English regime rested upon British ministers' ability to manage the House of Commons. They maintained that mastery through their control of patronage—what some called influence, and British opponents and Americans called corruption. In the mid–eighteenth century, more than a third of commoners held Crown-appointed offices and about 5 percent held Crown contracts. Appointment of thousands of "excise offices" also gave the sitting ministry the opportunity to appoint the favorites of house members. The ministry's domination of the Commons was never so secure as these numbers might imply, but American colonists believed such practices "corrupted" the Commons.[27]

Colonists' concerns were heightened because their own governors possessed vast formal patronage powers. Practice did not equal theory, for most governors had few favors to confer, but even a few well-placed appointments raised the specter of corruption.[28] Furthermore, Benning and John Wentworth in New Hampshire, and Francis Bernard and Thomas Hutchinson in Massachusetts, carefully dispensed offices and other considerations to build a substantial core of officeholding supporters.[29]

Not only did governors seem to wield dangerous patronage power, but the provinces offered little defense against the corruption of legislators. Among the colonies, only New Jersey had a place bill, a replica of the English Place Act of 1707, which excluded a few officeholders from the Commons and required others to seek reelection after appointment. Only

Maryland banned all proprietary appointees from the assembly. In 1775, one New Yorker declared it "a scandal" that the province had "no place bill to exclude such from the house of Assembly as after an election render themselves dependent upon the Crown for offices held during pleasure."[30] The New York provincial congress, at a reception to honor General George Washington, offered the following toast: "May placemen and pensioners never find seats in American senates."[31]

The fear of executive manipulation of the legislature influenced state constitution makers, but it neither encompassed what the revolutionaries meant by a separation of powers nor fully explained their concerns about plural officeholding. They feared both the magistrate's manipulation of the legislature through patronage and the dangerous accumulation of both executive and legislative powers in the same hands. The Virginia constitution, in the same paragraph that asserted the primacy of departmental government, prohibited persons in one branch from exercising "the powers properly belonging to the other."

Convention delegates did not seek merely to prohibit a man from holding more than one office; they prevented officials in one branch from also becoming officials in another. They hoped thereby to avoid concentrations of power in any one branch of government or any group of men. New York's "An Independent Whig" explicitly ignored the threat of executive manipulation of the legislature through the patronage, "taking it for granted, that the public will not leave with him the disposal of very profitable ones, or will by bills of exclusion, secure the Independence of the House and Council." Rather he brooded about the power of legislators to appoint themselves to office.[32] The Massachusetts constitution of 1780 was explicit: "In the government of this Commonwealth, the legislative department shall never exercise the executive and judicial powers, or either of them: The executive shall never exercise the legislative and judicial powers, or either of them: The judicial shall never exercise the legislative and executive powers, or either of them: to the end it may be a government of laws and not of men."[33]

Constitution writers assumed that if executive officials served in the legislature they would bring to it interests incompatible with the public good and their responsibilities as representatives, and ultimately acquire arbitrary power.[34] If representatives and executive officials were the same persons, they would pursue their own interests at the expense of the public's. One defender of the Pennsylvania constitution charged that critics objected to it because it prevented a few representatives from controlling the province's most lucrative offices. "Now a Judge of Admiralty must entirely give up the privilege of prescribing rules for his own conduct, or relinquish his post," he wrote. "This separation of Legislative and Executive power, and the amazing precautions taken to prevent the inveteration of power, are the really obnoxious articles in the Constitution."[35] A New Yorker worried that if the state's lower house or council could remove officers at will and replace them with members of the legislature, "it necessarily endangers, tho' it may not destroy, the Independency of the Members."[36] "An Observator" therefore recommended the exclusion of virtually all officeholders from the Massachusetts General Court, "which ought to be as pure as the element we breath."[37] By preventing legislators from choosing themselves for executive offices, delegates to the New Jersey provincial congress similarly hoped to preserve the legislature "from all suspicion of corruption."[38]

Time and again, writers noted the relationship between corruption and tyranny.[39] Rev. William Gordon of Massachusetts, a prolific writer on constitutional issues, argued that judicial, executive, and legislative powers must "be preserved separate and distinct" and "being thus divided, the people are the better secured in the possession of their liberties." Each branch of government had enough work to keep it busy; by focusing on its individual tasks, it could act expeditiously; "and being thus separated the guardians of the publick are increased, and dangerous encroachments upon the Constitution become the less probable." Therefore, he urged that judges be kept out of legislature and legislators out of the executive council. "The [legislative] Council should be solely legislative," he declared, "and the executive power be entrusted with other individuals."[40]

Like Gordon, the citizens of Orange County, North Carolina, sniffed tyranny in plural officeholding. Fearing the potential for despotism when the functional powers of government were undivided, they instructed their delegates to the provincial congress to try to organize a government with three separate branches. Then, delegates should attempt to bar any person from holding office in "any more than one of these branches at the same time lest they should fail of being the proper checks on each other and by their united influence become dangerous to any individual who might oppose the ambitious designs of the persons who might be employed in such power."[41]

The fear of such "united influence" became reality in the government established by New Hampshire delegates in 1776. Unlike most of the other charters, the sparse, temporary constitution of New Hampshire paid little heed to any separation of powers, or much of anything else.[42] Meschech Weare served as both president of the New Hampshire council and chief justice of the state supreme court, which made him the state's chief executive, judicial, and legislative official.[43] The aggrandizement of so much power by Weare and his fellow councillors aroused considerable fear and anger. Responding to the consolidation of power under John Wentworth's governorship and to the temporary constitution's failure to divide governmental powers, a New Hampshire citizen asserted: "The ambition of men is unbounded, and no man breathing should be intrusted with too much power nor with offices and places opposite in their institutions, incompatible with each other."[44] During the Wentworth era, "Amicus Respublica" continued, people had denounced the council, which they called "the *family compact*" for taking all of the provincial offices for councillors and their families. But "we could have wished" that the constitution "condemned the dangerous consequences of lodging the legislative and executive power in the same persons, which is a political *solecism*."

The solution was simple, "Amicus" contended; allow a person to hold only one office at a time. Another New Hampshire resident argued that because plural officeholding enabled one or a few men to monopolize power in the state, "the powers of government ought to be divided as much as possible." Indeed, "too great a power . . . should not be lodged in any one man, or body of men: by such investments their *influence* extends over too many departments."[45] The town meeting of Portsmouth instructed its representatives "that they do not consent that any Person should hold more than one place in Government at a time."[46] "Instead of a legislature grasping after unlimited authority, seeking their private interest," a New Hampshire "Cato" wished for one dedicated to "preserving it to the public emolument."[47]

New Hampshire's citizens remedied this problem when they adopted a permanent constitution in 1784. The constitution provided the president and executive council with patronage powers comparable to those of Massachusetts' governor and council, and reserved to the legislature the selection of secretary, treasurer, and commissary-general. Then it barred all of those officeholders from seats in the legislature or executive council.[48]

The revised constitution's prohibition of plural officeholding resembled the provisions in other states; all aimed to save legislators and executive officers from corruption and prevent them from becoming tyrants. This was true in states like Delaware, Maryland, Massachusetts, and Pennsylvania, where the executive and the legislature both held substantial patronage powers. It was also true in states like New Jersey, North Carolina, Virginia, and Georgia, where the assemblies dispensed virtually all of the offices. The only exceptions were New York, where the governor and legislature shared appointive power, and in the 1776 temporary constitutions of South Carolina and New Hampshire.

In those states in which the governor and the legislature held broad appointive powers, the new frames of government carefully excluded from the assembly all public officials appointed by either branch of government. In Maryland, the governor, with the approval of the executive council, appointed the chancellor, "all Judges and Justices," the attorney general, a variety of military officers, "and all civil officers of government (Assessors, Constables, and Overseers of the roads only excepted)."[49] The House of Delegates alone appointed the state's two treasurers and two commissioners of the loan office (one for each shore). The entire general assembly elected the state's governor, the executive council, and the congressional delegates. Using a broad brush, the state constitution excluded from the legislature any one who "shall hold or execute any office of profit, or receive the profits of any office exercised by any other person, during the time for which he shall be elected."[50]

Historians have generally treated Pennsylvania's constitution as if it made the unicameral legislature omnipotent, but such a conclusion is vastly overstated, at least on the crucial question of patronage. The House of Representatives selected the treasurer, the register of wills, and the recorder of deeds. But the president and council appointed all judges, naval officers, the attorney general "and all other officers, civil and military." The constitution excluded all officeholders, not only those appointed by the executive, from the House of Representatives, with the phrase, "nor shall any member, while he continues such, hold any other office, except in the militia."[51] Framers reaffirmed the point by excluding a long list of officeholders (including some who were popularly elected) from the legislature, executive council, and Continental Congress.[52]

In neighboring Delaware, the constitution also divided appointive powers between the legislature and the executive, but granted them different authority in choosing officers. It assigned to the general assembly the power to appoint army and navy officers and (with the president casting one vote) to elect all members of the state's judiciary except justices of the peace. It bestowed on the executive the authority to appoint, with the approval of the privy council, "the Secretary, the Attorney-General, Registers for the Probate of Wills, Registers in Chancery, Clerks of the Court of Common Pleas and of the Peace," and to select justices of the peace, sheriffs, and coroners from nominations made by the House of Delegates.

No matter whom it empowered to make the appointments, the constitution included a comprehensive article prohibiting officeholders from the legislature. It enumerated justices of the supreme court and of common pleas, the secretary, trustees of the loan office, court clerks, and "all Persons concerned in any Army or Navy Contracts." Any legislator who accepted any of those positions automatically vacated his seat.[53]

The Massachusetts constitution, paralleling Pennsylvania's, vested the executive with considerable appointive powers. With the executive council's approval, the governor appointed "ALL judicial officers, the Attorney-General, the Solicitor-General, all Sheriffs, Coroners, and Registers of Probate" and the officers for Massachusetts troops in the Continental army. The general court's elective authority was also substantial: it designated the secretary, treasurer, receiver-general, commissary-general, notaries public, naval officers, and the major generals of the militia. Whether appointed by the governor and council or by the legislators, judicial (except justices of the peace) and executive officeholders were excluded from the legislature. Also, in an early statement of the idea that professors should remain in their "ivory tower" (which actually stemmed from state support of Harvard), the constitution excluded from the legislature any "President Professor, or Instructor of Harvard-College."[54]

That the provincial congressmen intended by their exclusionary rules more than limitation of the governor's influence over the legislature is strikingly evident in constitutions that lodged virtually all appointive powers in the legislature. In Virginia, the governor played a role in the appointment of justices of the peace. But the general assembly wielded the lion's share of state power; it elected the governor, privy council, delegates to the Continental Congress, all state judges, secretary of state, and attorney general. Those officers, "together with all others, holding lucrative offices" were ineligible for a seat in the legislature.[55]

Similar patterns prevailed in New Jersey and North Carolina. New Jersey legislators elected the governor, supreme and inferior court judges, the attorney general, the provincial treasurer, the militia's general and field officers, court clerks, and justices of the peace.[56] The constitution then excluded from the legislature all but justices of the peace.[57] The North Carolina constitution granted vast appointive powers to the state's general assembly. It empowered the legislature to elect: the governor, the secretary of state, the council of state, supreme and admiralty court judges, the attorney general, the militia's generals and field officers, and the state treasurer. Then, the constitution carefully barred each of those officeholders from the general assembly, at the same time excluding court clerks, army and navy officers, "receivers of public monies," and army and navy contractors (but not militia officers or justices of the peace).[58]

In Georgia, the unicameral legislature elected the governor, executive council, justices of the peace, and registers of wills, and, without an explicit constitutional provision, the state's chief justice and four justices from each county to assist him. Aside from the unusual provisions permitting delegates to the Continental Congress to sit in the assembly but excluding "any person who holds any title of nobility," the constitution banned from the legislature anyone holding "any post of profit under this State," or a state military commission. It exempted militia officers.[59] In states that entrusted legislatures to wield vast patronage power but prohibited plural officeholding—like Georgia, North Carolina, Virginia, and New Jersey—constitution makers revealed their fear of legislative tyranny.

South Carolina's experience was somewhat different, but it again revealed fears of the accumulation of power in the hands of any body of men. The constitution of 1776 gave legislators the entire appointive power but required a legislator to vacate his seat if chosen for an executive office. Nevertheless, he could return to the legislature if reelected. Such eligibility for reelection was unique among the new states, but reminiscent of the English Place Act of 1707. The constitution of 1778 confirmed legislative control of patronage and reaffirmed lawmakers' eligibility for reelection to the legislature once they had vacated seats in favor of other offices. But, in a departure from 1776, it barred from the legislature a long list of officeholders, ranging from secretary of state to "powder-reviewer."[60]

Only New York made a minimal effort to prevent men from gaining power in different branches of the government. It vested a council of appointment—composed of the governor and four senators chosen by the assembly—with the power to choose most government officials. The composition of the council itself suggests inattention to the idea of a separation of powers. The exclusionary articles confirm this view. They only prohibited the chancellor and supreme court justices from serving in any office other than delegate to Congress and sheriffs from holding any other office.[61] Of the states writing constitutions, New York was the exception to the general constitutional rule that officeholders be excluded from legislature, whether they had been chosen by the executive, the legislature, or the electorate.

Constitution makers were primarily concerned about legislative and executive tyranny, not judicial tyranny. Responding to their colonial experience, when judges held office at the pleasure of the Crown or proprietor, they desired a judiciary independent of the executive and the legislature, yet restrained by law. The framers hoped to achieve that goal by keeping judges out of the executive and legislative branches, establishing terms of good behavior, and making judges subject to a process of impeachment and removal by the legislature. Such terms, they believed, gave judges the desired independence but still subjected them to legislative restraint. Only New Jersey (where the legislature selected judges) and Pennsylvania (where the president and council appointed them) limited judges' terms, in both cases to seven years, the longest term of office in either state. The constitutions also required legislators to provide judges with regular and adequate salaries so that they could not influence judicial decisions by manipulating salaries.[62]

The Gubernatorial Veto

Although curiously neglected by scholars, the gubernatorial veto played a crucial role in American thinking about a separation of powers. Because the veto was such an obvious exercise of the royal prerogative, granting the veto to the governors of the new states has seemed unimaginable. The presumption is surely correct. But the denial of a veto also revealed the framers' sense of a functional separation of powers and requires the careful analysis that contemporaries gave it.[63]

The veto empowered the governor to participate directly in the legislative process. In effect, it made the governor a separate house of the legislature. By depriving him of the veto, the constitutions denied him any legislative role. The citizens of Anne Arundel County, Maryland, demanded "that the persons appointed to hold the executive power, have no share or negative in the legislature."[64] As the author of "The Interest of America" explained, it was "a great absurdity that one branch of a Legislature, that can negative all the rest, should be the principal Executive power in the State." Because there could be "but little chance for proper freedom, where the making and executing the laws of a State lie in the same hand," he insisted that executive and legislative powers "ought to be kept as distinct as possible."[65] "Democraticus," writing in Purdie's *Virginia Gazette*, demanded the exclusion of the governor from legislation on the grounds that "it is a solecism in politick[s] to invest the different power of legislation and the execution of the laws in the same hands."[66]

Opposition to the gubernatorial veto cut across ideological divisions. The electors of Mecklenburg County, North Carolina, instructed their delegates to the provincial congress to ensure "that Legislation be not a divided right, and that no man or body of men be invested with a negative on the voice of the People duly collected."[67] The Mecklenburg instructions represented the radical end of North Carolina's political spectrum; but even the province's conservative congressional delegate, William Hooper, opposed a gubernatorial veto. Hooper worried much about popular power. The people had good intentions, he conceded, but they often fell "short in the means made use of to obtain them." "A Warmth of Zeal" induced them to make errors. Therefore, North Carolina's new constitution needed checks upon the people's representatives.

Nevertheless, Hooper opposed a gubernatorial veto. In a long letter to the provincial congress offering recommendations for the new constitution, he confessed that he "once thought it would be wise to adopt a double check as in the British Constitution." But now he worried about "the Abuses which power in the hand of an Individual is liable to, & the unreasonableness that an individual should abrogate at pleasure the acts of the Representatives of the people, refined by a second body." For those reasons, a gubernatorial veto was "unnecessary."[68]

In general, until 1780, the states carefully excluded or minimized the governors' participation in the legislative process. Virginia, North Carolina, Georgia, New Jersey, Maryland, and Delaware deprived their executives of a veto.[69] Pennsylvania and Vermont each made its chief executive officer the president of the council but did not allow the president or the council a negative on the actions of the assembly. The governor of New Jersey acted as president of the legislative council and received one vote on legislation. New Hampshire's temporary constitution of 1776 also authorized the president of the council, the state's executive officer, to cast a vote as a member of the council. In 1784, the new constitution made the presidency an independent office but designated the president as the senate's presiding officer and granted him a vote. It also gave him a second vote "in case of a tie."[70]

Among the first state constitutions, only South Carolina's of 1776 gave the governor a veto, indeed an absolute veto, over all legislation.[71] But two years later, state legislators brushed aside Governor John Rutledge's rejection of a new state constitution, compelled his resignation, and happily witnessed his successor's endorsement of the new constitution, which eliminated the governor's veto.

Although few embraced the idea of a gubernatorial veto, many feared the untrammeled power of the state legislature. As a result, the states produced hybrid institutions. In Pennsylvania, the convention created the council of censors to meet every seven years to review the constitution and the actions of the legislature under that constitution and "to recommend to the legislature the repealing [of] such laws as appear to them to have been enacted contrary to the principles of the Constitution."[72] More timely action could be expected from New York's council of revision—a standing body composed of the governor, chancellor, and supreme court justices. The constitution created the council to review the constitutionality of legislation and suggest revisions to the legislature. The general assembly could override the council's veto only with a two-thirds majority in both houses. Constitution makers were reluctant to vest the governor with a role in legislation, but they also feared unbounded legislative power. Just as the congress did not entrust substantial patronage power to the governor, and instead made him a member of a council of appointment with only one vote, so too did it make him a member of the council of revision with no greater power than any other member.[73]

The Massachusetts constitution of 1780 was the first to give the governor a veto over legislation, and the story of the convention's adoption of the veto reveals the revolutionary commitment to a separation of powers. The convention had entrusted the drafting of the constitution to a committee of thirty, which entrusted the task to a subcommittee of three, which in turn entrusted it to John Adams. In 1776, in his influential *Thoughts on Government*, Adams had proposed three legislative branches for the new state governments, with the governor exercising an absolute veto. None of the framers heeded his advice. But Adams became increasingly convinced of the need for an executive veto. "I have considered this Question in every Light in which my Understanding is capable of placing it," he wrote to Elbridge Gerry, "and my Opinion is decided in favour of Three Branches." Only then would Massachusetts enjoy "Stability, Dignity, Decision, or Liberty." The state's "many Men of Wealth, of ambitious Spirits, of Intrigue, of Luxury and Corruption," would create "incessant Factions." The veto would enable the governor, "the Reservoir of Wisdom," to defend the public good and the executive's independence. The governor "without this Weapon of Defence will be run down like a Hare before the Hunters."[74] Adams thus defended the veto in two ways: by referring to the governor as the embodiment of wisdom, implicitly likening executive participation in the legislative process to the Crown's legislative role in England's mixed government; and by arguing for the governor's need to protect the executive branch from encroachments by the legislative, utilizing the doctrine of a separation of powers.

The drafting committee embraced only Adams's separation of powers defense of the veto, frustrating his wish to make "the Legislature consist of three Branches." Instead, the committee draft asserted that "the department of legislation shall be formed by two branches." The governor, said the group, needed an absolute veto not to exercise legislative powers, but "to preserve the independence of the executive and judicial departments."[75]

Convention delegates replaced the absolute veto with a suspensive veto that could be overridden by a two-thirds majority in each house of the legislature. They justified the veto on the grounds that the governor needed to preserve executive independence and curb the legislature's power, not to participate in the legislative process. In their address to the people, delegates argued that the veto secured the separation of powers in the state government. A governor needed the veto so that "a due balance may be preserved in the three capital powers of Government." As the convention reminded Massachusetts voters, "when the Man or body of Men enact, interpret and execute the Laws, property becomes too precarious to be valuable, and a People are finally borne down with the force of corruption resulting from the Union of those Powers." Without a gubernatorial veto, the legislature would seize all governmental power and oppress the citizens of Massachusetts.[76]

The Privy Council: Nature, Form, and Substance

Historians sometimes interpret the creation of upper houses in state legislatures as an attempt to recreate the colonial councils on popular authority. That view has much merit, for constitution makers designed the senates, in part, to stand above the parochial interests of the houses, much as the councils were supposed to do. But that interpretation also underestimates how the doctrine of a separation of powers transformed the role of the upper house in the government.[77]

Most states divided the powers of the old councils between executive or privy councils and senates or legislative councils.[78] The South Carolina provincial congress made the point explicitly when it named one the executive council and the other the legislative council. The choice of names suggests that Carolinians intended a functional separation of powers.[79]

An examination of both eligibility for and the powers of the privy or executive councils reveals much about the constitution makers' understanding of the distribution of powers in the government. On one extreme was New Jersey, where the constitution established distinct privy and legislative councils but then stipulated that members of the upper house also serve as members of the executive council. In this way, the constitution both divided the functions of the old council into two institutions (a significant assertion of the idea of a separation of powers), and then reunited them in the same persons. As if to affirm continuity with the colonial past, the executive council and governor retained their power to act as New Jersey's final court of appeals and to pardon criminals.

No other state attempted to reproduce the colonial council, but South Carolina came close. The legislative council did not replicate the executive council, but representatives and legislative councillors who were elected to the executive council could retain their seats in the legislature.[80] At the same time, the constitutions excluded from the legislature the executive council's presiding officer, the vice president (1776) or the lieutenant governor (1778). By distinguishing between the presiding officer and other councillors, the constitutions clearly defined the presiding officer as an executive officer who needed to be isolated from the legislature. The status of the others was uncertain because they could retain their seats in the legislature, and because the legislative bodies were not required to elect persons from their own bodies. Also, in contrast to New Jersey, only a few legislators could serve on the executive council, whereas all members of the New Jersey legislative council also served on the privy council.[81] South Carolina's executive council was the only other such body outside of New Jersey to maintain a judicial function: it acted as the state's court of chancery. Councillors also performed the old council's advisory tasks, which shriveled because the constitution eviscerated the powers of the governor. Council members advised the governor on laying temporary embargoes and on the appointment of new offices when the method for appointment was not determined by the general assembly.[82]

Constitution makers in other states walled off the executive council more effectively. Virginia established a privy council or council of state of eight members elected by a joint ballot in the legislature. Members of the legislature were eligible for election but, upon election, vacated their seats in the legislature. The council carried out the executive functions of the old council. It advised the governor on the appointment of militia officers, sheriffs, coroners, and justices of the peace, after receiving nominations from the county courts; on interim appointments; on suspending a militia officer; and on calling out the militia. Every three years, the assembly required two councillors to retire for at least three years. Because convention delegates omitted any method for rotation, a councillor in theory could serve indefinitely.[83]

In North Carolina, legislators elected a seven-member council of state for a term of one year. It advised the governor on temporarily summoning the militia, initiating embargoes, and making interim appointments. The constitution also contained a separate article to exclude members of the council of state from the assembly.[84]

Delaware similarly established a privy council of four members, two chosen by the legislative council and two by the House of Assembly. If a member of either house were elected, then he would "lose his Seat." As in Virginia, the council advised the president on mustering the militia and on summoning the assembly for an early session. But unlike in Virginia, where the legislature elected most officials, the Delaware convocation granted substantial patronage power to the executive branch. The council and president shared the authority to make regular appointments of numerous officials and interim appointments of the rest. After serving a two-year term, a councillor was ineligible for the next three years.[85]

Maryland's constitution granted many of the same powers to its council.[86] As in other states, the council advised the governor on calling up the militia, convening an early session of the legislature, and making interim appointments. In Delaware and other states the executive retained substantial appointive power; Maryland's council similarly became a partner in the appointment process. Its "advice and *consent*" were required for the governor's major judicial appointments.[87] As in most other states, the framing text banned council members from holding any other office.[88]

Massachusetts provided that electors choose forty councillors and senators by district. Then, the house and the councillors and senators, by a joint ballot, selected nine of the forty to serve as the council and the remainder as the senate. If nine did not accept, then the legislature could choose the remainder "from among the people at large."

Once established, the council possessed considerable power. It formally offered only advice to the governor about executive pardons, proroguing the general court, and summoning it for an early meeting. But the council's advice and consent also were required for the governor to make appointments and initiate emergency expenditures of money for defense. Especially by compelling the governor to share the appointive power, convention delegates made clear their desire to curb the governor's powers.[89]

New Hampshire, with no independent executive in 1776, had no need for an executive council. But that changed in 1784. When constitutional convention delegates established the office of president, they also took steps to curb the president. By a joint ballot, the legislature elected two senators and three representatives to a council, with all of them meeting the qualifications of senators. The failure to require councillors to abdicate their seats in the general court blurred divisions between the executive and legislative branches; constitution makers seem to have viewed the council as a *legislative* curb on the president. All of the executive's many appointments were made jointly by "the president and council" and required the approval of at least three councillors. The constitution required the president to obtain the council's consent for the emergency expenditure of money for defense and its advice on ending a session of the general court.[90]

The states with unicameral legislatures faced different problems distributing powers to the executive councils. Pennsylvania's executive council of twelve was the only such council popularly elected. It was also the only executive council to participate in the election of a state's chief executive officer, the president. The council joined the house in a ballot to elect one of the councillors as president. After serving a three-year term, a councillor was technically ineligible for four years, but because elections were held triennially, a former councillor was effectively barred from the council for six years. The council also joined the president in exercising the executive's ample patronage powers. Together, they carried out all of the other executive tasks of government. The council acted as an upper house only when it served as a court of impeachment.[91]

Georgia operated with a unicameral legislature and an executive council to the governor. The constitution provided that the house annually elect to the executive council two members from each county entitled to ten representatives. Those remaining composed the legislature. Voting by county, the council, as in other states, advised the governor about calling emergency sessions of the house and making interim appointments. Councillors also served a legislative function. They reviewed, commented upon, and suggested amendments to bills sent to them by the house.[92]

New York was the only state not to create an executive council to advise the governor. Instead, the provincial congress established the councils of appointment and revision. The general assembly elected one senator from each of New York's four "great" senatorial districts to serve with the governor as members of the council of appointment, which selected most of the state's officials. The governor also served as a member of the council of revision with the chancellor and supreme court justices. The council possessed a suspensive veto, which could be overridden only with a two-thirds vote in each house of the legislature. In both councils, the governor could cast only one vote.[93]

The creation of executive councils reveals much about the framers' understandings of the contours of government and of the separation of powers. Neglect of these bodies is understandable: they were designed to curb governors who held diminished power, and they receded quickly from the political and constitutional scene. But their very formation indicated a desire to divide the functions of the old colonial councils. All of the constitutions, except those of New Jersey and South Carolina, affirmed the commitment to a separation of powers by stripping the councils of their traditional judicial functions. And all states but New Jersey, South Carolina, and New Hampshire carefully excluded councillors from seats in the legislatures.

By dividing the old councils' labors between executive and legislative councils, the framers furthered their effort to divide the powers of government among the different branches. The constitutions assigned the old councils' executive functions to executive councils and its legislative ones to the legislatures. They excluded the executive from the legislative process by eliminating the gubernatorial veto, though in New Jersey and New Hampshire they granted the executives a vote in the upper houses. When Massachusetts constitutional convention delegates adopted a suspensive gubernatorial veto, they defended it on the twin grounds that it would protect executive independence and strengthen the separation of powers. Framers also prohibited executive and judicial officeholders from sitting in the legislature. Anything less than a rigorous separation of powers would place unlimited power in the hands of one man or group of men. As the Boston town meeting instructed its representatives in early 1776: "It is essential to liberty that the legislative, judicial, and executive powers of Government be, as nearly as possible, independent of, and separate from each other; for where they are united in the same person or number of persons, there would be wanting that mutual check which is the principal security against the making of arbitrary laws, and a wanton exercise of power in the execution of them."[94]

Power Should Be

a Check to Power

Bicameralism and the

Reinvention of Mixed

Government

7

    Just as the fear of tyrannical power shaped how constitution makers understood the rule of law, the suffrage, and the separation of powers, so too did it influence the contours of the state legislatures. Despite the cry of a few unicameralists for an unchecked single assembly, all of the state constitutions established constitutional controls over the various assemblies, whether unicameral or bicameral.

    Support for bicameralism sprang from two pockets of concern: the danger that the legislature would represent the people too well and the threat that it would establish legislative tyranny. In traditional mixed-government theory, the house of representatives embodied "the people," who were virtuous and honest, but who were also passionate and acted in haste. Unchecked, a body of representatives was presumed incapable of tyranny but disposed to licentiousness. Therefore, a legislature required a second, "upper" house to impart wisdom to all legislative measures. Such a council or senate would have to be populated by individuals replete with wisdom and with interests different from those of the mass of people. But even men who advocated bicameral legislatures on the conventional grounds of mixed government also founded their pleas on the more basic dread of legislative tyranny. Joined by bicameralists who drew no social distinctions between the two houses and even by unicameralists, they believed that an unchecked single assembly would establish arbitrary government.

Mixed Government

The theory of mixed government built upon the classical belief that there were three simple forms of government—monarchy, aristocracy, and democracy. Each had its positive and negative attributes. Monarchies allowed government to act with power and dispatch, but, if unchecked, they turned to despotism. Aristocrats—in England, the Lords Temporal and Spiritual—lent wisdom to government but, if unlimited, transformed government into an oligarchy ruling for its own benefit. A democratic government had virtue and honesty but, if not hindered, degenerated into anarchy, mob rule, and licentiousness.

England's mixed government, so the argument went, mixed and balanced three forms of government. But it was especially effective because it purportedly embodied English society. The three parts of government represented the three social estates of the realm—the king, the nobility, and the people. The people checked the nobility and the nobility checked the people; the king checked both, as both checked the king. As a result, the government balanced so carefully the interests of society's estates that it displayed all of the good attributes of each but minimized the evil ones; it blended, in the words of one revolutionary, "virtue, wisdom, and power."[1] The constitution seemed to keep the estates of the realm in careful equipoise and thereby preserved the liberties of the people.

Colonists touted the virtues of English mixed government and assumed that their provincial governments emulated the English system. Colonies, after all, boasted equivalents of the monarch (the governor), aristocracy (the council), and democracy (the houses of representatives). To be sure, the likenesses were inexact, but many assumed that, over time, the systems would become increasingly alike.[2] And throughout much of the colonial era, the lower houses attempted to assume powers in the colonies like those the House of Commons enjoyed in England.[3]

In the eighteenth century, colonists worried about and sought to reduce the governors' extensive formal powers, which seemed greater than those of the Crown in England after the Glorious Revolution of 1688–89. The Crown could not create courts or remove judges at pleasure, but governors could. The Crown could not prevent new parliamentary elections every seven years; nor could it terminate that body. But governors could call elections and convene assemblies whenever they wished. The Crown confronted an independent aristocracy, as well as the House of Commons; in royal colonies, officials chose councillors who served at the pleasure of the Crown. And, finally, whereas the Crown had relinquished the veto in the early eighteenth century, governors retained absolute vetoes over provincial legislation.[4]

The governors' powers were more formidable on paper than in practice, for they substantially depended upon the assemblies. Most important, their salaries often required annual legislative authorization. Governors also lacked the informal powers of the king's ministers, especially patronage and control of minuscule electorates.

Both colonists and the governors also fretted about the absence of an independent aristocracy. Colonists regarded councillors as too dependent upon the governors, and governors believed them too reliant upon the people. Councillors served at the pleasure of the Crown or proprietor and therefore could not fulfill the role of an independent middle power. But the members of the councils were also wealthy men whose interests often lay in their colonies, not with the Crown and governor. Governors therefore could not rely upon councillors to do their bidding.

For different reasons, then, both royal administrators and colonists wrestled with the problem of cultivating a nobility to balance the powers of the governors and the people. Where councillors held office at royal pleasure, the lower houses tried to detach them from the governor, and where they were appointed locally (as in Massachusetts), the governors sought to free them from popular authority. Assuming that the colonies were too immature to sustain or warrant a hereditary aristocracy, some colonial officials proposed a lifetime peerage and membership in the council for the wealthiest colonists. Others advocated the lifetime appointment of councillors.[5]

Revolutionaries responded to their colonial experience by transforming the role of the magistracy. First, they made executives dependent upon the legislatures or the electorates for their offices. Then, although framers did not render the executive entirely powerless, they eliminated the governor's veto power and substantially reduced or eradicated his patronage power. By drastically weakening the governors, constitutionalists undermined their own efforts to devise balanced and mixed governments; nonetheless, they retained their commitment to such governments. As one of Maryland's congressional delegates, Benjamin Rumsey, asked of the new state government: "What sort of a Constitution have they framed? How far monarchical, aristocratick, or democratick? how far a mixture? how balanced each power? It is a matter of great importance to a subject of a State that power should be well and equally balanced."[6]

Defenders of mixed government predicated their arguments on the traditional gentry belief that ordinary people were honest and well meaning but gullible and easily swayed by others.[7] General Nathanael Greene urged the Continental Congress "to render the poorer sort of people as easy and happy . . . as possible; for they are creatures of a day, and present gain and gratification, though small, has more weight with them than much greater advantages at a distance."[8] Pennsylvania's Provost William Smith, writing as "Cato," declared that "the people generally judge right, when the whole truth is plainly laid before them; but through inattention in some, and fondness for novelty in others," were easily deceived and would "adopt what cooler reflection and future dear-bought experience may prove to be ruinous."[9] Because the people were "more influenced by their passions than by their reason," one Virginia defender of an established church warned, they would not voluntarily support good ministers.[10] Nor could judicial power be entrusted to "the honest, but too often misinformed multitude."[11] The mass of men, Alexander Hamilton asserted in late 1775, "have not a sufficient stock of reason and knowlege [*sic*] to guide them." When "the unthinking populace" became "loosened from their attachment to ancient establishments and courses, they seem to grow giddy and are apt more or less to run into anarchy."[12]

Mixed-government advocates, who assumed that delegates would act just as ardently and as heedlessly as the people they represented, argued that if an aristocracy did not check "the people," the resulting democratic government would inevitably sink into licentiousness.[13] These views were most fully articulated by opponents of Pennsylvania's unicameral legislature. Forced to make explicit their assumptions, they explained why simple governments crumbled and mixed governments flourished. Just after the Pennsylvania constitutional convention completed its work, one member, Benjamin Rush, denounced his colleagues' production for being "too much upon the democratical order, for liberty is as apt to degenerate into licentiousness as power is to become arbitrary. Restraints therefore are as necessary in the former as the latter case."[14] Another opponent of the Pennsylvania constitution agreed: "From the weakness and depravity of human nature power is apt to become absolute, and liberty to run into licentiousness. The perfection of government consists in laying both under proper restraints."[15] Repeating the mixed-government litany, Philadelphians meeting to oppose the constitution instructed their representatives to the first Pennsylvania state legislature to "consider well, that all Government is founded in the weakness and depravity of human nature, and that the perfection of Government consists in forming its powers in such a manner as shall most effectually guard against arbitrary power on the one hand and licentiousness on the other."[16]

"Demophilus" of Pennsylvania developed the case for a mixed government in which the people participated but did not dominate. He contended that a single legislature was potentially "fatal." Good government required "*wisdom*" and "*vigilance*," virtues that could be found only in compound governments, and which ordinary citizens did not possess. "Men busied with the common concerns of rural or mercantile life can hardly find leisure to acquaint themselves with all the requisites which render men judges of the expedience or danger of every article proposed to form a code of laws." An assembly of farmers, merchants, and mechanics could never perform that task. Such men, "Demophilus" asserted, were "honest" and would follow their ample fund of common sense in writing legislation, but they would not and could not weigh the consequences of their actions. As honest citizens, though, they possessed the requisite vigilance to protect themselves and "the people's purse-strings" against a greedy government of the wealthy, which, if unchecked, would "saddle" the people with "placemen and pensioners."[17]

More troublesome than agreeing upon the need for a "wise" upper house was identifying sage men in a society composed of weakly ranked men. Who would constitute "the aristocratical department" of the legislature when there was no securely aristocratic class?[18] Republicans rejected summarily an inherited aristocracy, but looked toward the existence of a natural aristocracy of able and wise men.

But who were natural aristocrats? "Owners of substantial property," answered the wealthy. William Hooper urged the North Carolina provincial congress to create an upper house "selected for their Wisdom, remarkable Integrity, or that weight which arises from property and gives Independence and Impartiality to the human mind."[19] In a critique of the proposed Massachusetts constitution of 1778, an Essex County meeting demanded an upper house composed of people with "the greatest wisdom, firmness, consistency, and perseverance." Such qualities, the *Essex Result* concluded, would be found "among gentlemen of education, fortune and leisure." Only such people would have both the ability and time for reading and contemplation. "Among gentlemen of education, fortune and leisure, we shall find the largest number of men, possessed of wisdom, learning, and a firmness and consistency of character."[20]

The authors of constitutions in most bicameral states agreed that property evidenced a measure of wisdom. They required senators to own substantial amounts of property, more than demanded of representatives. They also distinguished between the houses by giving them different electoral bases, by making the upper houses much smaller than the houses of representatives, and by giving senators longer terms.

Nevertheless, the state constitutions often revealed the framers' qualms about mixed government. The property requirements were sometimes (though not always) higher for senators than representatives, but were usually low enough to admit many of the merely well-to-do into the senates. The terms of office were sometimes (though not always) longer for senators but not substantially so. And while the apportionment of senators differed from the apportionment of representatives, the similarities were often more striking than the differences. Finally, and most importantly, although the constitution makers were committed to the idea of an independent senate, they also feared such a senate. In the end, virtually all opted for safety from the senate, *not* safety from the people, and made senators dependent upon voters for election at regular intervals.

The framers in five states rejected the association between senatorial wisdom and considerable property holding. Virginia and Delaware simply required that members of both houses be eligible voters. New York's constitution and the temporary constitutions of New Hampshire and South Carolina (both ratified in 1776) demanded that senators be freeholders ("reputable freeholder[s]" in New Hampshire), although the permanent constitutions of South Carolina (1778) and New Hampshire (1784) included special senatorial property qualifications.[21]

Virginia convention delegates spurned a hierarchy of property qualifications for officeholders. Convention president Edmund Pendleton desired a senate composed of men who held "great property to secure their Attachment." But he "never mentioned it" at the convention, where it "seemed so disagreable to the temper of the times."[22] He was right. When George Mason, the primary author of the Virginia constitution, proposed steep property qualifications for members of the senate (£2,000 in real estate) and the house (£1,000), the delegates summarily rejected them. And the men who subsequently served in the senate and House of Delegates were substantially less wealthy than those who had been members of the council or House of Burgesses before the Revolution.[23]

The unicameral states—Pennsylvania, Georgia, and Vermont—obviously had no senates and therefore no special property requirements for nonexistent senates. But they require consideration because, when added to Delaware, New York, New Hampshire (in 1776), South Carolina (in 1776), and Virginia, eight of the twelve constitution-writing states rejected the idea of singling out "the senatorial part" of society for an upper house.

Only three states—Maryland, New Jersey, and South Carolina (in 1778)—demanded considerable wealth of their senators. In South Carolina, house members met the same qualifications as voters, but senators needed a freehold worth £2,000 "currency clear of debts." The constitution also allowed nonresidents to serve in the senate if they owned a freehold in the district worth £7,000.[24] The New Jersey constitution insisted upon the possession of a £500 estate for representatives and a £1,000 estate for senators.[25] Like New Jersey's, Maryland's house members had to own property (real or personal) worth £500 and its senators property valued at £1,000, both calculated in depreciating "current money."[26]

Even in those three states, constitution makers set minimum requirements for senators substantially *lower* than the actual wealth of colonial councillors and even assemblymen. According to Jackson Turner Main's careful analysis, in New Jersey and Maryland, four out of every five assemblymen were what Main calls "well-to-do" or "wealthy"—that is, men worth at least £2,000. In South Carolina, all of the representatives possessed at least £2,000 estates, and two-thirds held estates valued at £5,000 or more. Main also judges that men owning 500 acres, "for the time not a big estate," would satisfy the requirements in Maryland and New Jersey, though South Carolina's criteria were "much more restrictive."[27]

The requirements in Massachusetts, New Hampshire (in 1784), and North Carolina were much lower. Massachusetts specified that a house member own a £100 freehold or a £200 personal estate and a senator possess a freehold valued at £300, a personal estate worth £600, or some combination of wealth amounting to at least £600. In 1784, New Hampshire required senators to own £200 freeholds (the same as required of representatives in 1776) and representatives £100 estates. In North Carolina, house members claimed freeholds of at least 100 acres and senators 300 acres.[28]

The framers of state constitutions understood the implications of these choices for upper houses. They surely did not have at hand Main's tabulations. Yet they recognized that, in order to replicate the elite status of colonial councillors, they had to raise the requirement dramatically. They acted otherwise. Constitution writers knew that they were opening the upper house to a substantial minority of the electorate, not the handful of individuals presumed to belong to a natural aristocracy.[29]

In addition to establishing different standards of wealth for senators, two states sought mixed governments by means of unique senatorial electorates. The North Carolina constitution enfranchised male taxpayers in house elections, but required senate electors to own fifty-acre freeholds. In New York, senate electors needed to own freeholds valued at £100 "clear of debts," five times the property requirement for house electors but low enough to allow most farmers to vote. Special property qualifications for senate electors, constitution makers hoped, would establish a separate artificial estate in society.[30]

Maryland's provincial convention delegates tried to attain a mixed government through indirect election. It created an intermediate electorate between ordinary voters and senators. Voters in each county chose two senatorial electors; Baltimore and Annapolis voters selected one each. The electors (whose wealth equaled that demanded of representatives) then selected the state senate.

Of perhaps greater significance than those three isolated efforts were decisions in all other states to allow qualified electors to vote in every popular election. In the other bicameral states, any inhabitant eligible to vote in house elections could also vote directly for senators. Virginia convention delegates rejected George Mason's proposal for indirect election of senators and insisted upon a direct, popular vote.[31]

The size and apportionment of representation in the upper houses also revealed the constitution makers' ambivalence about the nature of the senate. In theory, smaller senates would have enabled senators to represent larger, and therefore different, constituencies than those of members of houses of representatives. The framers did distinguish senates from houses by making the upper house much smaller than the lower. For example, New York's senate had 24 members; its house had 70. South Carolina's senate had 13 members in 1776 and 29 in 1778, compared to 202 members of the house under both constitutions. The New Hampshire Senate had 12 and, though representation varied in the house according to how many towns sent representatives, in 1786 there were 88 house members. North Carolina's senate accommodated slightly less than half of the house's membership; Delaware's was three-sevenths; and New Jersey's legislative council was one-third the size of the house.[32]

In several states, revolutionaries minimized the distinctive characteristics of their smaller senates by using the same representative units that they employed for the lower houses. The New Jersey and North Carolina constitutions gave one senator to each county, but New Jersey voters chose three representatives and North Carolinians two. Delaware's constitution assigned three senators and seven delegates to each county. With a few exceptions, the South Carolina constitution of 1778 allocated one or two senators to each parish or district, which had substantially larger numbers of representatives, usually six or ten.[33]

More significant differences in the apportionment of senators and representatives appeared in Virginia, New York, and Maryland. New York and Virginia, in the absence of special property qualifications for senators, constructed senatorial districts comprising several counties. To create Virginia's twenty-four-member senate, the constitution divided the state into twenty-four districts and authorized each district to elect a senator. Each Virginia district was created from two or more counties, a method not substantially different from the one delegate allotted to each county. New York went further. It grouped its counties into four "great districts" and apportioned representation among the districts roughly by population. It also provided that the legislature reapportion representation in the senate according to the number of senate electors (£100 freeholders) in each district after each septennial census. Maryland's constitution required electors to choose nine senators from the western shore and six from the eastern.[34]

Massachusetts and New Hampshire (in 1784) deviated sharply from the practices of other states. Although convention delegates in those states adopted the traditional view that an upper house should embody the aristocratic wisdom of propertied men, they transformed the argument into the assertion that property itself required protection and therefore representation. Both Massachusetts and New Hampshire (in 1784) apportioned senatorial representation among electoral districts according to taxes paid, a method rejected in every other state.[35] Thus, four of the states—Maryland, New York, Massachusetts, and New Hampshire (1784)—created senates with substantially different constituencies than those of their houses of representatives.

Nevertheless, efforts to create "aristocratic" senates failed miserably. And senators acted much like representatives. Scholars have treated the similar apportionment of representation in the senates and the houses, the popular election of senators, the inadequate effort to distinguish senate and house constituencies, and the relatively low pecuniary qualifications for senators as mistakes—as if the framers simply miscalculated in their efforts to create truly independent, cosmopolitan senates.[36]

On the contrary, those decisions were conscious choices made by an elite roughly knowledgeable about the sorts of men who could meet different property qualifications. Their decisions expressed the ambivalence of many. Torn between faith in mixed government and a pervasive, deep-seated fear of any unrestrained power, they reinterpreted the meaning of mixed government for the American polity and thereby transformed it.

Constitution makers revealed their ambivalence about the nature of the senate when they considered the independence of the upper house of the state legislature. If an upper house were to serve its purpose as a middle power, it had to be independent of the monarch and of the people. By definition, an upper house could not represent the people. And since governors were so weakened by the constitutions, the biggest concern was fashioning a senate truly independent of the people. But, if the people were the source of all governmental authority, as virtually all revolutionary leaders acknowledged, then how could constitution writers create an independent upper house?

Some, like Virginia's Thomas Jefferson and Edmund Pendleton, recognized that the length of a senator's term would dictate his independence. Committed to the idea of mixed government, both men were unhappy about the constitution's apparent failure to establish the Virginia senate's institutional independence. Jefferson, in the first of three drafts of a state constitution, had proposed that senators be elected by representatives, but "when appointed shall be in for life."[37] As he began the second draft, he initially retained the senators' life tenure, but then struck it out and opted for a nine-year term, with one-third of the body vacating every three years. Senators, he added, "shall be for ever incapable of being reappointed to that house."[38]

Pendleton was disturbed by Jefferson's final draft, as well as the convention's. "You proposed their Election by the House of Representatives," he wrote, "making them the mere creatures of that body and of course wholly unfit to correct their Errors or Allay casual heats which will at times arise in all large bodies." Pendleton worried that, even in a popular election, "delegates will have too much influence in the Senate Elections." He wished the two houses "totally independant of each other and to say the truth of the people too, after Election"—that is, a senate of wealthy men holding lifetime appointments.[39]

With Pendleton, Jefferson sought a senate of "the wisest men," (though not the wealthiest) who would be "perfectly independent when chosen." He despised the idea of direct popular election of senators: "I have ever observed that a choice by the people themselves is not generally distinguished for it's wisdom. This first secretion from them is usually crude and heterogeneous." It was better to "give to those so chosen by the people a second choice themselves, and they generally will chuse wise men." Yet a nine-year, nonrenewable term, he insisted, would make senators entirely independent of their electors. If eligible for reelection, "they would be casting their eyes forward to the period of election (however distant) and be currying favor with the electors, and consequently dependent on them." He proposed a nine-year term rather than life so "that they might have an idea that they were at a certain period to return into the mass of the people and become the governed instead of the governors which might still keep alive that regard to the public good that otherwise they might perhaps be induced by their independance to forget." Committed though he was to a term limit, he "could submit, tho' not so willingly to an appointment for life, or to any thing rather than a mere creation by and dependance on the people."[40]

Such recommendations, had they been adopted, might have secured senatorial independence. But they were vigorously and often angrily denounced by others and ignored by the authors of the state constitutions. Virginia convention delegates rejected Carter Braxton's proposal for a senate with lifetime tenure and ousted him from the province's Continental Congress delegation.[41] And they ignored Jefferson's proposal for a single nine-year term. Pendleton, the convention's presiding officer and a man of enormous influence, did not even present his plan for lifetime tenure because he was certain the delegates would disregard it.[42]

Constitution makers were obviously torn between their desire to fashion upper houses independent of the people and their apprehensions about making them truly independent. Maryland came closest with five-year terms and the provision that senators elect interim members to fill vacant seats.[43] Three other states established terms longer than the one year served by lower house members. Virginia and New York senators held their positions for four years, and in Delaware the number was three. But four states—Massachusetts, New Hampshire (in 1784), New Jersey, and North Carolina—stipulated annual elections for their upper houses. South Carolina's first constitutions specified biennial elections for both houses. Of the constitution-writing states, only four gave senators longer terms than representatives.

In those four states, some hoped that the longer terms would, in Richard Henry Lee's phrase, "answer the purpose of an independant middle power,"[44] but theirs was a wish unfulfilled. However much longer senate terms might be than those in the house, the terms were relatively short. Constitution makers distrusted a truly independent senate with a lifetime tenure or even the kind of nine-year, nonrenewable term suggested by Jefferson.[45] Because senators faced reelection by the voters, they became effectively dependent upon and representative of the people.

Even the most vigorous advocates of mixed government wanted to deny genuine independence to the upper houses. In Pennsylvania, a "Farmer" asserted that the genius of Americans "is of a monarchical spirit; this is natural from the government they have ever lived under." Therefore, he claimed, they rejected the idea of a "simple Republick." They also repudiated simplicity because of "the great distinction of persons, and difference in their estates or property, which cooperates strongly with the genius of the people in favour of monarchy." Thus, a mixed government was best. Most states had adopted one, "but in some of them too much power is delegated from the people."

Although "Farmer" recommended a mixed government "like what they have always been use to, viz: a supreme executive magistrate (with a necessary check) and two orders in the body of legislation," his plan diverged markedly from colonial antecedents. The closest he came was to suggest that members of the Continental Congress, in place of the king or proprietor, appoint the governor. Otherwise, the executive would be president of the legislative council and cast only one vote, a far cry from the absolute gubernatorial veto. "Farmer" also proposed a paltry three-year term for legislative councillors and insisted that both houses "derive their authority from the people only, and in a different manner from what has been usual."

Why did such an ardent advocate of mixed government depart so widely from its tenets? The answer lay in his conviction that any power unchecked by the people imperiled their liberties. As "Farmer" himself asserted: "It should be constantly in mind that the government of these States are founded on the authority of the people only; and therefore, that there should be sufficient power left in their hands always to prevent the delegated power from becoming dangerous to their liberty."[46]

This concern about unrestrained legislative power impelled many advocates of mixed government to urge the creation of an upper house.[47] If power were consolidated in a single body of representatives, tyranny would inevitably follow. North Carolina's William Hooper denounced a unicameral legislature as "a many headed Monster which without any check must soon defeat the very purposes for which it was created." Inevitably, it would "become a Tyranny dreadful in proportion to the numbers which compose it." Once "possessed of power uncontrolled," legislators would "put themselves free from the restraint of those who made them, and . . . make their own political existence perpetual." Unrestrained by an upper house, representatives of the people would become their oppressors.[48] "Democraticus" of Virginia also advocated mixed government to protect the people from a self-aggrandizing legislature, as well as to protect them from themselves. Because he apprehended that "an arbitrary representative body may find means of imposing partial temporary laws on the people," he recommended an indirectly elected small upper house composed "of the ablest men in the nation."[49] In Massachusetts, the *Essex Result* rejected the idea of a single assembly not only because its "judgments" would be "frequently absurd and inconsistent," but because it would be inclined to make itself perpetual, "to be avaricious, and to exempt itself from the burdens it lays upon it's constituents."[50]

In Massachusetts, a prolific analyst of state constitutions, the Rev. William Gordon, also examined various reasons why a republic required a complex legislature. He warned that a unicameral legislature would inevitably lead to legislative tyranny. Then, he urged the retention of a legislative council "as an essential branch of the Legislature," so that laws "may be the more matured for publick service." "Should the Assembly fall into the vices, follies, and frailties of individuals, they may have the assistance of the Council to recover them before they have rendered themselves ridiculous, or have thrown the State into a convulsion." But Gordon assumed that, because the council's members were "as much the Representatives of the people as the House," they should be chosen annually by popular election.[51]

Gordon, Hooper, "Democraticus," and the Essex County convention revealed an important strain in mixed-government theory that departed from traditional thinking. Americans dreaded tyranny and tried to restrain governmental power by recreating mixed governments. But they contorted the original idea so much that they created something altogether new. They eliminated the governor from the legislature or otherwise weakened the office; they also rendered the senate both dependent upon and representative of the people. They curbed the dangerous lower house with an upper house not only because an unchecked lower house would lead to licentiousness and anarchy, but because, if unchecked, it would establish arbitrary government.

Such conclusions led the revolutionary generation toward a rationale for bicameralism that departed from traditional mixed-government ideas and embraced the view that two houses, both representing the people, acted as checks upon each other. Richard Henry Lee, who as late as May 1776 had proposed an upper house elected by the assembly for a seven-year term and retention of the gubernatorial veto, jubilantly declared a month later that the Virginia constitution was "very much of the democratic kind, altho' a Governor and second branch of legislation are admitted. . . . Both the Houses of the Legislature are chosen by the whole body of the people." With his contemporaries, Lee understood that the popular election of senators in effect made members of both houses representatives of the people. Thus, even though the North Carolina constitution imposed a 300-acre freehold qualification for senators (compared to 100 acres for commoners) and a special fifty-acre freehold qualification for senatorial electors, it nevertheless asserted "that the legislative authority shall be vested in two distinct branches, both dependent on the people," and that both the senate and the house "shall be composed of Representatives" chosen in annual popular elections.[52]

John Adams summarized the mixed motives underlaying the creation of senates in his *Thoughts on Government*, a treatise largely responsible for the widespread adoption of bicameral legislatures. Adams greatly distrusted "a Single Assembly" because it was "liable to all the Vices, Follies, and Frailties of an Individual—subject to fits of Humour, Transports of Passion, Partialities of Prejudice." As a consequence, it would "make hasty Results and Absurd Judgments." Adams also expressed the mixed-government concern about future conflict "if the legislative power is wholly in one Assembly, and the executive in another, or in a single person." The republic would collapse, he predicted, in "a downright civil War, between the Legislative and Executive," after which the victor would gain "the whole power." He therefore recommended adoption of "a distin[c]t Assembly . . . as a mediator" between the two.[53]

But Adams was equally concerned about the dangers posed by an unbounded, potentially arbitrary legislature. Such a body was "apt to grow Avaricious, and in Time would not Scruple to exempt itself from Burdens, which it would lay upon its Constituents, without Sympathy." Even worse, a "Single Assembly will become ambitious, and after Some Time will vote itself perpetual." He pointedly recalled England's Long Parliament and the example of Holland, where assemblymen granted themselves seats for life and power to fill vacancies "without any application to constituents at all."[54]

Adams thus advocated a second house of the legislature, both to provide a balance between democracy and monarchy and to curb the potentially tyrannical power of an unchecked single assembly. His uneasiness arose from his apprehension that a unicameral legislature would render illconsidered, vague, and potentially harmful decisions and establish legislative tyranny. A second house would defend the people against an assembly greedy for power and mediate between the executive and the lower house.

Bicameralism as a Check on Unlimited Power

Many revolutionaries dispensed altogether with the idea of mixed government and envisioned a senate simply as an institutional restraint on the power of the representatives. These men based their views on the assumption that, in a republic, there could be only one interest—that of the people. To organize government around conflicting estates would encourage and even bless political disagreement. At the same time, the framers also assumed that when men held unchecked power they became dangerous. Therefore, they had little difficulty thinking of a bicameral legislature as two legislative bodies, both elected by and representative of the people, whose primary task was to contain one another's pretensions to unlimited power and together secure the common good.

Those bicameralists, as well as men who supported a single assembly, envisioned an undivided, harmonious polity. "Having no rank above that of freemen," the essayist "Salus Populi" declared, "she has but one interest to consult, and that interest, (blessed be *God* for it,) is the true and only interest of men as members of society."[55] Those who praised the English constitution, wrote another, denounced republican government. "Admitting the mixed government of Britain to be the best," he decided, "*we* cannot enjoy it, for want of its essential constituents."[56]

The assumption of homogeneity also informed General John Sullivan's understanding of a proper constitution for his home province, New Hampshire. Upon learning that the Continental Congress had granted New Hampshire the authority to form its own government, Sullivan, a former congressional delegate from the province, offered extensive recommendations to the provincial congress. Believing there was only one interest in society and assuming that government should promote "the Good of the People," he wrote from the field that a "Government which admits of contrary or clashing Interests, is imperfect, and must work its own Ruin." The eventual "Ruin" of England's "Empire," he predicted, would show "the Folly and Danger of establishing a government consisting of different Branches, having Seperate and distinct Interests." The theory of mixed government itself was wrong because the royal prerogative and "Checks upon the Licentiousness of the People, are only the Children of ambitious, or designing Men, no such Thing being Necessary." Indeed, when in the past "the people" have torn down governments by "Rage and Violence," invariably it was caused by placing in "their Rulers too extensive a Power." The "Tumults at Rome" arose when "Dictators and others were . . . made in some Sort independent of the People."[57]

Therefore, Sullivan argued, New Hampshire needed a government whose only goal was "the Good of the whole," attainable only if "one Interest should unite the several governing Branches." Concerned about "the incontrolable Power so much sought after by designing Men," he supported a complex government with a governor (who possessed a suspensive veto), council, and house of representatives. All officials would face frequent popular elections, which "should operate as a Check upon their Conduct." In effect, Sullivan proposed a government in which all branches depended directly upon and represented the people, and which the citizenry distrusted.[58]

Sullivan's argument struck a deep chord. The citizens of Orange County, North Carolina, instructed their delegates to the provincial congress to create a bicameral legislature, "each independent of the other and both dependent on the people."[59] The deputies of the militia battalions of Anne Arundel County, Maryland, insisted "that the Legislative may be so constituted as never to be able to form an interest of its own separate from the interest of the community at large, it is necessary its branches should be independent of, and balance, each other, and all dependent on the people."[60] Another Marylander asserted that any "government of a free people . . . consists of *authorities* derived from the people, and these *authorities* never cease to be conditional." He repudiated the mixed-government assumption of the need for an independent upper house, "for an independence of them [the people] destroys the idea of liberty."[61] A New Hampshire champion of a popularly elected bicameral legislature contended, "The more simple, and the more immediately dependent . . . the authority is upon the people the better, because it must be granted that they themselves are the best guardians of their own liberties."[62] Another writer urged that the Massachusetts lower house be called a house of assembly, not a house of representatives, because members of both houses represented the people.[63]

A bicameral legislature, composed of two equally representative branches, would ward off the dangers of an unrestrained single assembly. The English constitution, a Rhode Islander argued, created "*Parliaments*, as a curb on *kings and ministers*; but they neglected to reserve to *the people*, a regular and constitutional method of exerting their power in curbing of *parliaments*." In order "*to prevent the abuse of power*," he argued, "*it is neces-*

sary . . . that power should be a check to power." [64] Only two houses, both chosen by popular election and restraining one another, could protect the people's liberty.

The call for a second house to prevent the tyranny of a single assembly was heard up and down the coast and included constitutional radicals and conservatives. New York's conservative Gouverneur Morris, who brooded that New York's recently established bicameral legislature would make governance difficult, nevertheless concluded that his countrymen required a complex legislature "because a simple Legislature soon possesses itself of too much Power for the Safety of its Subjects." [65] He supported the creation of a senate not because a house of representatives would represent the people too well, but because it might become an exclusive institution pursuing interests contrary to the public good. "An Independent Whig," the New York writer who had supported Thomas Paine's call for independence, firmly opposed his plan for a large unicameral legislature to govern the new confederation. Its members eventually would "be overtaken with the same distemper, that has of late prevailed in the British Parliament, declare themselves omnipotent, and imagine they have a *right*, because they are the representatives of the continent, to alter the fundamental principles and articles of agreement." [66] As North Carolina's fourth provincial congress attempted to draft a constitution in April 1776, delegate Thomas Jones explained that the congress intended to establish a bicameral legislature in which the "two Houses are to be a check upon each other as no law can be made without the Consent of both." [67]

The fullest articulation of the need to divide legislative power among two bodies came from Thomas Burke, a North Carolina delegate to the Continental Congress. His experience in Congress, he told Governor Richard Caswell in March 1777, revealed "that unlimited power can not be safely trusted to any man, or set of men, on earth." No men, he asserted, were more disinterested than his fellow delegates, who left their homes and private affairs for the public's good and who, because they served briefly, would gain nothing from increasing congressional power. Yet they sought power for congress because "Power of all kinds has an irresistible propensity to increase a desire for itself. It gives the passion of ambition a velocity which increases in its progress; and this is a passion which grows in proportion as it is gratified." "No one," Burke concluded, "has entertained a concerted design to increase the power" of Congress. Delegates held no consistent position about the proper extent of congressional power; yet they endeavored to increase congressional power "from ignorance of what such a being ought to be, and from the delusive intoxication which power materially imposes on the human mind." The result inescapably would be "an abuse and corruption of power."

Burke pointed to Pennsylvania as a case in point. "I am told," he wrote, "Dr. Franklin persuaded them, by a simile, to reject a second branch of the Legislature. He said, two branches would resemble a wagon with two horses at the tongue two at the tail, who by pulling opposite ways would keep the machine still. I think the simile would have been more apt, had it represented four horses yoked to the tongue, whose business it is to assist one another in pulling on the plains, and up hill, and through all difficult places, but in going down hill the two hind-most should oppose the motion of the machine, and prevent its running too fast, to the prejudice—of horses themselves and all concerned."[68]

The two houses in Thomas Burke's legislature would cooperate in pursuit of the commonweal, but prevent one another from racing headlong toward tyranny.

Unicameralism: Checked and Unchecked

Unicameralists, who were just as concerned as Thomas Burke about arbitrary government, saw bicameral legislatures destroying the natural harmony of American society. For its instructions to its delegates to the Massachusetts constitutional convention of 1779, the town of Gorham, Massachusetts, rummaged through the Bible and the history of ancient Rome for examples of the evils of bicameralism. The Jews and Romans thrived as long as they had one legislature but became miserable after dividing it, declared Gorham's citizens. "The Roman Senate was a happy Constitution of government and the Romans a happy People while the Patricians considered their interest the same with that of the Plebiens, but when the Patricians made their interest distinct from the Plebiens confusion and misery insued."[69] From such examples, "Salus Populi" concluded that "two or more distinct interests can never exist in society without finally destroying the liberties of the people."[70]

If bicameralism fostered conflict in the legislative process, several writers concluded, then unicameral assemblies would promote unity. "Philo-Alethias" of Delaware, writing in the fall of 1776, evaluated the various state constitutions and offered suggestions for the composition of a congress of the states. He worried that each of Delaware's four separate governing bodies—president, privy council, council, and assembly—would struggle for preeminence "till one of these powers becomes an aristocracy, and like *Aaron's* serpent swallows up the rest, or betrays the whole to some foreign Power." As an alternative, he recommended the establishment of a "simple government" with a supreme unicameral congress. Americans could not "be afraid of our liberty in such hands"; all representatives would be "bound by every law they make" and would be restrained by annual election and by exclusion from the congress after three years of service. Such a congress would "have all the expedition of a monarchy, and the deliberate counsel of a republick." Unconcerned about congress's "absolute" power, he compared this congress to "a great court of chancery, governed only by the eternal laws of equity, patriotism, and reason, in order more effectually to promote the safety, equality, industry, union, virtue, and happiness of *America*." The result would be "harmony and joy."[71]

Few unicameralists so easily assumed legislators' virtue; indeed, these men often were among the most cautious, seeking to restrain legislators by requiring a near consensus for lawmaking. In 1775, the citizens of Mecklenburg County, North Carolina, instructed their deputies to the provincial congress to support a unicameral legislature. They vigorously opposed the creation of an upper house. "You are instructed to vote that Legislation be not a divided right," they said, "and that no man or body of men be invested with a negative on the voice of the People duly collected." But the instructions also specified a *four-fifths* house majority.[72] Mecklenburg's citizens hoped to prevent oppressive legislators by demanding a virtual consensus of them before acting.

Those less extreme than the Mecklenburg group expected to curb the appetites of power-hungry legislators by requiring a considerable majority. In *Common Sense*, Thomas Paine tried to assuage misgivings about independence by suggesting that Americans would easily make the transition to republican government by means of a national congress with 390 members, who would choose a president annually from each state delegation in succession. To ensure "that nothing may pass into law but what is satisfactorily just," Paine also recommended that "three fifths of the Congress . . . be called a majority."[73] One Massachusetts writer argued against bicameralism when he asked: "Are we not all one body, and one general interest? Is not the good of the whole, the good of all?" Then, citing the sizable majorities demanded of legislatures in the Netherlands, Switzerland, and Genoa, he recommended a two-thirds majority for lawmaking.[74]

Of the three states adopting unicameral legislatures, two responded to the demand for extraordinary legislative majorities. Pennsylvania and Vermont required the presence of two-thirds of the members to constitute a quorum.[75] Georgia required only a majority present, as in every bicameral state.[76] These three states also sought other ways to curb the assembly.

Their creation of unicameral legislatures expressed not a willingness to grant unlimited power to a single house but a belief in the divisive, anti-republican character of a second house.

The Pennsylvania constitution, the most notorious of the three, utilized numerous methods to restrict legislative power. The constitution opened the assembly's deliberations to the public, required weekly publication of "the votes and proceedings of the general assembly," and enabled only two representatives to force a roll-call vote on any measure. By means of these three provisions, voters kept a watchful eye on their representatives; annual elections allowed them to remove dangerous legislators. Further, the constitution established term limits for representatives. It permitted "no person" to serve in the house "more than four years in seven."[77] After four years, representatives would return to the citizenry to "mix with the mass of the people, and feel at their leisure the effects of the laws which they have made."[78] The constitution, which limited the assembly by entrusting most government appointments to the popularly elected executive council and its president, adhered more closely to the doctrine of a separation of powers than the fundamental law of any other state.[79]

In a unique and controversial effort to involve citizens in the legislative process, the constitution effectively turned Pennsylvania voters into a second house by requiring that "all bills of public nature shall be printed for the consideration of the people, before they are read in general assembly the last time for debate and amendment"; the assembly could pass no laws (except in emergencies) until after another legislative election. As one defender of the constitution reminded Pennsylvanians: "You have the perusal, and consequent approbation of every law before it binds you; so that you must consent to be slaves before you can be made such. By this means the whole State becomes its own council, and every freeman in it is a counsellor, and the negative lies in the whole body politic, and not in a few grandees."[80]

Opponents furiously denounced the provision, some because they believed it gave too much power to the people and others because they believed the provision an ineffective check on the assembly. "The Mob made a second branch of Legislation," seethed North Carolina Congressman William Hooper. "Laws subjected to their revisal in order to refine them a Washing in ordure by way of purification. Taverns and dram shops are the councils to which the laws of this State are to be referred for approbation before they possess a binding Influence." Equally unhappy were those who considered "the people" to be incapable of curbing the legislature. Inevitably the assembly would get its way; it would appeal to "*state necessity*" and ignore popular consultation.[81] Benjamin Rush brushed aside the provision when he decried the legislature as "the only *unaccountable body of men* that ever existed in a free country."[82]

An even more controversial curb on the legislature was the very powerful council of censors, which would meet every seven years to review the constitution, recommend constitutional revisions, and judge "whether the legislative and executive branches of government have performed their duty as guardians of the people, or assumed to themselves, or exercised other or greater powers than they are intitled to by the constitution."[83] Foes denounced the council as a tyrannical attempt to prevent the people from revising their constitution as often as they wished; its defenders claimed that opponents just did not want anyone looking over their shoulders while they embezzled the state's money.[84]

The Georgia constitution, which placed fewer restrictions on its House of Assembly, did delay the legislative process. Aside from a vigorously asserted article dissolving the assembly every year, the constitution required that all bills pass three readings on separate days. After the second reading, the assembly sent the bill to the executive council, which returned it within five days to the assembly with recommendations for approval or revision. In this way, Georgians hoped to discourage hasty action on the part of the assembly.[85]

Vermont patriots drew upon the Pennsylvania constitution, and possibly Georgia's, to ensure that laws would "be more maturely considered, and the inconveniency of hasty determination as much as possible prevented." Vermont's constitution required that "all bills of public nature" be printed and circulated among the people and that no act but temporary, emergency measures "shall be passed into laws" until the general assembly's next session. Also as in Pennsylvania, Vermont established a septennial council of censors. Like Georgia, Vermont demanded that all legislation be offered to the governor and council "for their perusal and proposals of amendment."[86]

Although constitution writers in the unicameral states, especially Pennsylvania and Vermont, radically eliminated an upper house, their pervasive fear of power placed them closer to the revolutionary mainstream than historians have seen. Like bicameralists elsewhere, advocates of unicameral assemblies worried about the tyranny of unchecked legislative power. Unicameralists sought to restrain the house of representatives but by different means than the bicameralists proposed. Everywhere, framers wrote sections of the constitutions to curb legislative power, whether by hemming in a single assembly or, more often, by a second house.

Historians of constitutional development in revolutionary America have placed great emphasis on the significance of the *Essex Result*—the outcome of an Essex County, Massachusetts, meeting to consider ratification of the proposed (and defeated) Massachusetts constitution of 1778. Drafted by attorney Theophilus Parsons, the *Essex Result* took the American defense of an upper house in a direction very different from where the framers of the state constitutions intended, and one that Americans supposedly followed.[87]

Parsons, who endorsed the widely held assumption that possession of property was a crude measure of wisdom, demanded an upper house composed of people with "the greatest wisdom, firmness, consistency, and perseverance. These qualities will most probably be found amongst men of education and fortune," who alone had the ability and time for reading and contemplation.[88] "Among gentlemen of education, fortune and leisure, we shall find the largest number of men, possessed of wisdom, learning, and a firmness and consistency of character."

Parsons then reconceived the function of the upper house by portraying property as a separate interest in society that needed special protection. Legislation aimed to protect persons and property. Hence, a law pertaining to persons had to be approved by a majority of persons, and one affecting property by a majority of property holders. If it involved both, then the approval of both would be necessary. "For the property-holder parts with the controul over his person," he said, "as well as he who hath no property, and the former also parts with the controul over his property, of which the latter is destitute."[89] The Essex meeting recommended that the number of senators be apportioned by the taxes paid and that senators own substantially more property than representatives. The Massachusetts convention followed the *Essex Result*'s ideas and recommendations basing senatorial representation on taxation and blending corporate and population representation in the house. "The House of Representatives," explained convention delegates, "is intended as the Representative of the Persons and the Senate, of the property of the Common Wealth."[90]

In part because the Massachusetts convention largely adopted Parsons's views, his essay has often been credited by historians and political theorists as a critical document in the history of American constitutional thought and practice.[91] Many writers subsequently accepted the *Essex Result*'s contention that government acted upon both persons and property and that property needed protection. After all, Parsons was simply articulating an age-old, common-law maxim. These notions lay at the heart of William Blackstone's influential *Commentaries*, which were divided into "Persons" and "Property."

But Americans of the founding era rejected the notion that the senate should represent property and the house, persons.[92] During the forty years after the adoption of the Massachusetts constitution, only one other state (New Hampshire in 1784) apportioned senatorial representation by taxes paid.[93] Most of the rest made senates smaller than the lower houses but apportioned them by population, or some variation thereof. Over the next two generations, politicians occasionally defended an upper house on the grounds it provided special protection for property.[94]

The main defense of bicameralism lay elsewhere. As Gordon Wood persuasively argues, Federalists primarily based the establishment of the United States Senate on the perceived need for a divided legislative power.[95] Even though the Federalists often spoke in the language of mixed government, as had the framers in 1776, they perceived the Senate as representative of and accountable to the people and deliberately established no distinctive property requirements for senators.

From the beginning of the Revolution, constitution writers distrusted the houses of representatives and were unwilling to grant unlimited power to them. Even those who created unicameral legislatures sought to restrain them. But most framers believed that the best way to check an assembly was with a second house of the legislature. In English theory, the second house would represent a separate, aristocratic estate mediating between the Crown and the people, and checking both. But in the new American states, there was no hereditary aristocracy, and the new governors or presidents held relatively little power. In 1776, some Americans sought to fashion mixed governments, constructing their senates somewhat differently from houses of representatives. But they also refused to make senates too different and too independent; senators, they decided, never should pursue separate interests at the expense of public harmony. Constitutionalists called the senates "upper" houses, but then erected them in the image of the "lower" houses. Some convention delegates required senators to possess greater wealth than representatives, though (except for Maryland and South Carolina) not much more. And a handful gave senators longer terms than representatives, but (except, once again, Maryland) not much longer. Finally, a few created special constituencies for their senates, but (except in New York and, of course, Maryland) they were constituencies that bore a striking resemblance to those of representatives. Most state constitutions did *not* require senators to possess greater wealth; most did *not* grant senators longer terms, and most did *not* create special senatorial constituencies. Constitution makers fashioned senates after the houses because they embraced both the republican idea that all branches of government were dependent upon and representative of the people and the republican fear of a genuinely independent upper house.

★　★　★　★　★　★　★　★　★　★　Conclusion

The Mechanical Polity

At the foundation of the first state constitutions lay a new American theory of politics that blended devotion to the commonweal and commitment to the security of individual rights. The framers assumed self-interest would animate people, but they did not conclude therefrom that politics merely expressed conflict between self-interested individuals and groups. Instead, they had in mind an identifiable and obtainable public good different from the aggregated interests of individuals. In 1776, in 1789, and beyond, Americans held fast to the idea that there was a public good and that legislators and magistrates—properly curbed by one another and by a politically active citizenry—were obligated to pursue it. Of course, they disagreed about both the means and ends of that quest, but they agreed that there was a common good to seek. In the late 1780s, as Gordon Wood concedes, "depreciations of public virtue were still sporadic and premature."[1] Indeed, such "depreciations" would remain "sporadic," but not "premature"; nineteenth-century Americans would reconceptualize and resituate the idea of civic virtue without abandoning it.[2]

Revolutionaries easily combined their understanding of the common good with a belief in the inviolability of at least a few individual rights. Those beliefs together reaffirmed but also altered the vital assumption that politics expressed conflict between rulers and the people. American patriots redefined "the rulers" to include all those who wielded governmental power, legislators as well as magistrates. Citizens—through their state constitutions and votes, declarations of rights, systems of representation, separation of governmental powers, and division of legislative power—would protect both the commonweal and individual rights from dangerous rulers.

The framers of the first constitutions, then, brought to their task a well-developed American theory of republican constitutionalism, rooted in the soil of English constitutionalism but partially uprooted by the stormy years of imperial conflict. This "American science of politics" did not emerge during the Revolution and triumph only in 1789, as Wood and others argue. Rather, it was largely in place by 1776. Americans did not forge their new understanding of the political order in the internal conflicts of the War of Independence, but in the years of imperial controversy. What happened later was refinement, not invention. They did not need to learn from state legislative conduct that legislators did not embody the will of the people; they had learned that lesson from Parliament's behavior. Nor did they need to learn the necessity for written, permanent fundamental law that surrounded and contained all of government, or for declarations of rights, whether prefatory to plans of government or incorporated into those plans. Parliament's arbitrary behavior had already taught them those lessons as well. The revolutionaries also had learned from parliamentary acts the importance of direct representation in the legislature of all parts of a state by men who resided among their electors. They knew, too, that representatives required restraint by frequent elections in which a broad, active citizenry participated.

Parliament's claims of unlimited constitutional power drove constitution makers to frame governments that limited the powers of the legislatures and the executives. The framers adopted the doctrine of a separation of powers not merely to hobble the magistrate but to prohibit the legislature or the governor from seizing all governmental powers. And while some revolutionaries sought the restoration of mixed governments in their bicameral legislatures, others did not. But virtually all, including advocates of unicameral legislatures, sought to avert the consolidation of all governmental power in a single assembly.

From the beginning of the Revolution, patriot leaders viewed the creation of political society through the lens of their distinctly American political theory and, as a consequence, established polities that relied upon the mechanics of government to protect liberty and promote the common good. They did not confirm thereby the hegemony of liberal ideology and the death of classical republicanism. No such dichotomy animated revolutionary minds. American patriots, taken collectively, were neither liberals nor classical republicans, but revolutionary republicans who drew eclectically from many political, legal, and constitutional traditions. Constitution makers identified their task as the establishment of viable, permanent, republican governments that preserved the individual's liberties and pursued the public's interest. They were concerned as much about liberty to participate in government as about liberty from arbitrary government, and they began to see the two as inseparable. When they tried to deter the emergence of arbitrary government, they hoped to secure popular liberty and avert the arbitrary ruler's propensity to seek self-interest at the expense of the public. They simultaneously sought individual liberty, the common good, and the antithesis of arbitrary government, the rule of law.

The years of imperial controversy prompted colonists to reaffirm their adherence to the English constitution of restraint and to transform it. As did the English, the American patriots believed that government needed to be restricted. But unlike the English, who saw monarchical prerogative as the greatest menace to popular rights and the House of Commons as the independent defender of those rights, American revolutionaries believed that the arbitrary power of the king-in-Parliament, including the House of Commons, imperiled their liberties. No part of government—not the executive and not the legislative—could be trusted with unlimited power.

The crisis of 1774–75—when Parliament made the danger of the Declaratory Act reality and destroyed the charter protection Americans imagined they enjoyed—focused the colonists' attention on the need to curb government. Parliament's assertion of boundless legislative power convinced constitution makers that the danger of arbitrary government lay not only in the magistracy but also in the legislature. They believed Parliament had become a tyrant. Parliament's unconstitutional course convinced many revolutionaries that even ostensibly representative state assemblies could act despotically. After Parliament apparently refused to change its policies in the face of colonial resistance, American patriots concluded that no political body would restrain itself within uncertain constitutional bounds; nor would it alter its behavior, even when confronted by its unconstitutional acts.[3] This understanding forged the beginnings of a new constitutional tradition and distinctively American polity.

Fear of tyranny led Americans to deny legislative authority to draft the constitutions that framed and constrained all of government, including the legislature. With only one exception, they relied upon provincial congresses and constitutional conventions to draft constitutions. The provincial congresses were not legislatures; rather, they were transitory institutions that wielded executive and judicial, as well as legislative, power. Only the members of such bodies or of temporary constitutional conventions, with no permanent interest in the frame of government, could be trusted to write a constitution. Even then, delegates to the congresses assumed the need for popular approval of constitution making. Therefore, virtually all congresses ordered new elections for new political bodies. New York's required voters to instruct their representatives as to whether they desired a state constitution, and, in 1776, the Massachusetts House of

Representatives asked the towns to approve its proposed method for drafting a constitution. In special elections, framers sought support from the whole people, whom all regarded as sovereign. In so doing, they effectively created constitutional conventions. Those specially elected congresses continued to perform governmental tasks, a reflection of the exigencies of war (not of the belief that constitution writing was but one of many legislative tasks). But they regarded constitution writing as their most important responsibility. In the face of imminent invasion, New Jersey's provincial congress reduced the number of delegates required for a quorum, except when the congress considered the constitution. For that task, delegates insisted upon the original quorum.

Republicans viewed provincial congresses as proper forums for drafting constitutions *because* they were not legislatures with entrenched interests potentially subversive of the public good. In the only three states in which sitting legislatures might have written constitutions—Pennsylvania, Delaware, and Massachusetts—delegates to constitutional conventions drafted the documents. Indeed, in Delaware, legislators explicitly asserted their incapacity to draft the state's fundamental law.

Whether delegates to provincial congresses or to constitutional conventions, those drafting state constitutions understood their task to be temporary. In most states, the delegates adjourned soon after adopting a constitution. They thereby isolated constitution writing from the exercise of ordinary governmental powers. Elsewhere, in those few states where the congresses or conventions resolved themselves into the new lower houses of the state legislatures, they substantially curtailed their power (sloughing off the congresses' judicial and executive functions, as well as a portion of their legislative authority) and retained reduced power for a limited time.

Moreover, American patriots allowed only delegates to congresses and conventions, not legislators, to write state constitutions because they viewed the documents as barriers against tyrannical power. They sought to restrain all branches of government, not only the magistrate. In declarations of rights, they articulated many of the principles of government and governmental restraint implemented in plans of government. The declarations were intended to protect the rights of individuals and of the community by restraining all of the branches of government. But they also protected common-law procedures from intrusions by legislators, executives, and judges, and prescribed the procedures by which the legislatures could tax the citizenry. In addition, the declarations delineated government's powers over matters of religion—protecting freedom of conscience, prohibiting the establishment of any single church, and, in many cases, collectively establishing Protestant churches. Some declarations prohibited the legislature from enacting ex post facto laws and bills of attainder and from establishing a hereditary aristocracy. Others guaranteed freedoms of the press and of assembly and the rights of instruction and petition.

Constitution makers attempted to fulfill the principles enunciated in the declarations of rights when they wrote plans of government that limited all parts of government. The constitutions, for example, dictated whether the legislature was composed of one house or two, whether the governor (if there was to be a governor) would participate in the legislature, who would elect individuals to office (and how votes would be cast), who could or could not hold public office, and the length of their terms. Constitution makers also contained legislative authority by restricting or prohibiting legislative amendment of the constitutions.

Emblematic of their distrust of all members of government and crucial to the protection of those rights was the revolutionaries' re-creation of the idea of representation. Since the end of the seventeenth century, the English had located government in the king-in-Parliament. In theory, the king was present when Parliament sat and Parliament spoke for the king. Within government, members of the House of Commons were representatives, independent of both the people and the Crown, who defended the people's liberties against monarchical prerogative.

During the revolutionary crisis, Americans reconsidered and recast the notion of representation. The traditional relationship of taxation and representation seemed to be shattered by Parliament's taxation of unrepresented Americans and by the Crown's exclusion of newly settled areas from representation in colonial assemblies. The struggle with England over tax policy after 1763 induced Americans to rearticulate their belief that representation meant direct representation of all areas in the new states. It also meant representation by men residing among constituents who elected them. Even then, such men could not be trusted entirely. Broad electorates would curb representatives through annual elections and instructions.

Americans brought the debate over representation home to its most elemental unit—the voter. Assuming that only a large electorate could escape corruption, constitution makers lowered property requirements. But as the relentless cry against taxation without representation came to be taken literally, revolutionaries increasingly viewed an individual who could not vote as unrepresented and suffrage rights and political participation as central to the meaning of the Revolution. In response, they began to liberate the suffrage from its centuries-long attachment to certain kinds of property and from privileges granted by the monarch. In other words, they ceased to conceive of the suffrage as a *franchise*. As some revolutionaries feared and others desired, the rethinking of suffrage rights unleashed a wide-ranging and far-reaching debate about voting. The new states experimented with taxpayer suffrage and female suffrage (in New Jersey), considered the right of free black men to vote, and linked the suffrage to loyalty (disfranchising propertied Loyalists). Nevertheless, the primary beneficiaries were white men. Only a few propertied women and a small minority of black men could vote.

The fear of governmental tyranny that compelled a reconsideration of representation and of the suffrage also led framers to restrain government by dividing governmental powers among the different branches and by establishing bicameral legislatures and recasting their roles. They did not conceive of the doctrine of a separation of powers merely as a means of preventing the governor from corrupting the legislature through the appointment of legislators to executive offices. Rather, they aimed to prevent the accumulation of arbitrary power in the hands of *any* man or group of men. Their experience with provincial congresses and the Continental Congress, which held the legislative, executive, and judicial powers in their hands, alerted American patriots to the dangers of untrammeled legislative power. So, in order to prevent the concentration of different powers in any one branch of government, the framers drafted constitutions that separated the different functions of government. Therefore, when constitution makers prohibited plural officeholding, they attempted to restrict legislative as well as magisterial power. They meant to prevent any man or political body from accumulating unchecked power, whether the intriguer be the executive, a legislator, or members of a legislative house. The framers also aimed to purge the polity of concentrated power by depriving the governor of a veto and by dividing the tasks of the old colonial council between an executive privy council and a legislative council or senate.

The framers not only separated the powers of government among different branches, they also generally divided legislative power into two houses. They retained an old English form but gave it a new rationale: to prevent a single assembly from seizing unbridled power. Bicameral legislatures, while bearing a superficial resemblance to the mixed governments of Commons and Lords in England or to the assemblies and councils of colonial America, no longer were to represent different orders in society. Now, Americans justified bicameralism on procedural grounds, as a check on the power of each house. Even the three states adopting unicameral legislatures restrained those assemblies.

In the end, constitution makers reinvented American political life by creating a mechanical polity—not in 1787, but in 1776. The English thought of political society as an organism in which all of the estates in society participated. The English constitution was also organic, an accretion of time-honored procedure, common law, custom, and parliamentary legislation. The English contended, in an argument embraced by the American revolutionaries, that their constitution restrained government by law and by the balanced government of monarch, lords, and commons. The constitution, it was presumed, prevented arbitrary government, especially monarchical tyranny, and limited Parliament's legislative authority. But the English carefully avoided describing just what those limits were and what could be done if rulers crossed the line.

Convinced that reliance upon such an amorphous constitution rendered their freedoms precarious, Americans found mechanisms, rules, and institutions to thwart tyranny. They established conventions to constitute and alter government, made representation of free men direct and actual, established an electoral system in which votes embodied the obligations of citizenship, separated the powers of government's different branches, and divided legislative authority into two bodies, both representative of the people.

The revolutionaries revealed their distrust of government by committing constitutions to writing. The idea that constitutions ought to be written explicitly challenged the customary English constitution and implicitly challenged the organic underpinnings of the English constitution. Precise definition of the limits of parliamentary authority supposedly endangered Parliament's independence; only a Parliament independent of the monarch and of the people could defend the people's liberties against monarchical power. Such a Parliament could not act arbitrarily, indeed was incapable of acting arbitrarily, because it was limited by what John Phillip Reid calls the "constraints" of trust, consent, contract, constitutionalism, liberty, law, and precedent.[4]

Americans embraced common-law precepts without embracing English forms; to secure trust, consent, the compact, or the rule of law, Americans committed the arrangement to writing. In the United States, the revolutionary state constitutions built restrictions on governmental power into the documents. The act of writing the constitutions, by itself, restricted the government and the exercise of governmental power. Many constitutions also restrained power by writing bills of rights with which no branch of government could interfere. Those without formal declarations of rights protected some rights in the texts of the constitutions. Only the formal apparatus of constitutions, the framers believed, would prevent tyranny; neither the unspecified constraints of the English constitution nor, as Gordon Wood argues, the civic virtue of political leaders would win the day.

The way the revolutionary generation thought about the suffrage also reflected the steady depreciation of the idea of an organic polity as a hedge against political slavery. The extraordinary interest in and debate over the suffrage and a broadened electorate, especially the taxpayer suffrage, signified unease with the idea of virtual representation of free men. The notion that people might be represented by a delegate not actually elected by them originated in the assumption of an organic, monarchical polity. Possession of the vote was unnecessary because others voted on your behalf and represented your interest, first on election day and then in the legislature. Voting, then, was a privilege reserved for a few. But state constitution makers began to regard voting as a right, and the act of voting became the hallmark of what they thought to be the only legitimate form of representation, direct representation. The mechanics of voting, not trusteeship and reliance upon the commonality of interests, established genuine representation.

The framers did not abandon the idea of a common good, but maintained that self-defense against tyranny by voting was the only way to secure the common good. The unchecked ruler threatened the commonweal. No matter how good a person was, once in power he became, in John Adams's words, "a ravenous beast of prey."[5] In order for men to pursue the common good, they would first need to curb the restless ambition of those who wielded power. As a consequence of exercising power, rulers developed interests and concerns at odds with the public interest. Therefore, it was imperative to prevent them from pursuing self-interest and to make them act for the benefit of all.

Similarly, whereas the English idea of bicameralism was rooted in the belief that different branches of Parliament embodied different estates or orders in society, bicameralism in the revolutionary states became an institutional means of stemming the potentially tyrannical behavior of assemblies. Constitution makers generally assumed that the different houses of the legislature both represented the people, though they bowed slightly in the direction of mixed-government theory by constituting the two houses somewhat differently. But they also believed that all men who wielded government power were potential tyrants. Two political bodies, a senate and a house of representatives, would check one another in defense of the people's liberties against legislative tyranny.

When congressional and convention delegates assembled to write new state constitutions, they marveled at their chance to create enduring republican governments. They rejected "the old channel" and "new-modelled" their governments on the assumption that only by constituting governments differently could republican government thrive. The constitutions they wrote sprang from traditional English hostility to arbitrary government and from their new understanding that tyranny lurked everywhere in government, in the legislature as well as the governor's residence. Without faith in legislators, the revolutionaries relied upon provincial congresses and conventions to create constitutions, which protected the people's liberties through the mechanics of governance. The framers, though, did not view the constitutions as machines that would go of themselves.[6] Instead, drawing upon different political and legal languages, they provided the machinery by which ordinary citizens and members of government could defend the public good and private rights against the designs of men intent upon abusing the public trust and securing arbitrary power. In so doing, the framers hoped to create republican polities that found the proper balance "between authority and liberty."[7]

Preface

1. In a critique of an early draft of this book, Professor Sandra VanBurkleo suggested that I was describing the revolutionary origins of what she calls "the mechanical political culture" of the 1830s and beyond. I want to thank her for allowing me to borrow the term.

2. On "republican" historiography, see especially Shalhope, "Toward a Republican Synthesis"; Shalhope, "Republicanism and Early American Historiography"; Kerber, "The Republican Ideology of the Revolutionary Generation"; and Rodgers, "Republicanism." For the most influential critiques of the concept of republicanism, see Appleby, *Liberalism and Republicanism*, and Kramnick, *Republicanism and Bourgeois Radicalism*.

3. Peter S. Onuf and Cathy Matson, "Republicanism and Federalism in the Constitutional Decade," in Klein, Brown, and Hench, *Republican Synthesis*, 119–41. Onuf and Matson extend their arguments in *A Union of Interests*.

4. Shalhope, *Roots of Democracy*, 27–52.

5. Banning, "Jeffersonian Ideology Revisited"; Wood, "Afterword," in Klein, Brown, and Hench, *Republican Synthesis*, 145.

Chapter 1

1. Resolution of May 10 and May 15, 1776, in Ford et al., *Journals of the Continental Congress*, 4:342, 357–58.

2. *New-York Journal*, May 9, 1776.

3. Ibid., February 29, 1776.

4. John Page to Thomas Jefferson, April 26, 1776, in Boyd, *Papers of Jefferson*, 1:288.

5. *Connecticut Journal*, May 8, 1776.

6. Dixon and Hunter's *Virginia Gazette*, May 11, 1776, extract from a letter from Charlestown, South Carolina.

7. See, for example, Marston, *King and Congress*, chap. 9 (quotation, 253). Also see Morey, "The First State Constitutions," which portrays continuity with the colonial past but discontinuity with the English experience, and Webster, "Comparative Study," 416.

8. See Boyd, *Papers of Jefferson*, 1:340–63.

9. Dixon and Hunter's *Virginia Gazette*, June 8 and 15, 1776.

10. Lee to [?], May 12, 1776, in Ballagh, *Letters of Lee*, 1:190; also see Selby, *Revolution in Virginia*, 116.

11. Patrick Henry to John Adams, May 20, 1776, in Taylor, *Papers of Adams*, 4:201.

12. William Fleming to Thomas Jefferson, July 27, 1776, in Boyd, *Papers of Jefferson*, 1:475.

13. On "new-modelling" governments, see, for example, "An Address Delivered at the Opening of the Election in Dover for the Choice of Members of Convention," August 19, 1776, in Force, *American Archives*, 5th ser., 1:1057; and "Letter to A. B.," *Connecticut Journal*, October 23, 1776.

14. Wood, *Creation*, 20–25.

15. Ibid., 48.

16. Ibid., 58.

17. Ibid., 268.

18. Ibid., 274.

19. Ibid., 272.

20. Ibid., 318.

21. Ibid., 154–58.

22. Ibid., 319.

23. Ibid., 168, 179.

24. Ibid., 135–72.

25. Ibid., 172.

26. Wood, *Representation in the American Revolution*, 25. This extended essay is an excellent distillation of the discussion of representation to be found in the same author's *Creation of the American Republic*.

27. Wood, *Creation*, 387–88; also see 409, 447.

28. Ibid., 409.

29. Reid, *Authority to Legislate*, 6.

30. Ibid., 32.

31. Ibid., 34–158.

32. For a good example of the idea of a self-correcting Parliament, see James Otis, "The Rights of the British Colonies Asserted and Proved" (Boston: Edes and Gill, 1764), in Bailyn, *Pamphlets of the American Revolution*, 1:418–82.

33. In his numerous studies, Reid often points out that the struggle in England between the customary constitution and the constitution of sovereign command persisted until the nineteenth century. Yet the logic of his defense of the constitutionality of American constitutional argument leads him to consider the Revolution as a conflict between the American defense of the customary constitution against the English assertion of the constitution of Parliament's command. For one particularly good example, see Reid, *Authority of Law*, 3–8.

34. Bailyn, *Ideological Origins*, 94–143.

35. Samuel Seabury, quoted in ibid., 119.

36. See especially Reid, *Authority to Tax*, and Reid, *Authority to Legislate*.

37. But see Richard Bland's 1764 insistence that only the colonial assemblies could pass legislation regarding the internal affairs of a colony. Bland, "The Colonel Dismounted: or the Rector Vindicated. . . . By Common Sense" (Williamsburg, Va.: Joseph Royle, 1764), in Bailyn, *Pamphlets of the American Revolution*, 1:320–23.

38. The Declaratory Act, March 18, 1766, in Morgan, *Prologue to Revolution*, 155–56.

39. Reid insists that American leaders ignored the act for constitutional, not politi-

cal, reasons. Yet much of his explanation for the response rests upon the notion that Americans were unconcerned because the Declaratory Act was "a declaration of constitutional principle, not the promulgation of a legislative program [i.e., a political act]." Reid, *Authority to Legislate*, 307. Also see VanBurkleo, review of *Authority to Legislate*, 390n.

40. See Morgan and Morgan, *Stamp Act Crisis*, 353–70.

41. Reid, *Authority to Legislate*, 309.

42. "Resolves of New Shoreham Town Meeting, March 2, 1774," quoted in ibid. Also see for the New York City and county grand jury, "To his Majesty's Justices assembled at the General Quarter Sessions of the Peace, for the city and county of New-York, February 10, 1775," *Pennsylvania Packet*, February 20, 1775. For an able study of the American response to the Coercive Acts, see Ammerman, *In the Common Cause*.

43. "From the County of Hampshire," *Essex Journal*, March 8, 1775.

44. "Speech of a Farmer to an Assembly of his Neighbours of Philadelphia County, on his engaging in the Continental service," in Force, *American Archives*, 4th ser., 4:1525.

45. This quotation is Laurens's report of the spokesman's words. Henry Laurens to William Manning, Charles Town, February 27, 1776, in Hamer, Chesnutt, et al., *Papers of Henry Laurens*, 11:125.

46. "Altering the Massachusetts Constitution: The Massachusetts Government Act (May 20, 1774)," in Greene, *Colonies to Nation*, 204–7.

47. Cf. Reid, *Authority to Legislate*, 172–91. See John Dickinson, "Address to Barbados," which argued that the charters simply confirmed natural rights, in Ford, *Writings of John Dickinson*, 262.

48. "From the County of Hampshire," *Essex Journal*, March 8, 1775. Also see John Pitts to Samuel Adams, October 16, 1774, quoted in Marston, *King and Congress*, 254.

49. Quoted in Jensen, *Founding of a Nation*, 622.

50. Resolution in response to King George III's speech to Parliament on October 27, 1775, in Maryland Convention Proceedings, January 18, 1776, in Force, *American Archives*, 4th ser., 4:762.

51. Gouverneur Morris to John Jay, June 30, 1775, in Morris, *John Jay*, 156.

52. Francis Alison et al., "An Address to the Ministers and Presbyterian congregations in North Carolina," Philadelphia, July 10, 1775, in Saunders, *Colonial Records of North Carolina*, 10:225–26.

53. Jay's Charge to the Grand Jury of Ulster County, in Johnston, *Correspondence of Jay*, 1:158–64.

54. "The Address and Instructions of the Freeholders of [Buckingham County, Virginia]," in Force, *American Archives*, 4th ser., 5:1207.

55. Judge Drayton's Charge to the Grand Jury of Charlestown, South-Carolina, April 23, 1776, in ibid., 1026.

56. Maryland Declaration of Rights (1776), in Thorpe, *Constitutions*, 3:1686.

57. South Carolina Constitution (1776), in ibid., 6:3241.

58. New Jersey Constitution (1776), in ibid., 5:2594.

59. Georgia Constitution (1777), in ibid., 2:777.

60. Thomas Jefferson, *A Summary View of the Rights of British America . . .* , in Boyd, *Papers of Jefferson*, 1:121–35 (quotation, 129).

Chapter 2

1. Palmer, *Age of Democratic Revolution*, 213–35 (quotations, 214). For a brief statement of the traditional view, see Murrin, "From Liberties to Rights," 63–64.

2. Conkin, *Self-Evident Truths*, 52, 55, 57.

3. Jefferson, *Notes on the State of Virginia*, 122.

4. Lutz, *Popular Consent*, 60. For a similar interpretation, see Johnson, "'Parliamentary Egotisms,'" 361.

5. Wood, *Creation*, 307.

6. Pole, *Political Representation*, 510.

7. Adams, *First American Constitutions*, 72, 74, 82.

8. New Hampshire Constitution (1776), in Thorpe, *Constitutions*, 4:2451–53; South Carolina Constitution (1776), in ibid., 6:3241; Henry Laurens to John Laurens, March 28, 1776, in Hamer, Chesnutt, et al., *Papers of Henry Laurens*, 11:194.

9. South Carolina Constitution (1776), in Thorpe, *Constitutions*, 6:3248; but see John Rutledge's argument that the legislature had no authority to alter the constitution, in Rutledge to Henry Laurens, March 8, 1778, in Hamer, Chesnutt, et al., *Papers of Henry Laurens*, 12:527–29.

10. The quotation is from the act of the Connecticut Assembly in Hoadly, *Records of the State of Connecticut*, 1:3–4. For Rhode Island, see "An ACT repealing an Act intituled, 'An Act for the more effectual securing to His Majesty the Allegiance of His Subjects in this His Colony and Dominion of Rhode-Island and Providence Plantations,' and altering the Form of Commisions . . . ," *Providence Gazette and Country Journal*, May 18, 1776. Also see Purcell, *Connecticut in Transition*, 113–14, 117.

11. Adams, *First American Constitutions*, 73, 82.

12. Five years later, the legislature repealed those requirements. McCormick, *Voting in New Jersey*, 70, 75, 75n.

13. Slade, *Vermont State Papers*, 287–88, 449; Wood, *Creation*, 307–8. Wood points out that legislators felt the need to legitimize the constitution by making it one of the laws of the state. But one must also consider the special circumstances of Vermonters, who found themselves repeatedly seeking legitimation. Not only did the Vermont legislature of 1779 feel that it needed to make the constitution part of the laws of the state, but the legislature of 1782 felt the need to do it again. That second decision revealed that Vermonters had questions not only about the legitimacy of the constitution but also about the legislature of 1779.

14. Wood offers a similar discussion of popular excitement about constituting new governments, but he draws conclusions different from those reached here. See Wood, *Creation*, 127–32. The American obsession with constitution making at the inception of the American Revolution undermines Theodore Draper's argument that the Revolution was primarily a struggle for power. See Draper, *A Struggle for Power*.

15. "The Address of the Deputies from the Committees of Pennsylvania, assembled in Provincial Conference, June 22," in Force, *American Archives*, 4th ser., 6:962.

16. *Continental Journal*, April 2, 1778.

17. "An Address Delivered at the Opening of the Election in Dover for the Choice of Members of Convention, August 19, 1776," in Force, *American Archives*, 5th ser., 1:1058.

18. "Resolution of the House to Empower the General Court to Frame a Constitution, April 4, 1777," in Taylor, *Colony to Commonwealth*, 50.

19. John Adams to Abigail Adams, Philadelphia, May 17, 1776, in Butterfield, *Adams Family Correspondence*, 1:411. Also see Henry Laurens to John Laurens, Charles Town, March 28, 1776, in Hamer, Chesnutt, et al., *Papers of Henry Laurens*, 11:195.

20. See, for example, the careful analysis of the New Jersey and Virginia constitutions in "Letter to A. B.," *Connecticut Journal*, October 23 and 30, 1776.

21. Ebenezer Hazard to Pierre Van Cortlandt, November 6, 1776, in Force, *American Archives*, 5th ser., 3:548; also see Josiah Bartlett to John Langdon, July 15, 1776, in ibid., 1:348.

22. Robert Morris to General Gates, October 27, 1776, in ibid., 2:1262.

23. Thomas Jefferson to Thomas Nelson, May 16, 1776, in Boyd, *Papers of Jefferson*, 1:292.

24. Ibid., 340–63. For a valuable recent discussion of Jefferson's constitutional thought, see Mayer, *Constitutional Thought of Thomas Jefferson*, 53–69.

25. William Hooper to Congress at Halifax, October 26, 1776, in Saunders, *Colonial Records of North Carolina*, 10:862.

26. John Adams, *Thoughts on Government*, in Taylor, *Papers of Adams*, 4:86.

27. "The Address of the Deputies from the Committees of Pennsylvania, assembled in Provincial Conference, June 22," in Force, *American Archives*, 4th ser., 6:962.

28. "The Interest of America," in ibid., 481.

29. A Watchman, "To the People of Massachusetts-Bay, June 12, 1776," in ibid., 831.

30. "Resolution of the House to Empower the General Court to Frame a Constitution, April 4, 1777," in Taylor, *Colony to Commonwealth*, 50–51 (quotation, 50).

31. *Boston Gazette*, April 13, 1778.

32. James Bowdoin to The Gentlemen of the Convention, November 20, 1779, *Continental Journal*, December 2, 1779.

33. R. H. Lee to Charles Lee, July 6, 1776, in Ballagh, *Letters of Lee*, 1:205.

34. North Carolina Committee of Safety, August 9, 1776, in Saunders, *Colonial Records of North Carolina*, 10:996.

35. Benevolus, "Thoughts on Government, No. III," *Continental Journal*, May 27, 1779. For a different view, see Plain Truth, "To the Justices in Massachusetts Empowered by the Court to Deal with the Tories," July 11, 1776, in Force, *American Archives*, 5th ser., 1:211.

36. Pittsfield town meeting, March 9, 1777, *Connecticut Courant*, March 31, 1777.

37. On the role of the Continental Congress, see the excellent discussions in Adams, *First American Constitutions*, 49–62, and Marston, *King and Congress*, 251–96.

38. South Carolina Constitution (1776), 33, in Thorpe, *Constitutions*, 6:3247.

39. John Adams to James Warren, May 15, 1776, in Taylor, *Papers of Adams*, 4:186.

40. Resolution of May 10 and May 15, 1776, in Ford et al., *Journals of the Continental Congress*, 4:342, 357–58.

41. Resolution of the Maryland Provincial Convention, July 3, 1776, in Papenfuse and Stiverson, *Decisive Blow*, n.p.

42. *New-York Journal*, May 23, 1776.

43. New York Provincial Congress, May 27 and 31, 1776, in Force, *American Archives*, 4th ser., 6:1338, 1351–52. Also see Carl Becker, *Political Parties*, 266–70.

44. For another example of a special election, see the Georgia council of safety's call for the election of a convention to frame a constitution, and council president Archibald Bulloch's call for the election as delegates of "men whose depth of political judgment qualified them to frame a constitution for the future government of the country" (quoted in Saye, *Constitutional History of Georgia*, 98; the council of safety's call for an election is summarized on 96–97).

45. New York Convention Proceedings, August 20, 1776, in Force, *American Archives*, 5th ser., 1:525. Edward Countryman identifies Kings County as "overwhelmingly royalist." Countryman, *A People in Revolution*, 104.

46. Cf. Wood, *Creation*, 332.

47. North Carolina Committee of Safety, August 9, 1776, in Saunders, *Colonial Records of North Carolina*, 10:696.

48. North Carolina Constitution (1776), in ibid., 1010.

49. See Chapter 4 below. Also see Countryman, *A People in Revolution*, 165; Ganyard, *Emergence of North Carolina's Revolutionary State Government*, 35; Proceedings of the New Jersey Provincial Congress, July 2, 1776, in Force, *American Archives*, 4th ser., 6:1635–36.

50. See, for example, Adams, *First American Constitutions*, 63–64.

51. Proceedings of the New Jersey Provincial Congress, June 29, 1776, in Force, *American Archives*, 4th ser., 6:1633.

52. Henry Laurens to John Laurens, Charles Town, March 19, 1776, in Hamer, Chesnutt, et al., *Papers of Henry Laurens*, 11:181.

53. South Carolina Constitution (1776), i, ii, in Thorpe, *Constitutions*, 6:3243–45.

54. New Hampshire Constitution (1776), in ibid., 4:2452–53; Daniell, *Experiment in Republicanism*, 110–11; Proceedings, New Hampshire Provincial Congress, December 28, 1775, in Bouton, *Provincial Papers*, 7:703–4.

55. Selby, *Revolution in Virginia*, 121, 138.

56. Stevens, *History of Georgia*, 2:298, 300.

57. Gerlach, *Prologue to Independence*, 348, 357.

58. Ganyard, *Emergence of North Carolina's Revolutionary State Government*, 88.

59. Ryerson, *Revolution Is Now Begun*, 208.

60. Resolution of May 10 and May 15, 1776, in Ford et al., *Journals of the Continental Congress*, 4:342, 357–58. Also see Ryerson, *Revolution Is Now Begun*, 211–12.

61. Ryerson, *Revolution Is Now Begun*, 212–16. Also see Foner, *Tom Paine*, 126–29.

62. "Four Letters on Interesting Subjects" (Philadelphia, 1776), in Hyneman and Lutz, *American Political Writing*, 1:385, 387. Internal evidence indicates that this document was written after the May 20 meeting.

63. "The Alarm: or, an Address to the People of Pennsylvania on the Late Resolve of Congress" (Philadelphia, 1776), in ibid., 322; also see Meeting of the Associators of Northampton, May 29, 1776, in Force, *American Archives*, 4th ser., 6:614.

64. Ryerson, *Revolution Is Now Begun*, 219–26.

65. Even associators could be asked to take an oath of allegiance. Associators also could vote if they had been rated for, but had not yet paid, taxes.

66. Provincial Conference, June 20, 1776, in Force, *American Archives*, 4th ser., 6:953–54.

67. The problem of representation is discussed in Chapter 4 below.

68. Ryerson, *Revolution Is Now Begun*, 12–13.

69. The assembly attempted to answer criticism of malapportionment by adding many new members from the more recently settled counties.

70. Selsam, *Pennsylvania Constitution of 1776*, 151–55, 159–60.

71. Address of the Pennsylvania Convention, September 28, 1776, in Force, *American Archives*, 5th ser., 2:585–86.

72. Caesar Rodney to John Haslet[?], May 17, 1776, in Ryden, *Letters to and from Rodney*, 80.

73. See the assembly's resolution of June 15, 1776, in Bushman, Hancock, and Homsey, *Proceedings of Delaware*, 199–200.

74. Ibid., 201.

75. Caesar Rodney to Thomas Rodney, August 28, 1776; Thomas Rodney to Caesar Rodney, September 4, 1776; Caesar Rodney to John Haslet, September 12, 1776; Thomas McKean to Caesar Rodney, September 19, 1776, in Ryden, *Letters to and from Rodney*, 105, 111, 116, 124.

76. Caesar Rodney to Thomas Rodney, August 28, 1776; Caesar Rodney to Thomas Rodney, September 11, 1776; Caesar Rodney to John Haslet, September 12, 1776, in ibid., 105, 114, 116. See convention proceedings for September 7, 12, 14, 20, 21, 1776, in Bushman, Hancock, and Homsey, *Proceedings of Delaware*, 209–10, 214–16, 218, 226–30. Also see Caesar Rodney to Thomas Rodney, Philadelphia, September 11, 1776, in Ryden, *Letters to and from Rodney*, 114.

77. Most of the following on Massachusetts was derived from Taylor, *Colony to Commonwealth*. On the assumption of power in Massachusetts, see Adams, *First American Constitutions*, 33–37.

78. "The House of Representatives Offers to Draft a Constitution, September 17, 1776," in Taylor, *Colony to Commonwealth*, 41.

79. For a defense of the general court's authority to write a constitution, see the comments of T. M. of Braintree, *Continental Journal*, October 17, 1776. But also see *Continental Journal*, May 29, 1777, for the instructions of the Boston town meeting, for which the alterations made by the general court were insufficient and which demanded a convention whose exclusive task would be the drafting of a state constitution.

80. See, for example, Wood, *Creation*, 340–41, and Adams, *First American Constitutions*, 87–91. Stephen Patterson notes the distinction made between the general court and the convention and points out that the general court acted as a convention when it drafted the constitution. See Patterson, *Political Parties in Massachusetts*, 166, 169, 173, 182–85. For support of legislative authority to draft the constitution, see the returns of Ashfield, October 4, 1776; Warwick, October 4, 1776; Newburyport, October 8, 1776; and Bradford, October 31, 1776, in Handlin and Handlin, *Popular Sources*, 111–13, 128, 156.

81. Few imagined women as participants or even considered children and the unfree, slaves and apprentices (though many of the towns objected to slavery itself). See James Sullivan to Elbridge Gerry, May 6, 1776, and John Adams to James Sullivan, May 26, 1776, in Taylor, *Papers of Adams*, 208–12, 212–13n.

82. Returns of Concord, October 21, 1776. Also see returns of Norton, October 7, 1776; Middleborough, October 7, 1776; Attleborough, October 14, 1776; Lexington, October 21, 1776; Acton, November 4, 1776; and Resolution of the Worcester County

Towns, November 26, 1776, in Handlin and Handlin, *Popular Sources*, 153, 124–27, 143–44, 149–51, 157–58, 164–66.

83. "Resolve of May 5, 1777," in ibid., 174–75. Also see "Resolution Authorizing the General Assembly to Frame a Constitution, April 4, 1777," in ibid., 171–73.

84. Committees generally had a chairman and two to four members. See Zemsky, *Merchants, Farmers, and River Gods*, 13.

85. "Journal of the Convention, June 17, 1777–March 6, 1778," in Handlin and Handlin, *Popular Sources*, 177–89; Patterson, *Political Parties in Revolutionary Massachusetts*, 166–75, 183–94.

86. "Resolve on the Question of a Constitution," February 20, 1779, in Handlin and Handlin, *Popular Sources*, 383–84.

87. "The Call for a Convention, [June 15] 1779," in ibid., 402–4.

88. Consideration, "Remarks on the Proceedings and Resolutions of the Meeting in the State-House Yard, on Monday and Tuesday, October 21 and 22, 1776" (Philadelphia, October 30, 1776), in Force, *American Archives*, 5th ser., 2:1153.

89. Daniell, *Experiment in Republicanism*, 164–79; Dodd, *Revision and Amendment of State Constitutions*, 62–65; Rodgers, *Contested Truths*, 87.

Chapter 3

1. Wood, *Creation*, 132–61.

2. For legislative assumption of judicial powers, see Goebel, *Antecedents and Beginnings*, 98–100.

3. Ibid., 100; also see Lutz, *Popular Consent*, 68.

4. See Rakove, "Parchment Barriers," 129–42. For different interpretations of the first declarations of rights and state constitutions, see Nelson and Palmer, *Liberty and Community*, 61–86; and Tomlins, *Law, Labor, and Ideology*.

5. For valuable discussions of rights in the colonies and the revolutionary states, see the essays in Conley and Kaminski, *Bill of Rights and the States*. On the influence of Magna Carta, see Howard, *Road from Runnymede*. More generally, see the excellent essay by Rakove, "Parchment Barriers," 98–143.

6. The constitution placed beyond the legislature's vast powers of revision annual elections, the article opposing church establishment and that giving all Protestants equal civil rights, and trial by jury. The New Jersey constitution's statement of "charter rights" was, like the other states', placed near the end of the document, but it was more scattered and included articles 18, 19, and 22. Those three articles constitute three-fourths of the articles that the constitution declared unamendable by the legislature. New Jersey Constitution (1776), in Thorpe, *Constitutions*, 5:2595, 2597–98.

7. Georgia Constitution (1777), arts. 56–62 (excepting 57). The articles provided "free exercise of religion" (56); "the liberty to plead his own cause" in court (58); ban on excessive fines and bail (59); the principles of habeas corpus (60); freedom of the press and trial by jury "to remain inviolate forever" (61). Art. 57 provided the design for the state seal. Ibid., 2:784–85.

8. New York Constitution (1777), 38–41. Art. 40, the militia article, like those con-

cerning rights, dealt with the relationship between citizens and the state, but in terms of obligations, not rights. Ibid., 5:2636–37.

9. South Carolina Constitution (1778), 38–43. The articles dealt with liberty of conscience and establishment of the "Christian Protestant religion" (38); reform of penal laws and "less sanguinary" punishments (40); no imprisonment "but by the judgment of his peers or by the law of the land" (41); subordination of the military to the civil power (42); and "liberty of the press" (43). Art. 39 provided for the division of the state into districts and counties and for the establishment of county courts. Ibid., 6:3255–57.

10. See Donald Lutz's careful enumeration of the usage of "ought" and "shall" in the first state declarations of rights. Lutz, *Popular Consent*, 67.

11. Ibid., 58–68; Wood, *Creation*, 271–73.

12. Wood, *Creation*, 272.

13. Lutz, *Popular Consent*, 66. See also *An Essay upon Government*, which argued that it was acceptable for rulers to deprive people of rights if the rulers determine that it is in society's best interests.

14. Isaac Backus to Noah Alden, July 20, 1779, quoted in McLoughlin, *New England Dissent*, 1:600.

15. Cf. Lutz, *Popular Consent*, 64–65.

16. Selby, *The Revolution in Virginia*, 100–23 (quotation, 104). On the framing of the declaration of rights and the constitution, both of which were initially drafted by George Mason, see Rutland, *Papers of Mason*, 1:274–310, and "The Virginia Constitution," in Boyd, *Papers of Jefferson*, 1:329–86.

17. Bushman, Hancock, and Homsey, *Proceedings of Delaware*, 208, 210, 212–14, 217–24.

18. The proceedings of the Maryland Convention are in Papenfuse and Stiverson, *Decisive Blow*.

19. "The Journal of the Provincial Congress of North Carolina, Held at Halifax, November the Twelfth Day, Anno. Dom. 1776," in Saunders, *Colonial Records of North Carolina*, 10:918, 967, 973–74.

20. Pennsylvania Constitution (1776), in Thorpe, *Constitutions*, 5:3082. The statements in the Vermont and Massachusetts constitutions differ mostly in capitalization or italics. Vermont Constitution (1777), in ibid., 6:3739; Massachusetts Constitution (1780), in Handlin and Handlin, *Popular Sources*, 442.

21. Pennsylvania Constitution (1776), sec. 46, in Thorpe, *Constitutions*, 5:3091.

22. North Carolina Constitution (1776), 44, in ibid., 2794; Maryland Constitution (1776), 59, in ibid., 3:1701; Delaware Constitution (1776), art. 30, in Bushman, Hancock, and Homsey, *Proceedings of Delaware*, 224.

23. Delaware Constitution (1776), art. 25, in Bushman, Hancock, and Homsey, *Proceedings of Delaware*, 223. Cf. Lutz, *Popular Consent*, 65, 67 (see note to the table on 67).

24. New Hampshire Constitution (1784), in Thorpe, *Constitutions*, 4:2453, 2458. Massachusetts called the declaration "Part the First" and the form "Part the Second"; Massachusetts Constitution (1780), in Handlin and Handlin, *Popular Sources*, 442, 448.

25. Maryland Constitution (1776), in Thorpe, *Constitutions*, 3:1686.

26. Virginia Constitution (1776), in ibid., 7:3812. Also see the preamble to the Pennsylvania Constitution (1776), in ibid., 5:3082.

27. Cf. Wood, *Creation*, 271.

28. Virginia Declaration of Rights, secs. 1, 2, in Thorpe, *Constitutions*, 7:3813.

29. Maryland Declaration of Rights, 1, in ibid., 3:1686. Even the states that did not write separate declarations included statements about popular sovereignty and the origins and purpose of government. The preamble to the New Jersey constitution asserted that "all the constitutional authority ever possessed by the kings of Great Britain over these colonies . . . was, by compact, derived from the people, and held of them, for the common interest of the whole society." Ibid., 5:2594. The delegates to the Georgia Provincial Congress defended their authority to write a constitution on the grounds that they were "the representatives of the people, from whom all power originates, and for whose benefit all government is intended." Ibid., 2:778. The last paragraph of the lengthy New York preamble and the first article of the constitution announced that, because of the Declaration of Independence, "all power . . . hath reverted to the people" and that "no authority shall . . . be exercised over the people or members of this State but such as shall be derived from and granted by them." Ibid., 5:2628.

30. Maryland Declaration of Rights, 2, in ibid., 3:1686. Also see Pennsylvania Declaration of Rights, 3, in ibid., 5:3082, and Massachusetts Declaration of Rights, art. 4, in Handlin and Handlin, *Popular Sources*, 443.

31. New York Constitution (1777), 1, in Thorpe, *Constitutions*, 5:2628.

32. Maryland Declaration of Rights, 4, in ibid., 3:1687. For a similar statement, see Pennsylvania Declaration of Rights, 4, in ibid., 5:3082.

33. Maryland Declaration of Rights, 4, in ibid., 3:1687; Virginia Declaration of Rights, sec. 3, in ibid., 7:3813.

34. Pennsylvania Declaration of Rights, 5, in ibid., 5:3082–83. Also see the similar statement in the Massachusetts Declaration of Rights, art. 7, in Handlin and Handlin, *Popular Sources*, 444.

35. Delaware Declaration of Rights, 5, in Bushman, Hancock, and Homsey, *Proceedings of Delaware*, 213.

36. Maryland Declaration of Rights, 4, in Thorpe, *Constitutions*, 3:1687.

37. Virginia Declaration of Rights, sec. 5, in ibid., 7:3813.

38. Pennsylvania Declaration of Rights, 6, in ibid., 5:3083. Also see North Carolina Declaration of Rights, 20, in ibid., 2788. But see the different phrasing of the Delaware and Maryland declarations. Delaware, as did Maryland, guaranteed frequent election because "the Right in the People to participate in the Legislature, is the Foundation of Liberty and of all free Government." Delaware Declaration of Rights, 6, in Bushman, Hancock, and Homsey, *Proceedings of Delaware*, 213; Maryland Declaration of Rights, 5, in Thorpe, *Constitutions*, 3:1687.

39. Virginia Declaration of Rights, sec. 6, in Thorpe, *Constitutions*, 7:3813. Also see Pennsylvania Declaration of Rights, 7, in ibid., 5:3083; Maryland Declaration of Rights, 5, in ibid., 3:1687; Delaware Declaration of Rights, 6, in Bushman, Hancock, and Homsey, *Proceedings of Delaware*, 213. The North Carolina Declaration of Rights, 6, was limited to the insistence that elections be free. Thorpe, *Constitutions*, 5:2787.

40. North Carolina Declaration of Rights, 4, in Thorpe, *Constitutions*, 5:2787. The

theory and practice of a separation of powers is discussed in Chapter 6 below.

41. Maryland Declaration of Rights, 32, in ibid., 3:1689.

42. See, for example, Maryland Declaration of Rights, 8, 9, 10, in ibid., 1687.

43. Maryland Declaration of Rights, 21, in ibid., 1688; Virginia Declaration of Rights, sec. 8, in ibid., 7:3813; Pennsylvania Declaration of Rights, 9, in ibid., 5:3083. Also see Vermont Declaration of Rights, 10, in ibid., 6:3741, and Massachusetts Declaration of Rights, art. 12, in Handlin and Handlin, *Popular Sources*, 445.

44. See, for example, Maryland Declaration, 12, in Thorpe, *Constitutions*, 3:1687. Other declarations phrased the prohibition differently. See Virginia Declaration of Rights, sec. 6, in ibid., 7:3813; Pennsylvania Declaration of Rights, 8, in ibid., 5:3083; North Carolina Declaration of Rights, 16, in ibid., 2788; Vermont Declaration of Rights, 9, in ibid., 6:3740–41; Delaware Declaration of Rights, 10, in Bushman, Hancock, and Homsey, *Proceedings of Delaware*, 213; and Massachusetts Declaration of Rights, arts. 10 and 23, in Handlin and Handlin, *Popular Sources*, 444, 447.

45. Maryland Declaration of Rights, 20, in Thorpe, *Constitutions*, 3:1688.

46. Massachusetts Declaration of Rights, art. 14, in Handlin and Handlin, *Popular Sources*, 445.

47. Delaware Declaration of Rights, 19, in Bushman, Hancock, and Homsey, *Proceedings of Delaware*, 214. Also see Maryland Declaration of Rights, 26, in Thorpe, *Constitutions*, 3:1688, and Massachusetts Declaration of Rights, art. 17, in Handlin and Handlin, *Popular Sources*, 446. For the intellectual origins of this section, see Schwoerer, *No Standing Armies*.

48. Maryland Declaration of Rights, 28, in Thorpe, *Constitutions*, 3:1688; Massachusetts Declaration of Rights, art. 27, in Handlin and Handlin, *Popular Sources*, 447; Delaware Declaration of Rights, 21, in Bushman, Hancock, and Homsey, *Proceedings of Delaware*, 214.

49. Massachusetts Declaration of Rights, art. 28, in Handlin and Handlin, *Popular Sources*, 447.

50. Cf. Wood, *Radicalism of the American Revolution*, 188–89.

51. Virginia was unique in its requirement that *all* legislation originate in the house, but it made only money bills unamendable by the senate. Thorpe, *Constitutions*, 7:3816. New Jersey Constitution (1776), 6, in ibid., 5:2596; South Carolina Constitution (1776), 7, and (1778), 16, in ibid., 6:3244, 3252.

52. New Hampshire Constitution (1776), in ibid., 4:2452; Delaware Constitution (1776), art. 6, in Bushman, Hancock, and Homsey, *Proceedings of Delaware*, 219–20; Massachusetts Constitution (1780), pt. 2, chap. 1, sec. 3, art. 7, in Handlin and Handlin, *Popular Sources*, 455.

53. On the controversy over the tax to support the clergy, see Hoffmann, *A Spirit of Dissension*, 118–20. On taxation in colonial Maryland more generally, see Robert Becker, *Politics of American Taxation*, 89–94, 106.

54. "Instructions to the Delegates of Anne Arundel County, in Maryland Convention," *Maryland Gazette*, August 22, 1776.

55. Maryland Declaration of Rights, 13, in Thorpe, *Constitutions*, 3:1687.

56. Maryland Constitution (1776), 10, 11, in ibid., 1692–93.

57. Massachusetts Constitution (1780), pt. 2, chap. 1, sec. 1, art. 4, in Handlin and Handlin, *Popular Sources*, 449–50.

58. Pennsylvania Constitution (1776), sec. 41, in Thorpe, *Constitutions*, 5:3091; Vermont Constitution (1777), sec. 37, in ibid., 6:3747.

59. Pennsylvania Constitution (1776), sec. 47, in ibid., 5:3091; Vermont Constitution (1777), sec. 44, in ibid., 6:3748–49. The council's other functions are discussed in the last section of the present chapter.

60. Maryland Declaration of Rights, 19, in ibid., 3:1688; North Carolina Declaration of Rights, 7, 9, in ibid., 5:2787; Virginia Declaration of Rights, sec. 8, in ibid., 7:3813; Pennsylvania Declaration of Rights, 9, in ibid., 5:3083; New Jersey Constitution (1776), 22, in ibid., 2598; Georgia Constitution (1777), arts. 59–61, in ibid., 2:785; New York Constitution (1777), 41, in ibid., 5:2637; Delaware Declaration of Rights, 13, 14, in Bushman, Hancock, and Homsey, *Proceedings of Delaware*, 213. No persons in Delaware and Pennsylvania could be compelled to incriminate themselves. Delaware Declaration of Rights, 15, in ibid.; Pennsylvania Declaration of Rights, 9, in Thorpe, *Constitutions*, 5:3083. Maryland allowed the legislature to abrogate the prohibition of self-incrimination. Maryland Declaration of Rights, 20, in ibid., 3:1688.

61. On ex post facto legislation, see Maryland Declaration of Rights, 15, in Thorpe, *Constitutions*, 3:1689; North Carolina Declaration of Rights, 24, in ibid., 5:2788; Delaware Declaration of Rights, 11, in Bushman, Hancock, and Homsey, *Proceedings of Delaware*, 213; Massachusetts Declaration of Rights, art. 24, in Handlin and Handlin, *Popular Sources*, 447. The quotations are from the Maryland Declaration of Rights, 22, 23, in Thorpe, *Constitutions*, 3:1688. For same or similar language, see the Virginia Declaration of Rights, secs. 9, 10, in ibid., 7:3813–14; North Carolina Declaration of Rights, 11, in ibid., 5:2788; Pennsylvania Declaration of Rights, 10, in ibid., 3083; Delaware Declaration of Rights, 16, 17, in Bushman, Hancock, and Homsey, *Proceedings of Delaware*, 213–14; and Massachusetts Declaration of Rights, art. 26, in Handlin and Handlin, *Popular Sources*, 447.

62. Maryland Declaration of Rights, 16, in Thorpe, *Constitutions*, 3:1688; New York Constitution (1777), 41, in ibid., 5:2637.

63. North Carolina Declaration of Rights, 14, in ibid., 2788; Virginia Declaration of Rights, sec. 11, in ibid., 7:3814; Pennsylvania Declaration of Rights, 11, in ibid., 5:3083.

64. New Jersey Constitution (1776), 22, 23, in ibid., 2598.

65. Maryland Declaration of Rights, 39, in ibid., 3:1690; North Carolina Declaration of Rights, 23, in ibid., 5:2788.

66. Maryland Declaration of Rights, 40, in ibid., 3:1690; North Carolina Declaration of Rights, 22, in ibid., 5:2788; Virginia Declaration of Rights, sec. 4, in ibid., 7:3813; Massachusetts Declaration of Rights, art. 6, in Handlin and Handlin, *Popular Sources*, 443–44.

67. See North Carolina Declaration of Rights, 15, in Thorpe, *Constitutions*, 5:2788; Virginia Declaration of Rights, sec. 12, in ibid., 7:3814; Pennsylvania Declaration of Rights, 12, in ibid., 5:3083; Maryland Declaration of Rights, 38, in ibid., 3:1690; Georgia Constitution (1777), art. 61, in ibid., 2:785; South Carolina Constitution (1778), 43, in ibid., 6:3257; Delaware Declaration of Rights, 23, in Bushman, Hancock, and Homsey, *Proceedings of Delaware*, 214; Massachusetts Declaration of Rights, art. 16, in Handlin and Handlin, *Popular Sources*, 446. For valuable discussions, see Levy, *Emergence of a Free Press*, 3–219, and Buel, "Freedom of the Press," 59–98.

68. North Carolina Declaration of Rights, 18, in Thorpe, *Constitutions*, 5:2788; Pennsylvania Declaration of Rights, 16, in ibid., 3084; Delaware Declaration of Rights, 9, in Bushman, Hancock, and Homsey, *Proceedings of Delaware*, 213; Massachusetts Declaration of Rights, art. 19, in Handlin and Handlin, *Popular Sources*, 446.

69. North Carolina Declaration of Rights, 17, in Thorpe, *Constitutions*, 5:2788; Virginia Declaration of Rights, sec. 13, in ibid., 7:3814; Pennsylvania Declaration of Rights, 13, in ibid., 5:3085; Delaware Declaration of Rights, 19, in Bushman, Hancock, and Homsey, *Proceedings of Delaware*, 214. Delaware's declaration (art. 21) also forbade the housing of soldiers in private homes during peacetime.

70. Virginia Declaration of Rights, sec. 13, in Thorpe, *Constitutions*, 7:3814; Pennsylvania Declaration of Rights, 13, in ibid., 5:3083; Delaware Declaration of Rights, 20, in Bushman, Hancock, and Homsey, *Proceedings of Delaware*, 214.

71. For a summary of constitutional provisions regarding freedom of religion, see Stokes, *Church and State*, 1:366–446. For a fuller discussion, see Curry, *First Freedoms*, 134–92.

72. Virginia Declaration of Rights, sec. 16, in Thorpe, *Constitutions*, 7:3814.

73. North Carolina Declaration of Rights, 19, in ibid., 5:2788.

74. New Jersey Constitution (1776), 18, in ibid., 2597.

75. Pennsylvania Declaration of Rights, 2, in ibid., 3082; also see Vermont Declaration of Rights, 3, in ibid., 6:3740. The Delaware Declaration of Rights, 2, varies in capitalization and adds the plural to "understanding." Bushman, *Proceedings of Delaware*, 212.

76. Georgia Constitution (1777), art. 56, in Thorpe, *Constitutions*, 2:784.

77. New York Constitution (1777), 38, in ibid., 5:2636–37.

78. Massachusetts Declaration of Rights, art. 2, in Handlin and Handlin, *Popular Sources*, 442.

79. Pennsylvania Declaration of Rights, 8, in Thorpe, *Constitutions*, 5:3083; Vermont Declaration of Rights, 9, in ibid., 6:3740; New York Constitution (1777), 40, in ibid., 5:2637; Delaware Declaration of Rights, 10, in Bushman, Hancock, and Homsey, *Proceedings of Delaware*, 213; New Hampshire Declaration of Rights (1784), 13, in Thorpe, *Constitutions*, 4:2455.

80. South Carolina Constitution (1778), 38, in Thorpe, *Constitutions*, 6:3255–57.

81. Maryland Declaration of Rights, 33, in ibid., 3:1689–90.

82. New Jersey Constitution (1776), 19, in ibid., 5:2597.

83. Pennsylvania Declaration of Rights, 2, in ibid., 3082; Delaware Declaration of Rights, 2, in Bushman, Hancock, and Homsey, *Proceedings of Delaware*, 212.

84. North Carolina Constitution (1776), 34, in Thorpe, *Constitutions*, 5:2793. Georgia's constitution contained a similar provision. Georgia Constitution (1777), art. 56, in ibid., 2:784. For a different reading of the Georgia article, see McLoughlin, "Role of Religion," 215.

85. New York Constitution (1777), 35, in Thorpe, *Constitutions*, 5:2636.

86. Virginia Constitution (1776), in ibid., 7:3818; North Carolina Constitution (1776), 31, 32, in ibid., 5:2793; Maryland Constitution (1776), 37, in ibid., 3:1697; Delaware Constitution (1776), art. 29, in Bushman, Hancock, and Homsey, *Proceedings of Delaware*, 224; Georgia Constitution (1777), art. 62, in Thorpe, *Constitutions*,

2:785; New York Constitution (1777), 39, in ibid., 5:2637; and South Carolina Constitution (1778), 21, in ibid., 6:3253.

87. South Carolina Constitution (1778), 21, in Thorpe, *Constitutions*, 6:3253.

88. New Jersey Constitution (1776), 19, in ibid. 5:2597–98. Likewise, the Vermont declaration asserted that no "man who professes the protestant religion, be justly deprived or abridged of any civil right, as a citizen, or account of his religious sentiment." Vermont Declaration of Rights, 3, in ibid., 6:3740. Similarly, the South Carolina constitution of 1778 asserted that "all denominations of Christian Protestants in this State, demeaning themselves peaceably and faithfully, shall enjoy equal religious and civil privileges." South Carolina Constitution (1778), 38, in ibid., 3255–57.

89. Maryland Declaration of Rights, 33, in ibid., 3:1689–90.

90. Pennsylvania Declaration of Rights, 2, in ibid., 5:3082.

91. New Jersey Constitution (1776), 19, in ibid., 2597–98. For a description of religious tests for officeholding, see Gaustad, "Religious Tests."

92. Georgia Constitution (1777), art. 6, in Thorpe, *Constitutions*, 2:779; North Carolina Constitution (1776), 32, in ibid., 5:2793; Delaware Constitution (1776), art. 22, in Bushman, Hancock, and Homsey, *Proceedings of Delaware*, 223; and Vermont Constitution (1777), sec. 9, in Thorpe, *Constitutions*, 6:3743.

93. Pennsylvania Constitution (1776), sec. 10, in Thorpe, *Constitutions*, 5:3085; Maryland Declaration of Rights, 35, in ibid., 3:1690; Massachusetts Constitution (1780), pt. 2, chap. 2, sec. 1, art. 2, and chap. 6, art. 1 (Christian oath), in Handlin and Handlin, *Popular Sources*, 456, 467–68. The additional test oath, which was directed at Roman Catholics, is also in chap. 6, art. 1, in ibid., 468.

94. South Carolina Constitution (1778), 12, 13, in Thorpe, *Constitutions*, 6:3250, 3252; New Hampshire Constitution (1784), pt. 2, in ibid., 4:2460–63, 2465.

95. My discussion of general assessments for religion follows McLoughlin, "Role of Religion," 197–255.

96. Maryland Declaration of Rights, 33, 34, in Thorpe, *Constitutions*, 3:1689–90.

97. The doctrinal requirements included belief in "one eternal God," an afterlife, public worship of God, "the Christian religion is the true religion," both Old and New Testaments as "of divine inspiration" and that they provided the "rule of faith and practice," and "the duty of every man . . . called by those that govern, to bear witness to the truth." South Carolina Constitution (1778), 28, in ibid., 6:3255–57.

98. Massachusetts Declaration of Rights, art. 3, in Handlin and Handlin, *Popular Sources*, 442–43.

99. For a full discussion, see McLoughlin, *New England Dissent*, 1:591–635.

100. New Jersey Constitution (1776), 18, in Thorpe, *Constitutions*, 5:2597; North Carolina Constitution (1776), 34, in ibid., 2793.

101. Georgia Constitution (1777), art. 56, in ibid., 2:784.

102. Delaware Constitution (1776), arts. 2, 30, in Bushman, Hancock, and Homsey, *Proceedings of Delaware*, 219, 224.

103. New Jersey Constitution (1776), 4, in Thorpe, *Constitutions*, 5:2595.

104. Georgia Constitution (1777), art. 9, in ibid., 2:779.

105. Delaware explicitly permitted the legislature to alter the state's existing suffrage qualifications. See Delaware Constitution (1776), arts. 5, 30, in Bushman, Hancock, and Homsey, *Proceedings of Delaware*, 219, 224.

106. Maryland Constitution (1776), 16, 2, in Thorpe, *Constitutions*, 3:1694, 1691.

107. Pennsylvania Constitution (1776), sec. 7, in ibid., 5:3084; New Hampshire Constitution (1784), pt. 2, "Senate," in ibid., 4:2460.

108. Georgia Constitution (1777), arts. 23, 24, in ibid., 2:781.

109. See the summary table on terms of office in Adams, *First American Constitutions*, 245.

110. Ibid., 308–11, provides an excellent summary of requirements for rotation in office, which are discussed in this paragraph and the next.

111. Pennsylvania Constitution (1776), sec. 31, in Thorpe, *Constitutions*, 5:3089; New Jersey Constitution (1776), 13, in ibid., 2597.

112. New York Constitution (1777), 26, in ibid., 2634.

113. South Carolina Constitution (1778), 28, 29, in ibid., 6:3254–55.

114. Pennsylvania Constitution (1776), sec. 8, in ibid., 5:3084.

115. Maryland Constitution (1776), 2, in ibid., 3:1691; North Carolina Constitution (1776), 2, 3, in ibid., 5:2790; Pennsylvania Constitution (1776), sec. 9, in ibid., 3084–85; Georgia Constitution (1777), art. 13, in ibid., 2:780.

116. New York Constitution (1777), 6, in ibid., 5:2630.

117. On the American response to Wilkes's plight, see Maier, *From Resistance to Revolution*, 162–78; Maryland Constitution (1776), 10, in Thorpe, *Constitutions*, 3:1692; Pennsylvania Constitution (1776), sec. 9, in ibid., 5:3084–85.

118. North Carolina Constitution (1776), 46, in ibid., 2794; Pennsylvania Constitution (1776), sec. 10, in ibid., 3085; Maryland Constitution (1776), 8, 20, in ibid., 3:1692, 1694; South Carolina Constitution (1776), 12, in ibid., 6:3245; New Hampshire Constitution (1784), in ibid., 4:2460, 2462.

119. Massachusetts Constitution (1780), pt. 2, chap. 1, sec. 1, art. 1, in Handlin and Handlin, *Popular Sources*, 448.

120. North Carolina Constitution (1776), 40, in Thorpe, *Constitutions*, 5:2793–94. New York required a naturalization law but left the crucial details to the legislature. New York Constitution (1777), 42, in ibid., 2637–38.

121. See Georgia Constitution (1777), art. 51, in ibid., 2:784, which also allowed the legislature to alter rules of intestate estates; North Carolina Constitution (1776), 43, in ibid., 5:2794, which required the legislature to regulate entails to "prevent perpetuities"; and Pennsylvania Constitution (1776), sec. 37, in ibid., 3090.

122. For example, see South Carolina Constitution (1778), 8, in ibid., 6:3249.

123. Georgia Constitution (1777), art. 7, in ibid., 2:779. Also see Pennsylvania Constitution (1776), sec. 9, in ibid., 5:3084–85.

124. Massachusetts Constitution (1780), pt. 2, chap. 1, sec. 1, art. 4, in Handlin and Handlin, *Popular Sources*, 449–50.

125. New Jersey Constitution (1776), 23, in Thorpe, *Constitutions*, 5:2598; also see Vermont Constitution (1777), sec. 8, in ibid., 6:3742–43; New Hampshire Constitution (1784), "The General Court," in ibid., 4:2458.

126. For an excellent brief discussion of Locke and revolution, see Tully, "Locke," 616–52. For observations about the connection, or lack thereof, of Lockean thought to constitutional amendment, see Peterson, "Thomas Jefferson," 279, and Adams, *First American Constitutions*, 139.

127. Bernstein, "Italian Political Thought," 30–65 (41–58 on Machiavelli; quotation, 57).

128. Thomas Jefferson to Edmund Pendleton, August 13, 1776, in Boyd, *Papers of Jefferson*, 1:492.

129. See "Second Draft by Jefferson" in ibid., 347. In the third draft, Jefferson revised the language slightly. See "Third Draft by Jefferson," in ibid., 356.

130. George Mason included this phrase in his original draft of the declaration, and the convention adopted it in the final version. See "First Draft of the Virginia Declaration of Rights," in Rutland, *Papers of George Mason*, 1:276; Virginia Declaration of Rights, Preamble, in Thorpe, *Constitutions*, 7:3812.

131. Bushman, Hancock, and Homsey, *Proceedings of Delaware*, 212.

132. Pennsylvania Declaration of Rights, 5, in Thorpe, *Constitutions*, 5:3082–83; Vermont Declaration of Rights, 6, in ibid., 6:3740; also see the similar statements in the Massachusetts Declaration of Rights, art. 7, in Handlin and Handlin, *Popular Sources*, 444; Virginia Declaration of Rights, sec. 3, in Thorpe, *Constitutions*, 6:3813; Maryland Declaration of Rights, 4, in ibid., 3:1687; New Hampshire Declaration of Rights, 10, in ibid., 4:2455.

133. "Address of the Convention, March 1780," in Handlin and Handlin, *Popular Sources*, 435.

134. "Four Letters on Interesting Subjects" (Philadelphia, 1776), in Hyneman and Lutz, *American Political Writing*, 1:387.

135. Demophilus, *Genuine Principles*, in ibid., 361.

136. North Carolina Declaration of Rights, 21, in Thorpe, *Constitutions*, 5:2788.

137. Demophilus, *Genuine Principles*, in Hyneman and Lutz, *American Political Writing*, 1:363.

138. Pennsylvania Constitution (1776), sec. 47, in Thorpe, *Constitutions*, 5:3091–92.

139. Massachusetts Constitution (1780), pt. 2, chap. 6, art. 10, in Handlin and Handlin, *Popular Sources*, 471.

140. Demophilus, *Genuine Principles*, in Hyneman and Lutz, *American Political Writing*, 1:361.

141. Jefferson, *Notes on the State of Virginia*, 121–25.

142. John Rutledge to Henry Laurens, Charles Town, March 8, 1778, in Hamer, Chesnutt, et al., *Papers of Henry Laurens*, 12:527–29.

143. South Carolina Constitution (1778), 44, in Thorpe, *Constitutions*, 6:3257.

144. New Jersey Constitution (1776), 23, in ibid., 5:2598; for a different interpretation of this article, see Lutz, *Popular Consent*, 62–63.

145. New Jersey Constitution (1776), 23, in Thorpe, *Constitutions*, 5:2598; McCormick, *History of Voting in New Jersey*, 70, 75, 75n.

146. Delaware Constitution (1776), art. 30, in Bushman, Hancock, and Homsey, *Proceedings of Delaware*, 224.

147. Maryland Constitution (1776), 59, in Thorpe, *Constitutions*, 3:1701; see the convention's consideration of this article in "Proceedings, November 6, 1776," in Papenfuse and Stiverson, *Decisive Blow*, n.p.

148. Pennsylvania Constitution (1776), sec. 47, in Thorpe, *Constitutions*, 5:3091–92; Vermont Constitution (1777), sec. 44, in ibid., 6:3748–49.

149. "Meeting in the State-House Yard, Philadelphia, October 22, 1776," in Force, *American Archives*, 5th ser., 2:1152; also see K., "Remarks on the Constitution of Pennsylvania," *Pennsylvania Packet*, September 24, 1776; "Meeting at Philosophical Society

Hall, October 17, 1776, to oppose the Constitution but support independence," ibid., October 22, 1776.

150. Camillus, "To the Freemen of Pennsylvania," *Pennsylvania Packet*, October 29, 1776.

151. "Philadelphia meeting, November 2, 1776," ibid., November 5, 1776.

152. Consideration, "Remarks on the Proceedings and Resolutions of the Meeting in the State-House Yard, on Monday and Tuesday, October 21 and 22, 1776" (Philadelphia, October 30, 1776), in Force, *American Archives*, 5th ser., 2:1153–55 (quotations, 1153 and 1155).

153. "One of the People," *Pennsylvania Packet*, November 5, 1776; see also "The Considerate Freeman, No. II," ibid., November 19, 1776.

154. "Philadelphia Meeting of Citizens, Philosophical Society Hall, November 8, 1776," in Force, *American Archives*, 5th ser., 3:598–99; also see "Christophilus Scotus, October 22, 1776 (In the interior parts of Pennsylvania)," and "Union," *Pennsylvania Packet*, October 29 and November 19, 1776.

155. Georgia Constitution (1777), art. 63, in Thorpe, *Constitutions*, 2:785.

156. New Hampshire Constitution (1784), in ibid., 4:2470.

157. Massachusetts Constitution (1780), pt. 2, chap. 6, art. 10, in Handlin and Handlin, *Popular Sources*, 471.

158. The fear of legislative tyranny increased substantially as the war compelled the legislatures to pass numerous acts of positive legislation, legislation that intruded substantially on the lives of ordinary citizens. See Rakove, "Parchment Barriers," 124; Wood, *Creation*, 363–76.

Chapter 4

1. On English constitutional understandings of representation as restraint, see Reid, *Concept of Representation*, esp. 2.

2. On the Stamp Act controversy, see Morgan and Morgan, *Stamp Act Crisis*. On the special hostility Englishmen and Americans reserved for internal taxes, see Slaughter, "The Taxman Cometh," 566–91; and Slaughter, *Whiskey Rebellion*, 11–27.

3. *An Address to "Friends and Countrymen" on the Stamp Act*, November 1765, in Ford, *Writings of John Dickinson*, 202.

4. See Whately's lengthy pamphlet, *The Regulations lately Made concerning the Colonies and the Taxes Imposed upon Them, Considered* (London, 1765). Whately devoted most of the pamphlet to a defense of the Sugar Act. In the last section, he defended Parliament's right to tax the colonists. That section is reprinted in Morgan, *Prologue to Revolution*, 17–23 (quotations, 21). The same may also be found in Greene, *Colonies to Nation*, 46–51.

5. Wood, *Creation*, 174.

6. Dulany, "Considerations on the Propriety of Imposing Taxes in the British Colonies," in Bailyn, *Pamphlets of the American Revolution*, 1:615.

7. "A Letter from a Plain Yeoman," *Providence Gazette*, May 11, 1765, reprinted in Morgan, *Prologue to Revolution*, 75–76.

8. Labaree, *Royal Government in America*, 186–87 (quotation, 187).

9. South Carolina General Assembly to Governor John Rutledge, December 13, 1776, *South Carolina and American General Gazette*, January [?], 1777. For a different view of revolutionary understandings of "equal representation," see Adams, *First American Constitutions*, 236–39.

10. For a different explanation of developments discussed in this section, see Zagarri, *Politics of Size*, 36–60. Zagarri argues that small states retained corporate representation and that large states moved toward numerical representation. The evidence offered in this section has led me to different conclusions. For example, Massachusetts adopted a system of corporation representation modified by population size; so did its small neighbor, New Hampshire. A large state, South Carolina in 1778, promised regular reapportionment according to population and wealth, but did not deliver on the promise until 1808. A small state, New Jersey, also promised reapportionment related to population changes, and responded (though not systematically) by altering representation in several counties. Geography, not size, provides a better explanation of how the states apportioned representation. For example, all the states of the Chesapeake region, large and small, *but only those states*, retained a pure form of corporate representation.

11. Greene, *Quest for Power*, 181–82.

12. Ibid., 174–84; Ekirch, *"Poor Carolina,"* 86–111.

13. Ganyard, *North Carolina's Revolutionary State Government*, 68, 81.

14. Virginia Constitution (1776), in Thorpe, *Constitutions*, 7:3815–16; Selby, *Revolution in Virginia*, 117; Munroe, *Colonial Delaware*, 231.

15. "Maryland Convention Proceedings, September 6, 1776," in Papenfuse and Stiverson, *Decisive Blow*, n.p.; Barker, *Background of the Revolution in Maryland*, 172.

16. Daniell, *Experiment in Republicanism*, 26–32, 78.

17. "Publicus," *New Hampshire Gazette*, March 18, 1774, quoted in ibid., 78.

18. Daniell, *Experiment in Republicanism*, 78, 86–87, 89. Also see Wentworth's correspondence with the assembly on July 14 and 18, 1775, in Bouton, *Provincial Papers*, 7:383–86.

19. Daniell, *Experiment in Republicanism*, 107–8.

20. For an excellent discussion of the representation controversy in New Hampshire, see ibid., 145–52, 165–66. The arguments of the westerners may be traced in Bouton, *Documents Relating to the State of New-Hampshire*, 8:421–26, 451. On town representation and allowance of greater representation for large towns, see *A People the Best Governors* (New Hampshire, 1776), in Hyneman and Lutz, *American Political Writing*, 1:395–97.

21. New Hampshire Constitution (1784), in Thorpe, *Constitutions*, 4:2461.

22. Charter of Massachusetts Bay, 1691, in ibid., 3:1878; Brown, *Middle-Class Democracy*, 63–64.

23. Patterson, *Political Parties in Revolutionary Massachusetts*, 144–45, 155, 167.

24. Massachusetts Constitution of 1780, pt. 2, chap. 1, sec. 3, arts. 1 and 2, in Handlin and Handlin, *Popular Sources*, 454.

25. Address of the Convention, March 1780, in ibid., 438; see the excellent discussion of corporate and individual representation in Pole, *Political Representation*, 198–204.

26. Pole, *Political Representation*, 204. Neighboring Vermont more closely approxi-

mated such a state of nature, but it, too, blended corporate and numerical representation. The constitution granted two representatives to all towns with eighty taxable inhabitants "within . . . seven years, next." It granted one representative to "each other inhabited town," regardless of the number of its inhabitants, taxable or not. Vermont Constitution (1777), chap. 2, sec. 16, in Thorpe, *Constitutions*, 6:3744. On constitution making in Vermont, see Bellisles, *Revolutionary Outlaws*, 136–41.

27. Greene, *Quest for Power*, 383–84; Coleman, *American Revolution in Georgia*, 33. The first quotation is from Greene, 384; the second from Coleman, 33.

28. Klein, *Unification*, 41.

29. Greene, *Quest for Power*, 381–82.

30. Klein, *Unification*, 41, 74; also see Greene, *Quest for Power*, 382.

31. Weir, *Colonial South Carolina*, 279.

32. Greene, *Quest for Power*, 382–83.

33. Klein, *Unification*, 82.

34. South Carolina Constitution (1776), 11, in Thorpe, *Constitutions*, 6:3244–45; South Carolina Constitution (1778), 13, in ibid., 3251; Nadelhaft, *Disorders of War*, 30–31, 43. The percentage for the colonial era is from Main, "Government by the People," 334.

35. South Carolina Constitution (1778), 15, in Thorpe, *Constitutions*, 6:3252.

36. McCormick, *Voting in New Jersey*, 36.

37. Ibid., 54.

38. New Jersey Constitution (1776), 3, in Thorpe, *Constitutions*, 5:2595.

39. On colonial representation in New York, see Bonomi, *A Factious People*, 186n, 240n; and Countryman, *A People in Revolution*, 74–75.

40. New York Constitution (1777), 4, 5, in Thorpe, *Constitutions*, 5:2629–30.

41. Illick, *Colonial Pennsylvania*, 173, 174.

42. Ryerson, *Revolution Is Now Begun*, 12–13.

43. Ibid., 162–63.

44. Ibid., 231.

45. Pennsylvania Constitution (1776), sec. 17, in Thorpe, *Constitutions*, 5:3086.

46. Adams, *First American Constitutions*, 237.

47. Virginia Constitution (1776), in Thorpe, *Constitutions*, 7:3816.

48. Maryland Constitution (1776), 4, 5, in ibid., 3:1691–92.

49. Wood, *Creation*, 171.

50. See North Carolina Constitution (1776), 3, in Thorpe, *Constitutions*, 5:2790.

51. Georgia Constitution (1777), art. 4, in ibid., 2:779–80.

52. Historians have generally accepted Federalist contentions that local or direct representation automatically meant parochial representation. See, for example, Morgan, *Inventing the People*, 209–15, 266–77; Wood, *Creation*, 393–518.

53. Wood, *Representation in the American Revolution*, 17.

54. Morgan, *Inventing the People*, 209–23; Pole, *Political Representation*, 344, 441.

55. For a different view, see Morgan, *Inventing the People*, 209–23.

56. See especially Brown, *Revolutionary Politics in Massachusetts*, 24.

57. Samuel Chase to John Adams, Annapolis, June 21, 1776, in Taylor, *Papers of Adams*, 4:323.

58. Richard Henry Lee to Charles Lee, June 29, 1776, in Ballagh, *Letters of Lee*, 1:204.

59. "Instructions to Delegates in Convention for Anne Arundel County," in Force, *American Archives*, 4th ser., 6:1092.

60. Samuel Chase to John Adams, June 28, 1776, in Taylor, *Papers of Adams*, 4:351.

61. Chase explained his objections to these parts of the instructions when he resigned as a member of the state legislature in December 1777. See "Samuel Chase, Strawberry-Mount, December 1, 1777," *Maryland Gazette*, December 10, 1777.

62. Charles Carroll of Carrollton to Charles Carroll of Annapolis, [August 17, 1776], in Charles Carroll of Carrollton Papers. For a valuable discussion of Carroll of Carrollton, see Maier, *Old Revolutionaries*, 201–68.

63. Charles Carroll, Brice T. B. Worthington, and Samuel Chase, "To the ELECTORS of Anne-Arundel County, Aug. 19, 1776," *Maryland Gazette*, August 22, 1776.

64. Charles Carroll of Carrollton to Charles Carroll of Annapolis, August 20, 1776, and August 23, 1776, in Charles Carroll of Carrollton Papers.

65. Ibid.

66. Chase, though, did get back into the convention as a delegate from Annapolis.

67. "Instructions from Wrentham, Norfolk Co., June 5, 1776," in Force, *American Archives*, 4th ser., 6:699–700.

68. "Instructions to Nathan Cushing, Esq. Representative of the Town of Scituate, June 4, 1776," in ibid., 699.

69. "Freeholders of James City County to Delegates Robert Carter Nicholas and William Norvell: A Public Letter of Instruction," in Scribner and Tarter, *Revolutionary Virginia*, 6:458, originally published in Purdie's *Virginia Gazette*, April 26, 1776, supplement. Also see "Charlotte County Committee to Delegates Paul Carrington and Thomas Read," in ibid., May 10, 1776.

70. "To Charles Patteson and John Cabell, Gentlemen, Delegates for the County of Buckingham, in Virginia, now in General Convention: The Address and Instruction of the Freeholders of the said County," in Force, *American Archives*, 4th ser., 6:459.

71. "Town of Stoughton instructions to Thomas Crane, Town meeting, May 18, 1778," *Continental Journal*, June 18, 1778.

72. "The sentiments of the several companies of militia and freeholders of Augusta, in Virginia, communicated by the deputies from the said companies and freeholders to their representatives in the General Assembly of the commonwealth," Purdie's *Virginia Gazette*, October 18, 1776.

73. "A Planter," Dixon and Hunter's *Virginia Gazette*, April 6, 1776.

74. Thomas Rodney to Caesar Rodney, May 26 and June 2, 1776, in Ryden, *Letters to and from Rodney*, 84, 88; also see John Haslet to Caesar Rodney, [May 1776], in ibid., 87.

75. The quotation is from the Pennsylvania Declaration of Rights, 16, in Thorpe, *Constitutions*, 5:3084; for the same or similar assertions, see North Carolina Declaration of Rights, 18, in ibid., 2788; Vermont Declaration of Rights, 18, in ibid., 6:3741–42; Massachusetts Declaration of Rights, art. 19, in Handlin and Handlin, *Popular Sources*, 446.

76. Pole, *Political Representation*, 403; Pole, *Gift of Government*, 117–31. Pennsylvania Constitution (1776), secs. 13, 14, in Thorpe, *Constitutions*, 5:3085–86; North Carolina Constitution (1776), 45, 46, in ibid., 2794; Vermont Constitution (1777), secs. 12, 13, in ibid., 6:3744; New York Constitution (1777), 15, in ibid., 5:2632; New Hampshire Constitution (1784), in ibid., 4:2462; Massachusetts Constitution (1780), pt. 2, chap. 1,

sec. 1, art. 2, in Handlin and Handlin, *Popular Sources*, 448–49.

77. "Some Thoughts on Government, for the Consideration of the good people of the STATE of MASSACHUSETTS-BAY," *Providence Gazette*, November 23, 1776.

78. New Jersey Constitution (1776), 3, in Thorpe, *Constitutions*, 5:2595; Maryland Constitution (1776), 2, in ibid., 3:1691; North Carolina Constitution (1776), 6, in ibid., 5:2461; Vermont Constitution (1777), chap. 2, sec. 7, which required a "foreigner" to meet a one-year residency requirement, in ibid., 6:3742; Massachusetts Constitution (1780), pt. 2, chap. 1, sec. 1, art. 3, in Handlin and Handlin, *Popular Sources*; Georgia Constitution (1777), art. 6, in Thorpe, *Constitutions*, 2:779; Virginia Constitution (1776), in ibid., 7:3816; Pennsylvania Constitution (1776), sec. 7, in ibid., 5:3084; New Hampshire Constitution (1784), which required of representatives two years state residency and a 100-acre freehold in the town or parish represented "or the value of 100 pounds, one half of which to be a freehold," in ibid., 4:2461; South Carolina Constitution (1778), 13, in ibid., 3252.

79. N. B., "Some Thoughts on an important Subject, for the Consideration of all the Friends to Liberty, but more especially the Honorable House of Representatives of the State of Massachusetts-Bay" [Rehoboth, September 4, 1776]," *Providence Gazette*, September 7, 1776.

80. Greene, *Quest for Power*, 200–203. But the legislatures of Connecticut, Massachusetts, New York, Pennsylvania, Rhode Island, and South Carolina had regular terms of office. See, for example, Bonomi, *A Factious People*, 135; Greene, *Quest for Power*, 199–200.

81. For a brief summary of the purpose and nature of the Triennial Act, see Pole, *Political Representation*, 392.

82. For an excellent discussion of the debate over and the passage of the Septennial Act, see Pole, *Political Representation*, 408–12, 424.

83. Greene, *Quest for Power*, 199–203; Bailyn, *Origins of American Politics*, 68n; also see Labaree, *Royal Government*, 190, 207.

84. Benjamin Rumsey to Maryland Council of Safety, Joppa, September 18, 1776, in Force, *American Archives*, 5th ser., 2:363.

85. William Gordon, "To the Inhabitants of the Massachusetts-Bay," Roxbury, September 7, 1776, in ibid., 228; "To the AUTHOR of a Pamphlet, entitled, 'A Candid Examination of the mutual claims of GREAT BRITAIN and her COLONIES, &c.,'" *Pennsylvania Journal*, March 8, 1775. Also on the Septennial Act, see "Cassandra to Cato," in Force, *American Archives*, 4th ser., 5:1093, and "S. McClintock to William Whipple, Greenland, New Hampshire, August 2, 1776," in ibid., 5th ser., 1:736.

86. Samuel Johnston to James Iredell, April 20, 1776, in Higginbotham, *Papers of Iredell*, 1:350. Also on the Septennial Act see "One of the People," *Pennsylvania Packet*, November 5, 1776.

87. *The Federalist Papers*, No. 53, 331–32; also see the observations of Gerald Stourzh on the American concerns about the Septennial Act in the years after the Revolution, Stourzh, "Fundamental Laws and Individual Rights," 180.

88. Wood, *Creation*, 166–67; the fear of the independent government official is well described in Bushman, *King and People*.

89. Jacob Green, *Observations*, 23; Demophilus, *Genuine Principles*, in Hyneman and Lutz, *American Political Writing*, 1:340–67. For Massachusetts, see Pittsfield

instructions to delegates, and the returns of Bellingham (Aug. 6) and Dudley (Aug. 16) in 1779 on the question of calling a constitutional convention, all in Handlin and Handlin, *Popular Sources*, 411, 413, 428. Cf. A Native of this Colony [Carter Braxton], "An Address to the Convention of the Colony and Ancient Dominion of Virginia on the Subject of Government in General, and Recommending a Particular For to their Attention," Dixon and Hunter's *Virginia Gazette*, June 8 and 15, 1776, which opposed frequent election of the governor; on annual election see Demophilus, *Genuine Principles*, in Hyneman and Lutz, *American Political Writing*, 1:353–54; and Zabdiel Adams, *An Election Sermon* (Boston, 1782), in ibid., 543–44.

90. "Petition of the Privates of the First Battalion of Militia in CUMBERLAND County," Proceedings of the Pennsylvania Assembly, March 11, 1776, in Force, *American Archives*, 4th ser., 5:680.

91. *Maryland Gazette*, July 18, 1776.

92. Demophilus, *Genuine Principles*, in Hyneman and Lutz, *American Political Writing*, 1:353.

93. Plymouth Town Meeting, June 1, 1778, in Handlin and Handlin, *Popular Sources*, 290.

94. Samuel Johnston to James Iredell, April 20, 1776, in Higginbotham, *Papers of Iredell*, 1:350. Also see "Philanthropy," *Essex Journal*, June 7, 1776.

95. Democraticus, "Loose Thoughts on GOVERNMENT," Purdie's *Virginia Gazette*, June 7, 1776.

96. John Adams, *Thoughts on Government* (Philadelphia, 1776), in Taylor, *Papers of Adams*, 4:90.

97. For examples, see Pennsylvania Constitution (1776), sec. 9, in Thorpe, *Constitutions*, 5:3084; Virginia Constitution (1776), in ibid., 7:3815–16. On South Carolina, see Nadelhaft, *Disorders of War*, 32.

98. Georgia Constitution (1777), art. 3, in Thorpe, *Constitutions*, 2:778.

Chapter 5

1. Return of Spencer, June 8, 1778, in Handlin and Handlin, *Popular Sources*, 302. Also see Return of Sutton, May 18, 1778, and return of Westminster, May 15, 1778, in ibid., 231, 312.

2. See J. R. Pole, "The Ambiguities of Power," in Greene, *American Revolution*, 126; Greene, "All Men Are Created Equal: Some Reflections on the Character of the American Revolution," in Greene, *Imperatives, Behaviors, and Identities*, 238, 265–66; and Wood, *Creation*, 168. Chilton Williamson discusses, but does not fully exploit, most of the evidence considered in this chapter. See Williamson, *American Suffrage*, 76–91.

3. Wood, *Creation*, 162–96, esp. 168, 179.

4. Force, *American Archives*, 4th ser., 4:430n.

5. Demophilus, *Genuine Principles*, in Hyneman and Lutz, *American Political Writing*, 1:344.

6. *Pennsylvania Packet*, March 25, 1779.

7. Unnamed town meeting, September 1776, not printed until 1777 in *Connecticut*

Courant, September 15, 1777; also reprinted in Force, *American Archives*, 5th ser., 2:113.

8. *Pennsylvania Journal*, May 14, 1777.

9. *Pennsylvania Evening Post*, October 24, 1776.

10. John Adams to James Sullivan, May 26, 1776, in Taylor, *Papers of Adams*, 4:211–12.

11. See especially Reid, *Authority to Tax*; Reid, *Concept of Representation*; Harris, *Politics under the Later Stuarts*, 17–18; Hirst, *The Representative of the People?*, 12–105; Plumb, "Growth of the Electorate," 90–116; Pocock, *Machiavellian Moment*, 203–4, 385–90, and Blackstone, *Commentaries*, bk. 1, chap. 2, 164–69.

12. Blackstone, *Commentaries*, bk. 2, chap. 2, 165–66; John Adams to James Sullivan, May 26, 1776, in Taylor, *Papers of Adams*, 4:210; also see Charles Carroll of Carrollton to Charles Carroll of Annapolis, August 20, 1776, in Carrollton Papers. On women's severely limited access to property ownership, see Salmon, *Women and the Law of Property*.

13. For a different reading of Jewish and alien disfranchisement and a somewhat different interpretation of Catholic disfranchisement, see Greene, "All Men Are Created Equal," 256, 258–59. On Jewish political disabilities in provincial British North America, see Marcus, *Colonial American Jew*, 1:397–511.

14. Charles Carroll of Carrollton to Charles Carroll of Annapolis, August 20, 1776, in Carrollton Papers. The controversy that prompted Carroll's comments was discussed in Chapter 4.

15. John Adams to James Sullivan, May 26, 1776, in Taylor, *Papers of Adams*, 4:210.

16. See Countryman, *A People in Revolution*, 36–71; Nash, *Urban Crucible*, 339–84; Maier, *From Resistance to Revolution*, 51–76.

17. Elbridge Gerry to Massachusetts Delegates to the Continental Congress, Watertown, June 4, 1775, in Force, *American Archives*, 4th ser., 2:905.

18. "Address of the Constitutional Convention of 1780," in Handlin and Handlin, *Popular Sources*, 437.

19. Virginia Constitution (1776), in Thorpe, *Constitutions*, 7:3816; Delaware Constitution (1776), art. 5, in Bushman, Hancock, and Homsey, *Proceedings of Delaware*, 219.

20. John Adams to James Sullivan, May 26, 1776, in Taylor, *Papers of Adams*, 4:210.

21. "Jefferson's First Draft," in Boyd, *Papers of Jefferson*, 1:344.

22. Maier, "Transforming Impact"; Katz, "Republicanism and the Law of Inheritance."

23. New York Constitution (1777), 7, in Thorpe, *Constitutions*, 5:2630.

24. See Hoffman, *Spirit of Dissension*, 180–81. Massachusetts, Rhode Island, and Connecticut had long allowed men to meet the property requirements with a personal estate.

25. New Jersey Constitution (1776), 4, in Thorpe, *Constitutions*, 5:2595; McCormick, *History of Voting in New Jersey*, 60–62, 68; Georgia Constitution (1777), art. 9, in Thorpe, *Constitutions*, 2:779.

26. Edmund Pendleton to Thomas Jefferson, August 10, 1776, in Boyd, *Papers of Jefferson*, 1:490.

27. For suffrage qualifications, see Pennsylvania Constitution (1776), sec. 6, in Thorpe, *Constitutions*, 5:3084; New Hampshire Constitution (1776), in ibid., 4:2452; New Hampshire Constitution (1784), in ibid., 2459–61, 2463; North Carolina Constitution (1776), 7, 8, 9, in ibid., 5:2790; South Carolina Constitution (1776), 11, in ibid.,

6:3245; South Carolina Constitution (1778), 7, in ibid., 3251–52; Vermont Constitution (1777), sec. 6, in ibid., 3742. For the suffrage provision in the defeated Massachusetts constitution of 1778, see Handlin and Handlin, *Popular Sources*, 192–93. "Proceedings of the Maryland Provincial Convention, November 4, 1776," in Papenfuse and Stiverson, *Decisive Blow*, n.p. The same day, the convention defeated (34–20) a proposal to reduce the personal property qualification from £30 to £5.

28. "Jefferson's Third Draft," in Boyd, *Papers of Jefferson*, 1:358. George Mason's initial draft of the Virginia constitution did propose that the suffrage be extended to any man who held a lease to land with at least seven years remaining on the lease and to any housekeeper who had one year's county residence "and hath been the father of three children in this country." See "Mason's Plan for the Virginia Constitution of 1776," in Rutland, *Papers of Mason*, 1:300.

29. Pole, *Political Representation*, 272–73 (quotations, 273).

30. Maryland Declaration of Rights, 13, in Thorpe, *Constitutions*, 3:1687.

31. It is ironic that the regressive poll tax broadened the suffrage dramatically in a number of states. On the poll tax, see Robert Becker, *Politics of Taxation*.

32. Reid, *Concept of Representation*, 20–25; Reid, *Authority to Legislate*, 97–99.

33. On this point, I recognize that a substantial portion of free adult males were eligible to vote, but those men, whether they composed one-third or three-quarters of the total adult free males, were presumed to speak politically for the excluded males, as well as women, children, and the unfree. On the proportion of men eligible to vote, see Williamson, *American Suffrage*; Dinkin, *Voting in Provincial America*; Robert Brown, *Middle-Class Democracy*; and Brown and Brown, *Virginia*.

34. Bailyn, *Ideological Origins*, 172–74.

35. An Elector, "To the Free and Independent Electors of the City of Philadelphia," *Pennsylvania Packet*, April 29, 1776.

36. Return of Dorchester, May 16, 1780, in Handlin and Handlin, *Popular Sources*, 778.

37. Return of Lee, May 11, 1780, in ibid., 479.

38. Return of Colrain, May 26, 1780, in ibid., 550.

39. See Pole, *Political Representation*, 272–73.

40. "A Watchman," *Maryland Gazette*, August 15, 1776.

41. Nine Petitions of the Inhabitants of Orange County, [November 13, 1776], in Secretary of State Papers, North Carolina Division of Archives and History.

42. The provincial congress's responses may be found in the proceedings of the Provincial Congress of North Carolina, November 23 and 28, 1776, in Saunders, *Colonial Records of North Carolina*, 10:932–33, 945. The election was held on December 10. The full election returns, including all voters and the men for whom they voted, may be found in Secretary of State Papers, North Carolina Division of Archives and History.

43. James Sullivan to Elbridge Gerry, May 17, 1776, in Taylor, *Papers of Adams*, 4:212n. Although Sullivan endorsed the enfranchisement of free men, he recognized that governments acted upon people as persons and as owners of property. In his letter, he tried to imagine multiple votes for property owners scaled to the amount of property owned. Ultimately, his concerns were addressed by the Massachusetts con-

stitution of 1780, which ostensibly represented property in the senate and people in the house. However, it required all voters to meet a property qualification.

44. Return of Norton, May 8, 1780, in Handlin and Handlin, *Popular Sources*, 525; for another town demanding that Protestant be substituted for Christian, see Return of Southampton, April 24, 1780, in ibid., 600.

45. "Instructions to the Delegates from Mecklenburg to the Provincial Congress at Halifax in November, 1776," and "Instructions to the Delegates from Orange in the Halifax Congress, to be held in November, 1776," in Saunders, *Colonial Records of North Carolina*, 10:870d, 870g.

46. South Carolina Constitution (1778), 13, in Thorpe, *Constitutions*, 6:3251–52.

47. Nadelhaft, *Disorders of War*, 204. Also see Kettner, *American Citizenship*, 213–19.

48. Return of Boothbay, May 20, 1778, in Handlin and Handlin, *Popular Sources*, 248–49.

49. Kettner, *American Citizenship*, 219.

50. *Pennsylvania Packet*, March 4, 1776. Also see the council of safety's memorial to the legislature, in ibid., March 11, 1776. On the committee of privates, see Rosswurm, *Arms, Country, and Class*, 66–72.

51. "Resolutions directing the mode of levying Taxes on Non-Associators," Proceedings of the Pennsylvania Assembly, April 1776, in Force, *American Archives*, 4th ser., 5:705.

52. The convention resolution may be found in Papenfuse and Stiverson, *Decisive Blow*, n.p.; or the *Maryland Gazette*, July 4, 1776.

53. All of the quotations come from the reports of the provincial convention election committee. They are in the proceedings for August 15 and 16, 1776, in Papenfuse and Stiverson, *Decisive Blow*, n.p.

54. Ibid.

55. Compare the proceedings of August 23 and August 15, 1776, in ibid., n.p.

56. Compare proceedings of August 15, August 30, and September 4, 1776, in ibid., n.p.

57. Deposition of James Disney, Annapolis, August 27, 1776, in Maryland State Papers, Red Books, 11, 8; Disney's testimony was corroborated by the Deposition of Lt. Joseph Burgess of Capt. Daniel Dorsey's Company of the Flying Camp [August 27, 1776], in ibid.

58. Deposition of Thomas Henry Howard, August 27, 1776, in ibid.; also see Deposition of Samuel Godman (included with the deposition of James Disney), August 27, 1776, in ibid. Part of the resistance was connected to factional conflict in Anne Arundel politics between the Hammond family—Matthias and Rezin—and the established leadership of Charles Carroll of Carrollton, Samuel Chase, and others. For a full discussion of factional conflict in Anne Arundel County, see Hoffman, *Spirit of Dissension*, 126–28, 135–38, and 169–78, esp. 169–72.

59. Deposition of Thomas Harwood, August 27, 1776; see also Deposition of Lt. Joseph Burgess of Capt. Daniel Dorsey's Company of the Flying Camp [August 27, 1776]; and Deposition of James Disney, Annapolis, August 27, 1776, all in Maryland State Papers, Red Books.

60. On the suppression of loyalism, generally, see Calhoon, *Loyalists in Revolutionary America*, 281–311, 397–414, 448–71.

61. North Carolina Provincial Congress, April 29, 1776, in Saunders, *Colonial Records of North Carolina*, 10:549.

62. On loyalty oaths, see Michael G. Kammen, "The American Revolution as a *Crise de Conscience*: The Case of New York," in Greene, Bushman, and Kammen, *Society, Freedom, and Conscience*, 125–89.

63. Resolution of the Maryland Provincial Convention, July 3, 1776, in Papenfuse and Stiverson, *Decisive Blow*, n.p.; the resolution may also be found in the *Maryland Gazette*, July 4, 1776.

64. Resolution of the House of Representatives for the Counties of Newcastle, Kent, and Sussex, upon Delaware, at New-Castle, July 27, 1776, in Bushman, Hancock, and Homsey, *Proceedings of Delaware*, 201.

65. "An Ordinance for directing the mode and fixing the time for the Election of Deputies, to serve in Provincial Congress, for this Colony: and also to ascertain the qualifications of Electors," in Force, *American Archives*, 4th ser., 4:1619.

66. Ibid., 6:1645n.

67. Pennsylvania Conference, June 20, 1776, in *Proceedings relative to calling the Conventions of 1776 and 1790*, 38–39; on the test oath for all voters see proceedings for June 21, 1776, ibid., 39.

68. Thomas Burke to Nathanael Greene, March 28, 1782, in Clark, *State Records*, 16:565–69, quoted in Crow, "Liberty Men and Loyalists," 173; also see 176. On Toryism and political rights, see Whitaker, *Antidote against Toryism*, which urged legislatures to deprive Loyalists of the right to hold office and other ordinary rights.

69. Pennsylvania did drop the taxpayer qualification for associators from Westmoreland County, which had been excused from paying taxes during the previous three years. See Provincial Conference, June 20, 1776, in *Proceedings relative to calling the Conventions of 1776 and 1790*, 39.

70. See Kettner, *American Citizenship*, especially his discussion of the idea of volitional allegiance, 173–209.

71. See, for example, Pole, "Suffrage Reform," 188–89. The very fact that the revolutionaries believed that extending the suffrage to others would attach those men to the Revolution is evidence of the significance of the vote to revolutionary Americans.

72. *Pennsylvania Packet*, March 4, 1776.

73. Pennsylvania Constitution (1776), secs. 6 and 42, in Thorpe, *Constitutions*, 5:3084, 3091.

74. Ganyard, *North Carolina's Revolutionary State Government*, 54.

75. North Carolina Provincial Congress, September 9, 1775, in Saunders, *Colonial Records of North Carolina*, 10:211.

76. Wood, *Creation*, 183; Pole, "Suffrage Reform," 188–89.

77. Such a policy was not entirely unknown before the Revolution. In New York City, the common council hoped to encouraged skilled workers to remain in the city by granting them freemanship at a cost of a few shillings, or even for free. Dinkin, *Voting in Provincial America*, 39–40.

78. *Essex Result*, in Handlin and Handlin, *Popular Sources*, 340–41. Also see the endorsement of *Essex Result* on this point in Return of Northampton, May 22, 1778, in ibid., 580.

79. John Adams to James Sullivan, May 26, 1776, in Taylor, *Papers of Adams*, 4:211–12.

80. Kerber, *Women of the Republic*, 35–36.

81. Richard Henry Lee to Hannah Corbin, Chantilly, March 17, 1778, in Ballagh, *Letters of Lee*, 1:392–94 (quotations, 392–93).

82. "ESSEX to Common Sense, No. IV," *New-York Journal*, March 7, 1776.

83. See Gerlach, *Prologue to Independence*, 473 n. 63, for his guess that "Essex" may have been William DeHart.

84. New Jersey Constitution (1776), 4, in Thorpe, *Constitutions*, 5:2595.

85. Women voted in New Jersey in 1787. See Chinn, "An Early New Jersey Poll List," 77–81. But see *Acts of the [First] General Assembly of the State of New Jersey*, Act of June 4, 1777 (Burlington: Isaac Collins, 1777); *Acts of the Eighth General Assembly of the State of New Jersey*, Act of December 16, 1783 (Trenton: Isaac Collins, 1784). In both of the acts, the legislature used the male pronouns "he" and "his" to refer to voters. Klinghoffer and Elkis, "'The Petticoat Electors,'" 159–94; McCormick, *History of Voting in New Jersey*, 98–100; Turner, "Women's Suffrage in New Jersey," 165–87; Philbrook, "Woman's Suffrage in New Jersey Prior to 1807," 870–98; Pole, "Suffrage in New Jersey, 1790–1807," 39–61; Norton, *Liberty's Daughters*, 191–93. Also see Gunderson, "Independence, Citizenship, and the American Revolution," 59–77, esp. 63–66, whose interpretation is compatible with the one offered here. The New Jersey experience reinforces Kerber's argument that at least some men "claimed for women the responsibility of assuming the obligations of citizenship." See Kerber, "Paradox of Women's Citizenship," 349–78 (quotation, 378).

86. The fullest study of female voting and disfranchisement is Klinghoffer and Elkis, "'The Petticoat Electors,'" 159–94.

87. Berlin, *Slaves without Masters*, 8; Crow, "To the Editor," 696.

88. Return of Spencer, June 8, 1778, in Handlin and Handlin, *Popular Sources*, 302.

89. Return of Sutton, May 18, 1778, in ibid., 231.

90. Return of Westminster, May 15, 1778, in ibid., 312.

91. *Continental Journal*, January 8, 1778.

Chapter 6

1. Montesquieu, *Spirit of the Laws*, bk. 11, chap. 6, 156–66.

2. Ibid., 157. For a brief, valuable discussion of Montesquieu's analysis of English government, see Kammen, *Spheres of Liberty*, 39–41.

3. Virginia Constitution (1776), in Rutland, *Papers of Mason*, 1:304.

4. Wood, *Creation*, 157. One historian has argued that the first state constitutions expressed a vigorous modern commitment to the separation of the functional powers of the government among the different branches of government. Americans had rejected the traditional theory of mixed government, but had not yet developed a theory of checks and balances; therefore, so this argument runs, they were left only with the doctrine of separation of powers to guide their construction of state governments. But, as we have seen, Americans thought of numerous ways other than through a separation of powers to restrict government, believed the importance of "checks" upon

governmental power, and, as we shall see, still accepted but transformed the idea of mixed government. See Vile, *Constitutionalism and the Separation of Powers*, 119–75. Neither Wood nor Vile gives full consideration to the actual separation of powers embodied in the state constitutions.

5. Wood, *Creation*, 150–61.

6. For one of the few who believed that a governor should maintain his executive, judicial, and legislative functions, see Farmer, "For the Pennsylvania Packet," *Pennsylvania Packet*, November 5, 1776, arguing that the governor should have substantial patronage powers, sit as part of a court of last appeal, and have a vote in the senate.

7. Gerlach, *Prologue to Independence*, 277–81. The powers of the provincial congresses are also discussed in Chapter 2, above.

8. Selby, *Revolution in Virginia*, 93–95. For similar behavior by the New York provincial congress, which became the Convention of Representatives of the State of New York on July 10, 1776, see Mason, *Road to Independence*, 182–212.

9. Ryerson, *Revolution Is Now Begun*, 118–19.

10. Hoffman, *Spirit of Dissension*, 185.

11. Samuel Chase to John Adams, Annapolis, June 21, 1776, in Taylor, *Papers of Adams*, 4:323; on the success of the instructions, see Chase to Adams, Annapolis, June 28, 1776, in ibid., 351. The Maryland county instructions were also discussed in Chapter 4, above.

12. Force, *American Archives*, 4th ser., 6:923, 1093.

13. C. X., "For the Maryland Gazette," *Dunlap's Maryland Gazette*, March 26, 1776.

14. Force, *American Archives*, 4th ser., 6:1019–20.

15. "Upper district of Frederick County (Maryland), June 29, 1776," in ibid., 1130.

16. Ibid., 1094–95. "An American" warned Marylanders that, unless checked, legislators would elect themselves and their families and friends to office. See *Maryland Gazette*, July 18, 1776.

17. The facsimile edition of the proceedings has been published in Papenfuse and Stiverson, *Decisive Blow*; article 6 of the declaration of rights may be found there or in Thorpe, *Constitutions*, 3:1687.

18. Force, *American Archives*, 4th ser., 4:476.

19. *Pennsylvania Packet*, June 10, 1776.

20. *Pennsylvania Evening Post*, June 15, 1776.

21. C. X., "For the Maryland Gazette," *Dunlap's Maryland Gazette*, March 26, 1776.

22. "New York Provincial Congress, Resolutions by the Committee on a constitution, May 31, 1776," in Force, *American Archives*, 4th ser., 6:1351.

23. Willi Paul Adams makes this important point, but does not develop it. See Adams, *First American Constitutions*, 264.

24. See, for examples, Howe, *Changing Political Thought of John Adams*, 93–94; and Wood, *Creation*, 208–9.

25. Adams, *Thoughts on Government*, in Taylor, *Papers of Adams*, 4:88.

26. Ibid.

27. For a careful evaluation of the vast literature on British politics, the ministry, and the House of Commons, see Holmes and Szechi, *Age of Oligarchy*, 39–54, 277–300. See also Plumb, *Growth of Political Stability*; and Bailyn, *Origins of American Politics*, 28–29.

28. Bailyn, *Origins of American Politics*, 72–80; and Pole, *Political Representation*, 506.

29. Daniell, *Experiment in Republicanism*, 3–73; Gross, *Minutemen and Their World*, 37–40. See the critique of Bernard and Hutchinson by Cosmopolitan, "No. VI," in Force, *American Archives*, 4th ser., 4:864–66.

30. *Connecticut Courant*, April 10, 1775.

31. *Connecticut Journal*, June 26, 1776.

32. "To the Printer. From An Independent Whig. More on Common Sense," *New-York Journal*, February 29, 1776.

33. Massachusetts Declaration of Rights, art. 30, in Handlin and Handlin, *Popular Sources*, 447–48.

34. For the similarities of this view and those of the Levellers of the English Civil War, see Gwyn, *Separation of Powers*.

35. Consideration, "Remarks on the Proceedings and Resolutions of the Meeting in the State-House Yard, on Monday and Tuesday, October 21 and 22, 1776" (Philadelphia, October 30, 1776), in Force, *American Archives*, 5th ser., 2:1153. Also see Demophilus, "To the Printer of the Pennsylvania Packet," *Pennsylvania Packet*, October 22, 1776.

36. "To the Printer. From An Independent Whig. More on Common Sense," *New-York Journal*, February 29, 1776.

37. *Freeman's Journal*, June 8, 1776. Also see Amicus Respublica, in ibid., August 3, 1776, calling for an assembly "as pure and free as a living spring."

38. New Jersey Constitution (1776), 20, in Thorpe, *Constitutions*, 5:2598.

39. Alociapt, in *Boston Gazette*, May 25, 1778. One author argued that plural office-holding was necessary during the war because many of the most talented men were in the army, but he agreed that this should be considered a temporary exception from the general rule of preventing a man from holding more than one office and more specifically, keeping officeholders out of the assembly. See Demophilus, "To the Honorable Electors of Counsellors for the Colony of Massachusetts Bay," ibid., May 27, 1776. Also see ibid., July 19, 1779, and Unsigned, from Rehoboth, Massachusetts, November 20, 1776, *Providence Gazette*, November 23, 1776.

40. William Gordon, "To the Inhabitants of the Massachusetts-Bay," Roxbury, September 7, 1776, in Force, *American Archives*, 5th ser., 2:229.

41. "Instructions to the Delegates from Orange in the Halifax Congress, November 1776," in Saunders, *Colonial Records of North Carolina*, 10:870h.

42. In eleven brief paragraphs, the constitution outlined the government. The constitution composed less than one page in Thorpe's compendium of constitutions. See Thorpe, *Constitutions*, 4:2452–53.

43. The election of Weare to the council and the court may be found in the provincial congress's proceedings of January 6 and January 10, 1776, in Bouton, *Documents and Records Relating to the State of New-Hampshire*, 8:6, 10.

44. Amicus Respublica, *Freeman's Journal*, August 3, 1776; it was in the same spirit that "Marcus Aurelianus" warned Rhode Islanders "to choose no men into more than one civil office of importance at the same time; nor to continue any men too long in office, lest from dignified *servants*, they become your absolute *masters*, and lord it over you." *Providence Gazette*, July 26, 1776.

45. *Freeman's Journal*, June 8, 1776.

46. Portsmouth Instructions to their Representative, July 31, 1776, in Bouton, *Documents and Records Relating to the State of New-Hampshire*, 8:301.

47. Cato, "My Friends and Countrymen," *Freeman's Journal*, November 12, 1776.

48. New Hampshire Constitution (1776), in Thorpe, *Constitutions*, 4:2464, 2466.

49. Maryland Constitution (1776), 48, in ibid., 3:1699.

50. Maryland Constitution (1776), 13, 25, 26, 27, 37, in ibid., 1693, 1695, 1697.

51. Pennsylvania Constitution (1776), sec. 9, 20, 34, in ibid., 5:3084–85, 3087, 3090.

52. The officials excluded were the state treasurer, trustees of the loan office, naval officers, collectors of customs or excise, judge of the admiralty, attorneys general, sheriffs, and prothonotaries (sec. 19) and all judges (sec. 23); see ibid., 3086–88.

53. The Delaware constitution provided for a four-member privy council, two chosen by the legislative council and two by the House of Assembly. It excluded regular officers in the armed forces, and, unlike in South Carolina, if a member of the legislature were elected to the privy council, he would lose his seat. In an unusual effort to include the executive (in Delaware, "the President") in the process of judicial appointments, the constitution permitted the president to participate in a joint vote with the general assembly in the choice of three supreme court justices, a judge of admiralty, and twelve justices of the courts of common pleas. The general assembly alone appointed army and navy officers (art. 16). The president obtained much greater power over nonjudicial appointments. The House of Assembly nominated two men for every position of justice of the peace, sheriff, and coroner; the president and privy council then made the appointment.

The constitution's grant of substantial appointive powers to the president continued past practices. The president and privy council appointed the sheriff and coroners from two nominees chosen by the general assembly "in the same Manner that the Governor heretofore enjoyed this Power" (art. 15). Delaware Constitution (1776), arts. 15, 16, 18, in Bushman, Hancock, and Homsey, *Proceedings of Delaware*, 222.

54. The Massachusetts constitution excluded from the legislature all judges, the secretary of state, treasurer, receiver-general, commissary-general, "President Professor, or Instructor of Harvard-College," sheriffs, clerks of the supreme and inferior judicial courts and of the House of Representatives, the registers of probate and deeds, and customs officials (chap. 6, art. 2). A legislator who accepted any of those posts automatically vacated his seat. The same was true for a judge who accepted another appointment. Massachusetts Constitution (1780), pt. 2, chap. 2, sec. 1, arts. 9, 10; chap. 2, sec. 3, art. 2; chap. 2, sec. 4, art. 1; chap. 6, art. 2, in Handlin and Handlin, *Popular Sources*, 459–60, 463–64, 469–70.

55. Virginia Constitution (1776), in Thorpe, *Constitutions*, 7:3817–18.

56. New Jersey Constitution (1776), 7, 10, 12, 19, 20, in ibid., 5:2596–98. Eligible voters elected sheriffs, constables, coroners, and a tax appeal commission. See arts. 13, 14, in ibid.

57. New Jersey Constitution (1776), 20, in ibid., 2598.

58. North Carolina Constitution (1776), 13, 14, 24, 25, 26, 27, 28, 29, 30, 31, 35, in ibid., 5:2792–93. It also went further to prevent the control of executive power in a few hands by prohibiting persons from "hold[ing] more than one lucrative office, at any one time."

59. Georgia Constitution (1777), arts. 53, 16, 11, 2, 7, in ibid., 2:778–80, 784; Saye, *Constitutional History of Georgia*, 112.

60. South Carolina Constitution (1776), 10. In 1778 the list included secretary of state, treasurer, customs officers, register of mesne conveyances, court clerks, sheriffs, powder-reviewer, clerk of the senate, house, or privy council, the surveyor general, and commissary of military stores. But delegates to the Continental Congress retained their seats in the legislature. South Carolina Constitution (1778), 20, 22, in Thorpe, *Constitutions*, 6:3244, 3253.

61. New York Constitution (1777), arts. 23, 25, 26, in ibid., 5:2633–34.

62. The legislatures of Virginia, North Carolina, South Carolina, and Maryland chose judges for terms of good behavior. In New York, the council of appointments selected judges for the same term, or until they reached sixty years of age. In Massachusetts and New Hampshire (1784), the executive appointed, with the consent of the council, judges who served terms of good behavior. Virginia Constitution (1776), in ibid., 7:3817; North Carolina Constitution (1776), 13, in ibid., 5:2791; South Carolina Constitution (1778), 27, in ibid., 6:3254; Maryland Constitution (1776), 40, in ibid., 3:1697; New York Constitution (1777), 24, in ibid., 5:2634; Massachusetts Constitution (1780), pt. 2, chap. 2., sec. 1, art. 9; pt. 2, chap. 3, art. 1, in Handlin and Handlin, *Popular Sources*, 459, 464; New Hampshire Constitution (1784), in Thorpe, *Constitutions*, 4:2464, 2466; New Jersey Constitution (1776), 12, in ibid., 5:2596; Pennsylvania Constitution (1776), sec. 20, in ibid., 3087.

63. Wood devotes only one paragraph to discussion of the veto, Willi Paul Adams and Donald Lutz one page each. See Wood, *Creation*, 141; Adams, *First American Constitutions*, 273; Lutz, *Popular Consent*, 146. Lutz and Adams mention the veto elsewhere in their volumes.

64. "Instructions to the Delegates of Anne Arundel County, in Maryland Convention; signed by 885 freemen," *Maryland Gazette*, August 22, 1776.

65. "The Interest of America," in Force, *American Archives*, 4th ser., 6:843.

66. Purdie's *Virginia Gazette*, June 7, 1776.

67. "Instructions for the Delegates of Mecklenburg County proposed to the Consideration of the County," in Saunders, *Colonial Records of North Carolina*, 10:239; and in the "Mecklenburg Instructions to Provincial Congress Delegates, November, 1776," in ibid., 870c, they required their delegates to oppose any gubernatorial participation, except in cases where the council (the upper house) was evenly divided.

68. William Hooper to Congress at Halifax, Philadelphia, October 26, 1776, in ibid., 868.

69. See Richard Henry Lee's happy comment on the Virginia constitution: "I have had the pleasure to see our new plan of Government goes on well. . . . 'Tis very much of the democratic kind, altho' a Governor and second branch of legislation are admitted, for the former is not permitted voice in Legislation." R. H. Lee to Charles Lee, Williamsburgh, June 29, 1776, in Ballagh, *Letters of Lee*, 1:203.

70. New Hampshire Constitution (1784), in Thorpe, *Constitutions*, 4:2463.

71. South Carolina Constitution (1776), 7, in ibid., 6:3244.

72. Pennsylvania Constitution (1776), sec. 47, in ibid., 5:3091–92.

73. On the Council of Appointment, see John Jay to R. R. Livingston and

Gouverneur Morris, Fishkill, April 29, 1777, in Morris, *John Jay*, 397–98.

74. John Adams to Elbridge Gerry, November 4, 1779, in Taylor, *Papers of Adams*, 8:276.

75. "The Report of a Constitution . . . ," in ibid., 242. Also see the "Editorial Note," in ibid., 230. The committee draft resembled Elbridge Gerry's proposal for "a negative, only so far as the proceedings affect the . . . powers of the Executive?" Otherwise, he feared "that the Community will be endangered." Elbridge Gerry to John Adams, October 12, 1779, in ibid., 198.

76. "An Address of the Convention . . . to Their Constituents," [1780], in Handlin and Handlin, *Popular Sources*, 439.

77. See Morgan, *Inventing the People*, 248.

78. See Vile, *Separation of Powers*, 134.

79. The upper house will be considered in Chapter 7.

80. But the constitution of 1778 excluded from the privy council officers in the regular military service, judges, and, in the only antinepotism clause in any of the early constitutions, any "father, son, or brother to the governor." South Carolina Constitution (1778), 9, in Thorpe, *Constitutions*, 6:3249–50.

81. In 1776, the privy council was composed of six members, three chosen by each house of the legislature, and the state's vice president. Qualifications for the council were the same as those for the general assembly. In 1778, the new constitution expanded the size of the council to eight.

82. South Carolina Constitution (1776), 16, 25, in Thorpe, *Constitutions*, 6:3246–47; South Carolina Constitution (1778), 24, 32, 35, in ibid., 3254–55.

83. Virginia Constitution (1776), in ibid., 7:3817–18; also see Selby, *Revolution in Virginia*, 118.

84. North Carolina Constitution (1776), 14, 18, 19, 20, 28, in Thorpe, *Constitutions*, 5:2791–92.

85. Delaware Constitution (1776), arts. 8, 9, 10, 12, 21, in Bushman, Hancock, and Homsey, *Proceedings of Delaware*, 220–23.

86. It required its councillors, elected by a joint ballot of the two houses of the legislature, to be at least twenty-five years old and to possess a freehold of £1,000. Maryland Constitution (1776), 26, in Thorpe, *Constitutions*, 3:1695.

87. Maryland Constitution (1776), 33, 29, 41, 42, 47, in ibid., 1696–99. As in Delaware, and other states where the executive retained substantial appointive power, the council was a partner in the appointment process. Its "advice and *consent*" were required for the governor's major judicial appointments. But the constitution (art. 33) also authorized the governor to "alone exercise all other the executive powers of government, where the concurrence of the Council is not required" by law.

The constitution (art. 34) also gave the governor a seat in the council and a tie-breaking vote. Moreover, the council could replace on an interim basis any of its members who no longer qualified for a place on the council (art. 35).

88. Maryland Constitution (1776), 37, 38, 39, in ibid., 1697.

89. Massachusetts Constitution (1780), pt. 1, chap. 1, sec. 2, art. 1; chap. 2, sec. 1, arts. 5, 6, 8, 9, 10, 11; chap. 2, sec. 3, art. 1, in Handlin and Handlin, *Popular Sources*, 451, 457–60, 462.

90. New Hampshire Constitution (1784), in Thorpe, *Constitutions*, 4:2463–65.

91. Pennsylvania Constitution (1776), secs. 19, 20, in ibid., 5:3086–88.

92. Georgia Constitution (1777), arts. 2, 20, 21, 27, 28, in ibid., 2:778, 781–82.

93. New York Constitution (1777), 3, 23, in ibid., 5:2628, 2633.

94. Force, *American Archives*, 4th ser., 6:557.

Chapter 7

1. William Hooper to Congress at Halifax, Philadelphia, October 26, 1776, in Saunders, *Colonial Records of North Carolina*, 10:867. For a valuable discussion of the evolution of the English theory of mixed government, see Weston, *English Constitutional Theory*. On the "establishment Whig" interpretation of mixed and balanced government, see Dickinson, *Liberty and Property*, 142–59.

2. Bailyn, *Ideological Origins*, 67–76.

3. Greene, *Quest for Power*; Jordan, *Foundations of Representative Government*, 84–97, 164–77, 203–4; and Clarke, *Parliamentary Privilege*. More generally, see Greene, "The Role of the Lower Houses of Assembly," 86–109.

4. Morgan, *Inventing the People*, 140; Bailyn, *Origins of American Politics*, 24–27.

5. Bailyn, *Origins of American Politics*, 131–33; Bailyn, *Ideological Origins*, 274–80; Wood, *Creation*, 210–13.

6. Benjamin Rumsey to Daniel of St. Thomas Jenifer, Philadelphia, November 13, 1776, in Smith, *Letters of Delegates*, 5:479.

7. Gordon Wood offers an evocative discussion of eighteenth-century gentry attitudes toward ordinary folk in Wood, *Radicalism of the American Revolution*, 24–30.

8. General Nathanael Greene to Samuel Ward, Prospect-Hill, December 31, 1775, in Force, *American Archives*, 4th ser., 4:483.

9. Cato, "To the People of Pennsylvania—Letter 3," *Pennsylvania Packet*, March 25, 1776.

10. "A Member of the Established Church to Mr. Purdie," Purdie's *Virginia Gazette*, November 1, 1776.

11. Impartialis, *Continental Journal*, March 12, 1778.

12. Alexander Hamilton to John Jay, November 26, 1775, in Syrett and Cooke, *Papers of Hamilton*, 1:176–77.

13. "Philadelphia Meeting of Citizens, Philosophical Society Hall, 8 November 1776," *Pennsylvania Packet*, November 12, 1776; also reprinted in Force, *American Archives*, 5th ser., 3:599.

14. Benjamin Rush to Anthony Wayne, September 24, 1776, in Butterfield, *Letters of Benjamin Rush*, 1:115.

15. K., "Remarks on the Constitution of Pennsylvania," *Pennsylvania Packet*, September 24, 1776.

16. "Philadelphia Meeting of Citizens, Philosophical Society Hall, 8 November 1776," *Pennsylvania Packet*, November 12, 1776; reprinted in Force, *American Archives*, 5th ser., 3:599.

17. *Pennsylvania Journal*, September 25, 1776.

18. Benevolus, "Thoughts on Government, No. 5," *Continental Journal*, December 30, 1779.

19. William Hooper to Congress at Halifax, October 26, 1776, in Saunders, *Colonial Records of North Carolina*, 10:868.

20. *Essex Result*, in Handlin and Handlin, *Popular Sources*, 333–34.

21. New York Constitution (1777), 10, in Thorpe, *Constitutions*, 5:2631; New Hampshire Constitution (1776), in ibid., 4:2452.

22. Edmund Pendleton to Thomas Jefferson, August 10, 1776, in Boyd, *Papers of Jefferson*, 1:489.

23. George Mason, "A Plan of Government," 4, in Rutland, *Papers of Mason*, 1:299; Main, *Upper House*, 125–28.

24. South Carolina Constitution (1778), 12, in Thorpe, *Constitutions*, 6:3250.

25. New Jersey Constitution (1776), 3, in ibid., 5:2595.

26. Maryland Constitution (1776), 2, 15, in ibid., 3:1691, 1693–94.

27. Main, "Government by the People," 391–407; Main, *Sovereign States*, 196.

28. Massachusetts Constitution (1780), pt. 2, chap. 1, sec. 2, art. 5, and sec. 3, art. 3, in Handlin and Handlin, *Popular Sources*, 453–55; North Carolina Constitution (1776), 5, 6, in Thorpe, *Constitutions*, 3:2790; New Hampshire Constitution (1784), in ibid., 4:2460–61. The qualification for New Hampshire's house members represented a reduction of two-thirds from the colonial requirement of a £300 freehold. See Daniell, *Experiment in Republicanism*, 108.

29. Edmund Pendleton to Thomas Jefferson, August 10, 1776, in Boyd, *Papers of Jefferson*, 1:489.

30. New York Constitution (1777), 10, in Thorpe, *Constitutions*, 5:2631; Main, *Upper House*, 134.

31. George Mason, "A Plan of Government," 4, in Rutland, *Papers of Mason*, 1:299.

32. South Carolina Constitution (1776), 2, 11, in Thorpe, *Constitutions*, 6:3243–45; South Carolina Constitution (1778), 12, 13, in ibid., 3250–51; Virginia Constitution (1776), in ibid., 7:3815–16; New Jersey Constitution (1776), 3, in ibid., 5:2595; Maryland Constitution (1776), 2, 4, 5, 14, 15, 16, in ibid., 3:1691–94; North Carolina Constitution (1776), 2, 3, in ibid., 5:2790; New York Constitution (1777), 4, 12, in ibid., 2629, 2631; New Hampshire Constitution (1784), in ibid., 4:2460–61; Delaware Constitution (1776), arts. 3, 4, in Bushman, Hancock, and Homsey, *Proceedings of Delaware*, 219; Massachusetts Constitution (1780), pt. 2, chap. 1, sec. 2, arts. 1, 2; sec. 3, art. 2, in Handlin and Handlin, *Popular Sources*, 450–51, 454–55. Also see Main, *Upper House*, 101, 115, 125, 134, 149, 154, 164, 174; and Main, "Government by the People."

33. South Carolina Constitution (1778), 12, 13, in Thorpe, *Constitutions*, 6:3250–51.

34. Virginia Constitution (1776), in ibid., 7:3816; New York Constitution (1777), 12, in ibid., 5:2631; Maryland Constitution (1776), 15, in ibid., 3:1693–94.

35. For a further discussion of Massachusetts and New Hampshire, see the section below entitled "The Irrelevance of the *Essex Result*." The constitutions of both states required senators to obtain a majority of the votes in their districts. If there was no majority, then the elected senators and the representatives elected, on a joint ballot, the senators from the top vote getters. Massachusetts Constitution (1780), pt. 2, chap. 1, sec. 2, arts. 2, 3, 4, in Handlin and Handlin, *Popular Sources*, 451–53; New Hampshire Constitution (1776), in Thorpe, *Constitutions*, 4:2460.

36. See Morgan, *Inventing the People*, 248–54; Main, *Upper House*, 101–87.

37. "Jefferson's First Draft," in Boyd, *Papers of Jefferson*, 1:341.

38. "Jefferson's Second Draft," in ibid., 348–49.

39. Edmund Pendleton to Thomas Jefferson, August 10, 1776, in ibid., 489. For a similar view, see C. X., "For the Maryland Gazette," *Dunlap's Maryland Gazette*, April 2, 1776.

40. Thomas Jefferson to Edmund Pendleton, August 26, 1776, in Boyd, *Papers of Jefferson*, 1:503–4.

41. See Patrick Henry to John Adams, May 20, 1776, in Taylor, *Papers of Adams*, 4:200–201; and Edmund Pendleton to Thomas Jefferson, July 22, 1776, in Boyd, *Papers of Jefferson*, 1:472.

42. Edmund Pendleton to Thomas Jefferson, August 10, 1776, in Boyd, *Papers of Jefferson*, 1:489.

43. Maryland Constitution (1776), 19, in Thorpe, *Constitutions*, 3:1694. During its first twelve years, the senate selected one-third of its own members. Main, *Upper House*, 102.

44. Richard Henry Lee to Patrick Henry, April 20, 1776, in Ballagh, *Letters of Lee*, 1:179.

45. Jefferson soon retreated from his position. In 1783, he recommended, instead, indirect election of senators for two-year terms. See "Draught of a Fundamental Constitution for the Commonwealth of Virginia," in Jefferson, *Notes on the State of Virginia*, 211.

46. Farmer, "On the Present State of Affairs in America," Philadelphia, *Pennsylvania Packet*, November 5, 1776; also reprinted in Force, *American Archives*, 5th ser., 3:518.

47. Democraticus, "Loose Thoughts on GOVERNMENT," Purdie's *Virginia Gazette*, June 7, 1776.

48. William Hooper to Congress at Halifax, Philadelphia, October 26, 1776, in Saunders, *Colonial Records of North Carolina*, 10:866–68.

49. Democraticus, "Loose Thoughts on GOVERNMENT," Purdie's *Virginia Gazette*, June 7, 1776.

50. *Essex Result*, in Handlin and Handlin, *Popular Sources*, 343.

51. William Gordon, "Letter 1.—To the Inhabitants of the Massachusetts-Bay," Roxbury, August 31, 1776, in Force, *American Archives*, 5th ser., 1:1285–87 (quotation, 1286).

52. North Carolina Constitution (1776), 1, 2, 3, in Thorpe, *Constitutions*, 5:2790. Even in Maryland, where constitution makers went furthest to establish a truly mixed government, some assumed that the senators were as much representatives of the people as the delegates. See Rationalis, "To the People of Maryland," *Maryland Gazette*, July 17, 1777.

53. Adams, *Thoughts on Government*, in Taylor, *Papers of Adams*, 4:88–89, 76.

54. Ibid., 88.

55. Salus Populi, "To the People of North-America on the Different Kinds of Government," n.d., in Force, *American Archives*, 4th ser., 5:183.

56. E. F., Purdie's *Virginia Gazette*, May 17, 1776.

57. John Sullivan to Meshech Weare, December 12, 1775, in Hammond, *Letters of John Sullivan*, 1:142–43.

58. Ibid., 144–47.

59. The county did recommend, though, that one house be chosen by freeholders and householders, and the other just by freeholders. "Instructions to the Delegates from Orange in the Halifax Congress, November, 1776 (written by Gov. Thomas Burke)," in Saunders, *Colonial Records of North Carolina*, 10:870h.

60. "Meeting of the Deputies of the Several Battalions of Militia of Ann[e] Arundel County, June 26–27, 1776," *Maryland Gazette*, July 18, 1776.

61. A Watchman, "To the Printer," ibid., August 15, 1776. Here, "A Watchman" was referring to all rulers, but the general point was applicable to the upper houses specifically.

62. *The People the Best Governors: Or a Plan of Government Founded on the Just Principles of Natural Freedom* (New Hampshire, 1776), in Hyneman and Lutz, *American Political Writing*, 1:390–400, esp. 393 (quotation), 394, 397 (quotation).

63. William Gordon, "Letter 2, To the Freemen of Massachusetts-Bay," *Continental Journal*, April 9, 1778.

64. *Providence Gazette*, August 9, 1777.

65. Gouverneur Morris to Alexander Hamilton, May 16, 1777, in Syrett and Cooke, *Papers of Alexander Hamilton*, 1:254. On Morris's earlier support, in May 1776, for a unicameral "Congress," for which members were elected annually from "small districts" and eligible to serve one in every three years, see Sparks, *Life of Gouverneur Morris*, 1:103. For the dating of Morris's speech, see Mason, *Road to Independence*, 152, 152n.

66. "An Independent Whig, No. 4," *New-York Journal*, March 28, 1776.

67. Thomas Jones to James Iredell, April 28, 1776, in Higginbotham, *Papers of Iredell*, 1:352.

68. Burke did not offer his discussion of Pennsylvania as an answer to the problems of congressional power that he discussed earlier in the letter, but, in the context of the letter, bicameralism provides the solution to the unlimited power of a unicameral legislature. Thomas Burke to Richard Caswell, March 11, 1777, in Clark, *State Records of North Carolina*, 11:417–22 (quotations, 417–18, 422). Burke, as the author of the Orange County instructions of November 1776, suggested slightly different social bases for the two legislative bodies. The instructions recommended that the constitution enfranchise householders in house elections and freeholders in senate elections. "Instructions to the Delegates from Orange in the Halifax Congress, November 1776 (written by Gov. Thomas Burke)," in Saunders, *Colonial Records of North Carolina*, 10:870h.

69. Return of Gorham [1779], in Handlin and Handlin, *Popular Sources*, 429–30 (quotation, 430).

70. Salus Populi, "To the People of North-America on the Different Kinds of Government," n.d., in Force, *American Archives*, 4th ser., 5:181, 183.

71. Philo-Alethias, "On the Present State of America," Delaware, October 10, 1776, *Maryland Gazette*, October 31, 1776; also reprinted in Force, *American Archives*, 5th ser., 2:967–69.

72. Saunders, *Colonial Records of North Carolina*, 10:239, 241. Historians have often noted this call for a unicameral legislature, but they have ignored how even these instructions sought to curb the legislature. See Douglass, *Rebels and Democrats*, 116–17.

73. Paine, *Common Sense*, in Foot and Kramnick, *Thomas Paine Reader*, 91.

74. *Boston Gazette*, September 23, 1776.

75. Pennsylvania Constitution (1776), sec. 10, in Thorpe, *Constitutions*, 5:3085; Vermont Constitution (1777), sec. 9, in ibid., 6:3743. All of the other constitutions, except Virginia's (which failed to stipulate a quorum for its House of Delegates), required a majority or less for a quorum. See Maryland Constitution (1776), 8, in ibid., 3:1692; Georgia Constitution (1777), art. 2, in ibid., 2:778. The Massachusetts Constitution (1780), chap. 1, sec. 3, art. 9, required 60 for a quorum in the house; see Handlin and Handlin, *Popular Sources*, 455. New York Constitution (1777), 9, in Thorpe, *Constitutions*, 5:2631; North Carolina Constitution (1776), 46, in ibid., 2794; New Jersey Constitution (1776), 3, in ibid., 2595. South Carolina required 49 members in 1776 (art. 12) out of some 202 members and 69 out of 202 in 1778 (art. 14), ibid., 6:3245, 3252. New Hampshire stipulated no quorum for its house in 1776 but adopted a complicated quorum provision in 1784. It declared a majority to be a quorum "but when less than two-thirds of the representatives elected shall be present, the assent of two-thirds of those members shall be necessary to render their acts and proceedings valid"; ibid., 4:2462.

76. Georgia Constitution (1777), art. 2, in Thorpe, *Constitutions*, 2:778.

77. Pennsylvania Constitution (1776), sec. 8, in ibid., 5:3084.

78. "The Considerate Freeman, No. III," *Pennsylvania Packet*, November 26, 1776.

79. For a fuller discussion of the appointive power, see Chapter 6 above, "Separation of Powers," and Vile, *Separation of Powers*, 136.

80. Pennsylvania Constitution (1776), sec. 15, in Thorpe, *Constitutions*, 5:3086; "The Considerate Freeman, No. III," *Pennsylvania Packet*, November 26, 1776.

81. K., "Remarks on the Constitution of Pennsylvania," *Pennsylvania Packet*, October 15, 1776.

82. Benjamin Rush to Anthony Wayne, Philadelphia, April 2, 1777, in Butterfield, *Letters of Rush*, 1:137.

83. Pennsylvania Constitution (1776), sec. 47, in Thorpe, *Constitutions*, 5:3091.

84. *Pennsylvania Packet*, November 26, 1776.

85. Georgia Constitution (1777), arts. 8, 27, in Thorpe, *Constitutions*, 2:779, 782.

86. Vermont Constitution (1777), sec. 14, in ibid., 6:3744.

87. See, for example, Pole, *Political Representation*, 172; Patterson, *Political Parties*, 190–92, places the *Essex Result* in its political context.

88. *Essex Result*, in Handlin and Handlin, *Popular Sources*, 333–34.

89. Ibid., 492–93.

90. "An Address of the Constitutional Convention, to Their Constituents, 1780," in Taylor, *Colony to Commonwealth*, 125.

91. For example, J. R. Pole calls the *Essex Result* "a brilliant success which had lasting effects on American constitutional thought." He contends that its explanation of bicameralism "was rapidly accepted as a normal tenet of political thought." See Pole, *Political Representation*, 172, 186. Pole offers a superb analysis of the document in ibid., 182–89. Donald S. Lutz describes the *Essex Result* as "one of the finest political tracts" of the founding era for best articulating "a coherent theory of American politics." Lutz, *Origins of American Constitutionalism*, 70–82, 92. Yet Lutz recognizes that Parsons's explanation of bicameralism ultimately did not prevail. (See ibid., 132.) Also see Adams, *First American Constitutions*, 91. Stephen E. Patterson places the *Essex Result*

in the context of Massachusetts politics. Patterson, *Political Parties*, 190–92. For an interesting critique of the *Essex Result*'s account of representation, see Peters, *Massachusetts Constitution of 1780*, 143–46.

92. See Gordon Wood's conclusion: "No other state in the period so boldly interpreted the bicameral principle in this way." Wood, *Creation*, 576.

93. This conclusion is drawn from a review of apportionment provisions in all of the state constitutions written between 1784 and 1820. New Hampshire Constitution (1784), pt. 2, The Senate, in Thorpe, *Constitutions*, 4:2459. South Carolina in 1808 based representation in both houses upon a combination of population and taxes paid. Amendments ratified in 1808 to the South Carolina Constitution (1790), in ibid., 6:3266–67. In 1835, the North Carolina constitution based representation in the senate on taxes paid by each county. North Carolina Constitution (1776), amendment of art. 1, sec. 1, in ibid., 5:2794–95.

94. For a discussion of the defense of North Carolina's fifty-acre freehold requirement for senatorial electors, see Kruman, *Parties and Politics*, 87–88.

95. Wood, *Creation*, 553–62, 596–600.

Conclusion

1. Wood, *Creation*, 612.

2. See Kruman, "Second American Party System." Also see Watts, *Republic Reborn*. Cf. Wood, *Radicalism of the American Revolution*.

3. The revolutionaries' perception of a relentless, power-hungry Parliament must be measured against Parliament's repeated concessions in response to American resistance. See Thomas, *British Politics and the Stamp Act Crisis*; Thomas, *Townshend Duties Crisis*; and Thomas, *Tea Party to Independence*. But also see Ian Christie, "British Response to American Reactions to the Townshend Acts, 1768–1770," and Christie, "The British Ministers, Massachusetts, and the Continental Association, 1774–1775," in Conser, McCarthy, Toscano, and Sharp, *Resistance, Politics, and the American Struggle for Independence*, 193–214, 325–57.

4. Reid, *Authority to Legislate*, 87–158.

5. Adams, *Thoughts on Government*, in Taylor, *Papers of Adams*, 4:90.

6. This is a paraphrase of the title of Kammen, *A Machine That Would Go of Itself*.

7. The phrase "between authority and liberty" is from David Hume, "Of the Origin of Government," in Hume, *Essays: Moral, Political, and Literary*, 40.

★ ★ ★ ★ ★ ★ ★ ★ ★ ★ ★ ★ # Bibliography

Primary Sources

Printed Sources

The Alarm: Or, an Address to the People of Pennsylvania on the Late Resolve. . . . Philadelphia, 1776.

Bailyn, Bernard, ed. *Pamphlets of the American Revolution, 1750–1776.* 1 vol. to date. Cambridge, Mass., 1965– .

Ballagh, James Curtis, ed. *The Letters of Richard Henry Lee.* 2 vols. New York, 1911.

Blackstone, Sir William. *Commentaries on the Laws of England: in Four Books.* New York, 1822.

Bouton, Nathaniel, ed. *Provincial Papers: Documents and Records Relating to the Province of New-Hampshire, from 1764–1776.* . . . 7 vols. Nashua, N.H., 1873.

———. *Documents and Records Relating to the State of New-Hampshire During the Period of the American Revolution, From 1776 to 1783.* Vol. 8. Concord, N.H., 1874.

Boyd, Julian P., ed. *The Papers of Thomas Jefferson.* Vol. 1. Princeton, 1950.

Bushman, Claudia L., Harold B. Hancock, and Elizabeth Moyne Homsey, eds. *Proceedings of the Assembly of the Lower Counties on Delaware 1770–1776, of the Constitutional Convention of 1776, and of the House of Assembly of the Delaware State 1776–1781.* Newark, Del., 1986.

Butterfield, L. H., ed. *Adams Family Correspondence.* 3 vols. Cambridge, Mass., 1963.

———. *The Letters of Benjamin Rush.* 2 vols. Princeton, 1951.

Clark, Walter, ed. *State Records of North Carolina.* Vol. 11. Raleigh, 1895.

Demophilus. *The Genuine Principles of the Ancient Saxon, or English Constitution.* Philadelphia, 1776.

An Essay of a Frame of Government for Pennsylvania. Philadelphia, 1776.

An Essay upon Government, Adopted by the Americans, Wherein, the Lawfulness of Revolutions, are Demonstrated in a Chain of Consequences from the Fundamental Principles of Society. Philadelphia, 1775.

Foot, Michael, and Isaac Kramnick, eds. *The Thomas Paine Reader.* Harmondsworth, Eng., 1987.

Force, Peter, ed. *American Archives,* 4th and 5th ser. Washington, D.C., 1837–53.

Ford, Paul L., ed. *The Life and Writings of John Dickinson.* Philadelphia, 1895.

Ford, Worthington C., et al., eds. *Journals of the Continental Congress, 1774–1789.* 34 vols. Washington, D.C., 1904–37.

Green, Jacob. *Observations: On the Reconciliation of Great Britain and the Colonies.* Philadelphia, 1776.

Hamer, Philip, David Chesnutt, et al., eds. *The Papers of Henry Laurens.* 14 vols. to date. Columbia, S.C., 1968– .

Hamilton, Alexander, James Madison, and John Jay. *The Federalist Papers.* Edited by Clinton Rossiter. New York, 1961.

Hammond, Otis G., ed. *Letters and Papers of Major-General John Sullivan*. 2 vols. Concord, N.H., 1930.

Handlin, Oscar, and Mary Handlin, eds. *The Popular Sources of Political Authority: Documents on the Massachusetts Constitution of 1780*. Cambridge, Mass., 1966.

Higginbotham, Don, ed. *The Papers of James Iredell*. 2 vols. to date. Raleigh, 1976– .

Hoadly, Charles L., ed. *The Public Records of the State of Connecticut*. 3 vols. Hartford, Conn., 1894–1922.

Hume, David. *Essays: Moral, Political and Literary*. Edited by Eugene F. Miller. Indianapolis, 1987.

Hutchinson, William T., and William M. E. Rachal, eds. *The Papers of James Madison*. Vol. 1. Chicago, 1962.

Hyneman, Charles S., and Donald S. Lutz, eds. *American Political Writing during the Founding Era, 1760–1805*. 2 vols. Indianapolis, 1983.

Izard, Ralph. *Correspondence of Mr. Ralph Izard, of South Carolina, from the Year 1774 to 1804; with a Short Memoir*. 2 vols. New York, 1844.

Jefferson, Thomas. *Notes on the State of Virginia*. Edited by William Peden. New York, 1972.

Johnston, Henry P., ed. *The Correspondence and Public Papers of John Jay*. 2 vols. New York, 1890.

Journal and Correspondence of the Maryland Council of Safety, August 29, 1775–July 6, 1776. Archives of Maryland. Vol. 11. Baltimore, 1892.

Lee Papers. New-York Historical Society, *Collections*. Vols. 4–7. New York, 1871–74.

Mays, David John, ed. *The Letters and Papers of Edmund Pendleton, 1734–1804*. 2 vols. Charlottesville, Va., 1967.

Montesquieu, Charles de Secondat, Baron de. *The Spirit of the Laws*. Translated and edited by Anne M. Cohler, Basia C. Miller, and Harold Stone. Cambridge, 1989.

Morgan, Edmund S., ed. *Prologue to Revolution: Sources and Documents on the Stamp Act Crisis, 1764–1766*. Chapel Hill, 1959.

Morris, Richard B., ed. *John Jay: The Making of a Revolutionary, Unpublished Papers, 1745–1780*. New York, 1975.

Papenfuse, Edward C., and Gregory A. Stiverson, eds. *The Decisive Blow Is Struck: A Facsimile Edition of the Proceedings of the Constitutional Convention of 1776 and the First Maryland Constitution*. Annapolis, 1977.

Prince, Carl E., ed. *The Papers of William Livingston*. Vol. 1. Trenton, 1979.

Proceedings of the Maryland Convention, July 26–August 14, 1775. Archives of Maryland. Vol. 11. Baltimore, 1892.

The Proceedings relative to calling the Conventions of 1776 and 1790. Harrisburg, Pa., 1825.

Rutland, Robert A., ed. *The Papers of George Mason*. 3 vols. Chapel Hill, 1970.

Ryden, George Herbert, ed. *Letters to and from Caesar Rodney, 1756–1784*. Philadelphia, 1933.

Saunders, William L., ed. *Colonial Records of North Carolina*. 10 vols. Raleigh, 1886–90.

Scribner, Robert L., and Brent Tarter, comps. and eds. *Revolutionary Virginia: The Road to Independence*. Vol. 6, *A Time for Decision, 1776: A Documentary Record*. Charlottesville, Va., 1981.

Slade, William, Jr., comp. *Vermont State Papers; Being a Collection of Records and Docu-*

ments, Connected with the Assumption and Establishment of Government by the People of Vermont; Together with the Journal of the Council of Safety, the First Constitution, the Early Journals of the General Assembly, and the Laws from the Year 1779 to 1786, inclusive. To which are Added the Proceedings of the First and Second Councils of Censors. Middlebury, Vt., 1823.

Smith, Paul H., ed. *Letters of Delegates to Congress, 1774–1789*. 22 vols. to date. Washington, D.C., 1976– .

Syrett, Harold C., and Jacob E. Cooke, eds. *The Papers of Alexander Hamilton*. Vol. 1. New York, 1961.

Taylor, Robert J., ed. *Massachusetts, Colony to Commonwealth: Documents on the Formation of Its Constitution, 1775–1780*. Chapel Hill, 1961.

———. *The Papers of John Adams*. 8 vols. to date. Cambridge, Mass., 1977– .

Thorpe, Francis Newton, comp. and ed. *The Federal and State Constitutions, Colonial Charters, and Other Organic Laws of the States, Territories, and Colonies Now or Heretofore Forming the United States of America*. 7 vols. Washington, D.C., 1909.

Whitaker, Nathaniel. *An Antidote against Toryism*. Newburyport, Mass., 1777.

Yazawa, Melvin, ed. *Representative Government and the Revolution: The Maryland Constitutional Crisis of 1787*. Baltimore, 1975.

Newspapers

Boston Gazette and Country Journal

Connecticut Courant and Hartford Weekly Intelligencer

The Connecticut Journal, and the New-Haven Post-Boy

Continental Journal and Weekly Advertiser (Boston)

Dunlap's Maryland Gazette; or the Baltimore General Advertiser

Dunlap's Pennsylvania Packet, or, the General Advertiser (Philadelphia)

Essex Journal and Merrimack Packet: Or, The Massachusetts and New-Hampshire General Advertiser

The Freeman's Journal, or New-Hampshire Gazette (Portsmouth)

Georgia Gazette

Independent Chronicle and Universal Advertiser (Boston)

Maryland Gazette (Annapolis)

Massachusetts Spy Or, American Oracle of Liberty (Worcester)

The New Hampshire Gazette and Historical Chronicle (Portsmouth)

New-York Gazette and Weekly Mercury

New-York Journal; or, the General Advertiser

Norwich (Conn.) Packet and Connecticut, Massachusetts, New-Hampshire & Rhode-Island Weekly Advertiser

Pennsylvania Evening Post (Philadelphia)

Pennsylvania Journal; and the Weekly Advertiser (Philadelphia)

Providence Gazette and Country Journal

South Carolina and American General Gazette (Charleston)

Dixon & Hunter's *Virginia Gazette* (Williamsburgh)

Pinckney's *Virginia Gazette* (Williamsburgh)

Purdie's *Virginia Gazette* (Williamsburgh)

Manuscript Collections

Charles Carroll of Carrollton. Papers. Maryland Historical Society. Baltimore. Microfilm.

Maryland State Papers. Red Book. Maryland State Archives. Annapolis.

Secretary of State Papers. North Carolina Division of Archives and History. Raleigh.

Secondary Sources

Adams, Willi Paul. *The First American Constitutions: Republican Ideology and the Making of the State Constitutions in the Revolutionary Era*. Translated by Rita Kimber and Robert Kimber. Foreword by Richard B. Morris. Chapel Hill, 1980.

Ammerman, David. *In the Common Cause: American Response to the Coercive Acts of 1774*. Charlottesville, Va., 1974.

Appleby, Joyce. *Liberalism and Republicanism in the Historical Imagination*. Cambridge, Mass., 1992.

Bailyn, Bernard. *The Ideological Origins of the American Revolution*. Cambridge, Mass., 1967.

———. *The Ordeal of Thomas Hutchinson*. Cambridge, Mass., 1974.

———. *The Origins of American Politics*. New York, 1968.

Ball, Terence, and J. G. A. Pocock, eds. *Conceptual Change and the Constitution*. Lawrence, Kans., 1988.

Banning, Lance. "Jeffersonian Ideology Revisited: Liberal and Classical Ideas in the New American Republic." *William and Mary Quarterly*, 3d ser., 43 (1986): 3–19.

Barker, Charles Albro. *Background of the Revolution in Maryland*. New Haven, 1940.

Becker, Carl Lotus. *The History of Political Parties in the Province of New York, 1760–1776*. Foreword by Arthur M. Schlesinger. Madison, Wisc., 1968.

Becker, Robert A. *Revolution, Reform, and the Politics of American Taxation, 1763–1783*. Baton Rouge, 1980.

Beeman, Richard R. "Deference, Republicanism, and the Emergence of Popular Politics in Eighteenth-Century America." *William and Mary Quarterly*, 3d ser., 49 (1992): 401–30.

Beeman, Richard, Stephen Botein, and Edward C. Carter II, eds. *Beyond Confederation: Origins of the Constitution and American National Identity*. Chapel Hill, 1987.

Bellisles, Michael A. *Revolutionary Outlaws: Ethan Allen and the Struggle for Independence on the Early American Frontier*. Charlottesville, Va., 1993.

Berlin, Ira. *Slaves without Masters: The Free Negro in the Antebellum South*. New York, 1973.

Bernstein, Nicolai. "Italian Political Thought, 1450–1530." In *Cambridge History of Political Thought*, edited by J. H. Burns, 30–65. Cambridge, 1991.

Berthoff, Rowland. "Independence and Attachment, Virtue and Interest: From Republican Citizen to Free Enterpriser, 1787–1837." In *Uprooted Americans: Essays to Honor Oscar Handlin*, edited by Richard L. Bushman, Neil Harris, David Rothman, Barbara Miller Solomon, and Stephan Thernstrom, 97–124. Boston, 1979.

Billias, George Athan. *Elbridge Gerry: Founding Father and Republican Statesman*. New York, 1976.

Bogin, Ruth. *Abraham Clark and the Quest for Equality in the Revolutionary Era, 1774–1794*. Rutherford, N.J., 1982.

Bonomi, Patricia. *A Factious People: Politics and Society in Colonial New York*. New York, 1971.

Brown, Richard D. *Revolutionary Politics in Massachusetts: The Boston Committee of Correspondence and the Towns, 1772–1774*. Cambridge, Mass., 1970.

Brown, Robert E. *Middle-Class Democracy and the Revolution in Massachusetts, 1691–1780*. Ithaca, N.Y., 1955.

Brown, Robert E., and B. Katherine Brown. *Virginia, 1705–1786: Democracy or Aristocracy?* East Lansing, Mich., 1964.

Buel, Richard, Jr. *Dear Liberty: Connecticut's Mobilization for the Revolutionary War*. Middletown, Conn., 1980.

———. "Democracy and the American Revolution." *William and Mary Quarterly*, 3d ser., 21 (1964): 165–90.

———. "Freedom of the Press in Revolutionary America: The Evolution of Libertarianism, 1760–1820." In *The Press and the American Revolution*, edited by Bernard Bailyn and John B. Hench, 59–98. Boston, 1981.

Bushman, Richard L. *King and People in Provincial Massachusetts*. Chapel Hill, 1985.

Calhoon, Robert McCluer. *The Loyalists in Revolutionary America, 1760–1781*. New York, 1973.

Carpenter, William S. "The Separation of Powers in the Eighteenth Century." *American Political Science Review* 22 (1928): 32–44.

Chinn, H. C. "An Early New Jersey Poll List." *Pennsylvania Magazine of History and Biography* 44 (1920): 77–81.

Clarke, Mary P. *Parliamentary Privilege in the American Colonies*. New Haven, 1943.

Colbourn, H. Trevor. *The Lamp of Experience: Whig History and the Intellectual Origins of the American Revolution*. Chapel Hill, 1965.

Coleman, Kenneth. *The American Revolution in Georgia*. Athens, Ga., 1958.

Conkin, Paul. *Self-Evident Truths: Being a Discourse on the Origins and Development of the First Principles of American Government—Popular Sovereignty, Natural Rights, and Balance and Separation of Powers*. Bloomington, Ind., 1974.

Conley, Patrick T., and John P. Kaminski, eds. *The Bill of Rights and the States: The Colonial and Revolutionary Origins of American Liberties*. Madison, Wisc., 1992.

Conser, Walter H., Jr., Ronald M. McCarthy, David Toscano, and Gene Sharp, eds. *Resistance, Politics, and the American Struggle for Independence, 1765–1775*. Boulder, Colo., 1986.

Countryman, Edward. *A People in Revolution: The American Revolution and Political Society in New York, 1760–1790*. Baltimore, 1981.

Crow, Jeffrey J. "Liberty Men and Loyalists: Disorder and Disaffection in the North Carolina Backcountry." In *An Uncivil War*, edited by Ronald Hoffman, Thad Tate, and Peter J. Albert, 125–78. Charlottesville, Va., 1985.

———. "To the Editor." *William and Mary Quarterly*, 3d ser., 34 (1977): 696.

Curry, Thomas J. *The First Freedoms: Church and State in America to the Passage of the First Amendment*. New York, 1986.

Cushing, Harry A. *History of the Transition from Provincial to Commonwealth Government in Massachusetts*. New York, 1896.

Daniell, Jere R. *Experiment in Republicanism: New Hampshire Politics and the American Revolution, 1741–1794*. Cambridge, Mass., 1970.

Dickinson, H. T. *Liberty and Property: Political Ideology in Eighteenth-Century Britain.* New York, 1977.

Diggins, John Patrick. *The Lost Soul of American Politics: Virtue, Self-Interest, and the Foundations of American Liberalism.* New York, 1984.

Dinkin, Robert J. *Voting in Provincial America: A Study of Elections in the Thirteen Colonies, 1689–1776.* Westport, Conn., 1977.

———. *Voting in Revolutionary America: A Study of Elections in the Original Thirteen States, 1776–1789.* Westport, Conn., 1982.

Dodd, Walter Fairleigh. *The Revision and Amendment of State Constitutions.* Baltimore, 1910.

Douglass, Elisha P. *Rebels and Democrats: The Struggle for Equal Political Rights and Majority Rule during the American Revolution.* Chapel Hill, 1955.

Draper, Theodore. *A Struggle for Power: The American Revolution.* New York, 1996.

Ekirch, A. Roger. *"Poor Carolina": Politics and Society in Colonial North Carolina, 1729–1776.* Chapel Hill, 1981.

Erdman, Charles R., Jr. *The New Jersey Constitution of 1776.* Princeton, 1929.

Farrand, Max. "The Delaware Bill of Rights of 1776." *American Historical Review* 3 (1897–98): 641–50.

Fehrenbacher, Don E. *Constitutions and Constitutionalism in the Slaveholding South.* Athens, Ga., 1989.

Foner, Eric. *Tom Paine and Revolutionary America.* New York, 1976.

Ganyard, Robert L. *The Emergence of North Carolina's Revolutionary State Government.* Raleigh, 1978.

Gaustad, Edwin S. "Religious Tests, Constitutions, and 'Christian Nation.'" In *Religion in a Revolutionary Age*, edited by Ronald Hoffman and Peter J. Albert, 218–35. Charlottesville, Va., 1994.

Gerlach, Larry R. *Prologue to Independence: New Jersey in the Coming of the American Revolution.* New Brunswick, N.J., 1976.

Goebel, Julius, Jr. *Antecedents and Beginnings to 1801.* Vol. 1 of *The Oliver Wendell Holmes Devise History of the Supreme Court of the United States.* Edited by Paul A. Freund. New York, 1971.

Green, Fletcher M. *Constitutional Development in the South Atlantic States, 1776–1860: A Study in the Evolution of Democracy.* Chapel Hill, 1930.

Greene, Jack P. "Character, Persona, and Authority: A Study of Alternative Styles of Political Leadership in Revolutionary Virginia." In *The Revolutionary War in the South: Power, Conflict, and Leadership: Essays in Honor of John Richard Alden*, edited by W. Robert Higgins, 3–42. Durham, N.C., 1979.

———. *Imperatives, Behaviors, and Identities: Essays in Early American Cultural History.* Charlottesville, Va., 1992.

———. *Peripheries and Center: Constitutional Development in the Extended Polities of the British Empire and the United States, 1607–1788.* Athens, Ga., 1986.

———. "Political Mimesis: A Consideration of the Historical and Cultural Roots of Legislative Behavior in the British Colonies in the Eighteenth Century." *American Historical Review* 75 (1969–70): 337–67.

————. *The Quest for Power: The Lower Houses of Assembly in the Southern Royal Colonies, 1689–1776.* Chapel Hill, 1963.

————. "The Role of the Lower Houses of Assembly in Eighteenth-Century Politics." In *The Reinterpretation of the American Revolution, 1763–1789,* edited by Jack P. Greene, 86–109. New York, 1968.

————, ed. *The American Revolution: Its Character and Limits.* New York, 1987.

————. *Colonies to Nation: A Documentary History of the American Revolution.* New York, 1975.

Greene, Jack P., Richard L. Bushman, and Michael Kammen. *Society, Freedom, and Conscience: The American Revolution in Virginia, Massachusetts, and New York.* New York, 1976.

Gross, Robert A. *The Minutemen and Their World.* New York, 1976.

Gunderson, Joan R. "Independence, Citizenship, and the American Revolution." *Signs* 13 (1987): 59–77.

Gwyn, William B. *The Meaning of the Separation of Powers: An Analysis of the Doctrine from Its Origin to the Adoption of the United States Constitution.* New Orleans, 1965.

Hancock, Harold. "The Kent County Loyalists." *Delaware History* 6 (1954–55): 3–24, 93–139.

Harris, Tim. *Politics under the Later Stuarts: Party Conflict in a Divided Society, 1660–1715.* London, 1993.

Hatch, Nathan O. *The Democratization of American Christianity.* New Haven, 1989.

————. *The Sacred Cause of Liberty: Republican Thought and the Millennium in Revolutionary New England.* New Haven, 1977.

Hawke, David. *In the Midst of a Revolution.* Philadelphia, 1961.

Hirst, Derek. *The Representative of the People?: Voters and Voting in England under the Early Stuarts.* Cambridge, 1975.

Hoerder, Dirk. *Crowd Action in Revolutionary Massachusetts, 1765–1780.* New York, 1977.

Hoffman, Ronald. *A Spirit of Dissension: Economics, Politics, and the Revolution in Maryland.* Baltimore, 1973.

Hoffman, Ronald, and Peter J. Albert, eds. *Sovereign States in an Age of Uncertainty.* Charlottesville, Va., 1981.

Holmes, Geoffrey, and Daniel Szechi. *The Age of Oligarchy: Pre-industrial Britain, 1722–1783.* London, 1993.

Howard, A. E. Dick. *The Road from Runnymede: Magna Carta and Constitutionalism in America.* Charlottesville, Va., 1968.

Howe, John R., Jr. *The Changing Political Thought of John Adams.* Princeton, 1966.

Illick, Joseph E. *Colonial Pennsylvania: A History.* New York, 1976.

Jensen, Merrill. *The Founding of a Nation: A History of the American Revolution, 1763–1776.* New York, 1968.

Johnson, Richard R. "'Parliamentary Egotisms': The Clash of Legislatures in the Making of the American Revolution." *Journal of American History* 74 (September 1987): 338–62.

Jordan, David W. *Foundations of Representative Government in Maryland, 1632–1715.* Cambridge, 1987.

Kammen, Michael. *A Machine That Would Go of Itself: The Constitution in American Culture.* New York, 1986.

————. *Spheres of Liberty: Changing Perceptions of Liberty in American Culture*. Madison, Wisc., 1986.

Katz, Stanley N. "Republicanism and the Law of Inheritance in the American Revolutionary Era." *Michigan Law Review* 76 (1977–78): 1–29.

Kenyon, Cecilia M. "Republicanism and Radicalism in the American Revolution: An Old-Fashioned Interpretation." *William and Mary Quarterly*, 3d ser., 19 (1962): 153–82.

Kerber, Linda K. "The Paradox of Women's Citizenship in the Early Republic: The Case of *Martin vs. Massachusetts*, 1805." *American Historical Review* 97 (April 1992): 349–78.

————. "The Republican Ideology of the Revolutionary Generation." *American Quarterly* 37 (Fall 1985): 474–95.

————. *Women of the Republic: Intellect and Ideology in Revolutionary America*. New York, 1980.

Kettner, James H. *The Development of American Citizenship, 1608–1870*. Chapel Hill, 1978.

Klein, Milton M., Richard D. Brown, and John B. Hench, eds. *The Republican Synthesis Revisited: Essays in Honor of George Athan Billias*. Worcester, Mass., 1992.

Klein, Rachel N. *Unification of a Slave State: The Rise of the Planter Class in the South Carolina Backcountry, 1760–1808*. Chapel Hill, 1990.

Klinghoffer, Judith Apter, and Lois Elkis. "'The Petticoat Electors': Women's Suffrage in New Jersey, 1776–1807." *Journal of the Early Republic* 12 (Summer 1992): 159–94.

Kloppenberg, James T. "The Virtues of Liberalism: Christianity, Republicanism, and Ethics in Early American Political Discourse." *Journal of American History* 74 (1987): 9–33.

Kramnick, Isaac. *Republicanism and Bourgeois Radicalism: Political Ideology in Late Eighteenth-Century England and America*. Ithaca, N.Y., 1990.

Kruman, Marc W. *Parties and Politics in North Carolina, 1836–1865*. Baton Rouge, 1983.

————. "The Second American Party System and the Transformation of Revolutionary Republicanism." *Journal of the Early Republic* 12 (Winter 1992): 509–37.

Labaree, Leonard Woods. *Royal Government in America: A Study of the British Colonial System before 1768*. New Haven, 1930.

Levy, Leonard W. *Emergence of a Free Press*. New York, 1985.

Lovejoy, David S. *Rhode Island Politics and the American Revolution, 1760–1776*. Providence, R.I., 1958.

Lutz, Donald S. *The Origins of American Constitutionalism*. Baton Rouge, 1988.

————. *Popular Consent and Popular Control: Whig Political Theory in the Early State Constitutions*. Baton Rouge, 1980.

McCormick, Richard P. *The History of Voting in New Jersey: A Study of the Development of Election Machinery, 1664–1911*. New Brunswick, N.J., 1953.

McDonald, Forrest. *E Pluribus Unum: The Formation of the American Republic, 1776–1790*. Boston, 1965.

————. *Novus Ordo Seclorum: The Intellectual Origins of the Constitution*. Lawrence, Kans., 1985.

[McGiffert, Michael, ed.]. "The Creation of the American Republic: A Symposium of Views and Reviews." *William and Mary Quarterly*, 3d ser., 44 (1987): 549–640.

McKinley, Albert Edward. *The Suffrage Franchise in the English Colonies.* Philadelphia, 1905.

MacLeod, Duncan J. *Slavery, Race, and the American Revolution.* London, 1974.

McLoughlin, William G. *New England Dissent, 1630–1833: The Baptists and the Separation of Church and State.* 2 vols. Cambridge, Mass., 1971.

———. "The Role of Religion in the Revolution: Liberty of Conscience and Cultural Cohesion in the New Nation." In *Essays on the American Revolution*, edited by Stephen G. Kurtz and James H. Hutson, 197–255. Chapel Hill, 1973.

Maier, Pauline. *From Resistance to Revolution: Colonial Radicals and the Development of American Opposition to Britain, 1765–1776.* New York, 1972.

———. "John Wilkes and American Disillusionment with Britain." *William and Mary Quarterly*, 3d ser., 20 (1963): 373–95.

———. *The Old Revolutionaries: Political Lives in the Age of Samuel Adams.* New York, 1980.

———. "The Transforming Impact of Independence, Reaffirmed: 1776 and the Definition of American Social Structure." In *The Transformation of Early American History: Society, Authority, and Ideology*, edited by James A. Henretta, Michael Kammen, and Stanley Katz, 194–217. New York, 1991.

Main, Jackson Turner. "Government by the People: The American Revolution and the Democratization of the Legislatures." *William and Mary Quarterly*, 3d ser., 23 (1966): 391–407.

———. *The Sovereign States, 1775–1783.* New York, 1973.

———. *The Upper House in Revolutionary America.* Madison, Wisc., 1967.

Marcus, Jacob R. *The Colonial American Jew, 1492–1776.* 3 vols. Detroit, 1970.

Marston, Jerrilyn Greene. *King and Congress: The Transfer of Political Legitimacy, 1774–1776.* Princeton, 1987.

Mason, Bernard. *Road to Independence: The Revolutionary Movement in New York, 1773–1777.* Lexington, Ky., 1966.

Matthews, Richard K. *The Radical Politics of Thomas Jefferson: A Revisionist View.* Lawrence, Kans., 1984.

Mayer, David N. *The Constitutional Thought of Thomas Jefferson.* Charlottesville, Va., 1994.

Miller, Frank Hayden. "Legal Qualifications for Office in America, 1619–1899." American Historical Association, *Annual Report . . . for the Year 1899.* Vol. 1. 89–153. Washington, D.C., 1900.

Miller, William Lee. *The First Liberty: Religion and the American Republic.* New York, 1986.

Morey, William C. "The First State Constitutions." American Academy of Political and Social Science, *Annals* 4 (1893): 201–32.

Morgan, Edmund S. *American Slavery, American Freedom: The Ordeal of Colonial Virginia.* New York, 1975.

———. "Colonial Ideas of Parliamentary Power, 1764–1766." *William and Mary Quarterly*, 3d ser., 5 (1948): 311–41.

———. *Inventing the People: The Rise of Popular Sovereignty in England and America.* New York, 1988.

Morgan, Edmund S., and Helen M. Morgan. *The Stamp Act Crisis: Prologue to Revolution.* Rev. ed. London, 1962.

Morison, Samuel Eliot. "The Struggle over the Adoption of the Constitution of Massachusetts, 1780." Massachusetts Historical Society, *Proceedings* 50 (1916–17): 353–412.

Munroe, John A. *Colonial Delaware: A History.* Millwood, N.Y., 1978.

Murrin, John M. "From Liberties to Rights: The Struggle in Colonial Massachusetts." In *The Bill of Rights and the States: The Colonial and Revolutionary Origins of American Liberties,* edited by Patrick T. Conley and John P. Kaminski, 63–99. Madison, Wisc., 1992.

———. "The Great Inversion, or Court versus Country: A Comparison of the Revolution Settlements in England (1688–1721) and America (1776–1816)." In *Three British Revolutions: 1641, 1688, 1776,* edited by J. G. A. Pocock. Princeton, 1980.

———. "The Myths of Colonial Democracy and Royal Decline in Eighteenth-Century America: A Review Essay." *Cithara* 5 (1965): 53–69.

Nadelhaft, Jerome J. *The Disorders of War: The Revolution in South Carolina.* Orono, Me., 1981.

Nash, Gary B. *The Urban Crucible: Social Change, Political Consciousness, and the Origins of the American Revolution.* Cambridge, Mass., 1979.

Nelson, William E., and Robert C. Palmer. *Liberty and Community: Constitution and Rights in the Early American Republic.* New York, 1987.

Nevins, Allan. *The American States during and after the Revolution, 1775–1789.* New York, 1924.

Norton, Mary Beth. *Liberty's Daughters: The Revolutionary Experience of American Women, 1750–1800.* Boston, 1980.

Onuf, Peter S., and Cathy Matson. *A Union of Interests: Political and Economic Thought in Revolutionary America.* Lawrence, Kans., 1990.

Palmer, R. R. *The Age of Democratic Revolution: A Political History of Europe and America, 1760–1800: The Challenge.* Princeton, 1959.

Patterson, Stephen E. *Political Parties in Revolutionary Massachusetts.* Madison, Wisc., 1973.

Peters, Ronald M. *The Massachusetts Constitution of 1780: A Social Compact.* Amherst, 1978.

Peterson, Merrill D. "Thomas Jefferson, the Founders, and Constitutional Change." In *The American Founding: Essays on the Formation of the Constitution,* edited by J. Jackson Barlow, Leonard W. Levy, and Ken Masugi, 275–94. Westport, Conn., 1988.

Philbrook, Mary. "Woman's Suffrage in New Jersey prior to 1807." *Proceedings of the New Jersey Historical Society* 57 (1939): 870–98.

Plumb, J. H. "The Growth of the Electorate in England from 1600–1715." *Past and Present* 45 (November 1969): 90–116.

———. *The Growth of Political Stability in England, 1675–1725.* London, 1967.

Pocock, J. G. A. *The Machiavellian Moment.* Princeton, 1975.

———. *Politics, Language and Time: Essays on Political Thought and History.* New York, 1971.

Pole, J. R. *The Gift of Government: Political Responsibility from the English Restoration to American Independence.* Athens, Ga., 1983.

————. *Political Representation in England and the Origins of the American Republic.* Berkeley, 1971.

————. "Suffrage in New Jersey, 1790–1807." *Proceedings of the New Jersey Historical Society* 71 (1953): 39–61.

————. "Suffrage Reform and the American Revolution in New Jersey." *Proceedings of the New Jersey Historical Society* 74 (1956): 173–94.

Potter, Janice. *The Liberty We Seek: Loyalist Ideology in Colonial New York and Massachusetts.* Cambridge, Mass., 1983.

Purcell, Richard J. *Connecticut in Transition, 1775–1818.* Middletown, Conn., 1963.

Rakove, Jack N. *The Beginnings of National Politics: An Interpretive History of the Continental Congress.* New York, 1979.

————. "Parchment Barriers and the Politics of Rights." In *A Culture of Rights: The Bill of Rights in Philosophy, Politics, and Law—1791 and 1991,* edited by Michael James Lacey, 98–143. Cambridge, 1991.

Reed, H. Clay. "The Delaware Constitution of 1776." *Delaware Notes* 6 (1930): 7–42.

Reid, John Phillip. *The Concept of Representation in the Age of the American Revolution.* Chicago, 1989.

————. *Constitutional History of the American Revolution: The Authority of Law.* Madison, Wisc., 1993.

————. *Constitutional History of the American Revolution: The Authority to Legislate.* Madison, Wisc., 1991.

————. *Constitutional History of the American Revolution: The Authority to Tax.* Madison, Wisc., 1987.

Robbins, Caroline. *The Eighteenth-Century Commonwealthman: Studies in the Transmission, Development, and Circumstances of English Liberal Thought from the Restoration of Charles II until the War with the Thirteen Colonies.* Cambridge, Mass., 1959.

Rodgers, Daniel T. *Contested Truths: Keywords in American Politics since Independence.* New York, 1987.

————. "Republicanism: The Career of a Concept." *Journal of American History* 79 (1992): 11–38.

Rosswurm, Steven. *Arms, Country, and Class: The Philadelphia Militia and "Lower Sort" during the American Revolution, 1775–1783.* New Brunswick, N.J., 1987.

Ryerson, Richard Alan. *Revolution Is Now Begun: The Radical Committees of Philadelphia, 1765–1776.* Philadelphia, 1978.

Salmon, Marylynn. *Women and the Law of Property in Early America.* Chapel Hill, 1986.

Saye, Albert Berry. *A Constitutional History of Georgia, 1732–1945.* Athens, Ga., 1948.

Schwoerer, Lois G. *"No Standing Armies": The Antiarmy Ideology in Seventeenth-Century England.* Baltimore, 1974.

Selby, John E. *The Revolution in Virginia, 1775–1783.* Williamsburg, Va., 1988.

Selsam, J. Paul. *The Pennsylvania Constitution of 1776: A Study in Revolutionary Democracy.* Philadelphia, 1936.

Shalhope, Robert E. "Republicanism and Early American Historiography." *William and Mary Quarterly,* 3d ser., 39 (1982): 334–56.

————. *The Roots of Democracy: American Thought and Culture, 1760–1800.* Boston, 1990.

————. "Toward a Republican Synthesis: The Emergence of an Understanding of

Republicanism in American Historiography." *William and Mary Quarterly*, 3d ser., 29 (1972): 49–80.

Shaw, Peter. *American Patriots and the Rituals of Revolution*. Cambridge, Mass., 1981.

Slaughter, Thomas P. "The Taxman Cometh: Ideological Opposition to Internal Taxes, 1760–1790." *William and Mary Quarterly*, 3d ser., 41 (1984): 566–91.

———. *The Whiskey Rebellion: Frontier Epilogue to the American Revolution*. New York, 1986.

Sparks, Jared. *The Life of Gouverneur Morris*. 3 vols. Boston, 1832.

Steinfeld, Robert J. "Property and Suffrage in the Early Republic." *Stanford Law Review* 41 (1989): 335–76.

Stevens, William Bacon. *A History of Georgia, from its First Discovery by Europeans to the adoption of the Present Constitution in [1798]*. 2 vols. Philadelphia, 1859.

Stokes, Anson Phelps. *Church and State in the United States*. 3 vols. New York, 1950.

Stourzh, Gerald. *Alexander Hamilton and the Idea of Republican Government*. Palo Alto, 1970.

———. "Fundamental Laws and Individual Rights in the Eighteenth-Century Constitution." In *The American Founding: Essays on the Formation of the Constitution*, edited by J. Jackson Barlow, Leonard W. Levy, and Ken Masugi, 159–94. Westport, Conn., 1988.

Takaki, Ronald T. *Iron Cages: Race and Culture in Nineteenth-Century America*. New York, 1979.

Taylor, Robert J. *Western Massachusetts in the Revolution*. Providence, R.I., 1954.

Thomas, P. D. G. *British Politics and the Stamp Act Crisis: The First Phase of the American Revolution, 1763–1767*. Oxford, 1975.

———. *Tea Party to Independence: The Third Phase of the American Revolution, 1773–1776*. Oxford, 1991.

———. *The Townshend Duties Crisis: The Second Phase of the American Revolution, 1767–1773*. Oxford, 1987.

Tomlins, Christopher L. *Law, Labor, and Ideology in the Early American Republic*. Cambridge, 1993.

Tucker, Robert W., and David C. Hendrickson. *The Fall of the First British Empire: Origins of the War of American Independence*. Baltimore, 1982.

Tully, James. "Locke." In *The Cambridge History of Political Thought, 1450–1700*, edited by J. H. Burns, 616–52. Cambridge, 1991.

Turner, Raymond E. "Women's Suffrage in New Jersey." *Smith College Studies in History* 1, no. 4 (1916): 165–87.

Upton, Richard Francis. *Revolutionary New Hampshire: An Account of the Social and Political Forces Underlying the Transition from Royal Province to American Commonwealth*. Hanover, N.H., 1936.

VanBurkleo, Sandra F. Review of *Constitutional History of the American Revolution: Authority to Legislate* by John Philip Reid. *American Journal of Legal History* 38 (July 1994): 79–90.

Vile, M. J. C. *Constitutionalism and the Separation of Powers*. Oxford, 1967.

Walsh, Correa Moylan. *The Political Science of John Adams: A Study in the Theory of Mixed Government and the Bicameral System*. New York, 1915.

Watts, Steven. *The Republic Reborn: War and the Making of Liberal America, 1790–1820.* Baltimore, 1987.

Webster, William Clarence. "A Comparative Study of the State Constitutions of the American Revolution." American Academy of Political and Social Science, *Annals* 9 (1897): 380–420.

Weir, Robert M. *Colonial South Carolina: A History.* Millwood, N.Y., 1983.

———. *"The Last of American Freemen": Studies in the Political Culture of the Colonial and Revolutionary South.* Macon, Ga., 1986.

Weston, Corinne Comstock. *English Constitutional Theory and the House of Lords.* New York, 1965.

Wiebe, Robert H. *The Opening of American Society: From the Adoption of the Constitution to the Eve of Disunion.* New York, 1984.

Williamson, Chilton. *American Suffrage: From Property to Democracy, 1760–1860.* Princeton, 1960.

———. *Vermont in a Quandary: 1763–1825.* Montpelier, Vt., 1960.

Wills, Gary. *Inventing America: Jefferson's Declaration of Independence.* Garden City, N.Y., 1978.

Wood, Gordon S. *The Creation of the American Republic, 1776–1787.* Chapel Hill, 1969.

———. *The Radicalism of the American Revolution.* New York, 1992.

———. *Representation in the American Revolution.* Charlottesville, Va., 1969.

Wright, Benjamin Fletcher, Jr. "The Origins of the Separation of Powers in America." *Economica* 13 (1933): 169–85.

Young, Alfred F. *The Democratic Republicans of New York: The Origins, 1763–1797.* Chapel Hill, 1967.

Zagarri, Rosemarie. *The Politics of Size: Representation in the United States, 1776–1850.* Ithaca, N.Y., 1987.

Zemsky, Robert. *Merchants, Farmers, and River Gods: An Essay on Eighteenth-Century American Politics.* Boston, 1971.

Zuckerman, Michael. "The Social Context of Democracy in Massachusetts." *William and Mary Quarterly,* 3d ser., 25 (1968): 523–44.

instruction in, 80; legislature, 80, 201 (n. 75); suffrage in, 92–94, 106–7, 187 (n. 24); patronage in, 116, 128; separation of powers in, 117, 125, 128, 135; veto in, 125–26, 196 (n. 75); bicameralism in, 128, 139, 141; senators, terms of, 141; constitutional convention, 148, 158; colonial legislature of, 172 (n. 84); 195 (n. 62); elections in, 198 (n. 35). *See also* Adams, John; Parsons, Theophilus

Matson, Cathy, xi

May 10 and 15, 1776: resolutions of, 20, 80, 114

Middleton, Arthur, 56

Mixed government: proposed for states, 2–3; of England, 4, 132; theory of, 132, 143; colonial emulation of, 132–33; colonial councillors in, 133; and executives, 133–34; aristocracy in, 133, 135; and the people, 134–35; and natural aristocracy, 135; and property, 135–36; rejection of, 136–37, 160–61; modification of, 137–39; failure of, 139, 141–45; upper houses in, 140–41. *See also individual states*

Monarchy, 132. *See also* Mixed government

Montesquieu, Charles de Secondat, Baron: *The Spirit of the Laws*, 109

Morgan, Edmund S., 74

Morris, Gouverneur, 13, 147; on unicameralism, 200 (n. 65)

Morris, Robert, 18

Navigation Acts, 62

Nepotism, 196 (n. 80)

New Hampshire: constitution of 1776, 16, 43, 118–19; constitution making in, 20, 33; provincial congress, 23; declaration of rights, 37; constitution of 1784, 39, 43, 44; taxation in, 43–44; officeholding in, 48, 51, 118–19, 136–37; church establishment in, 48–49; suffrage in, 50, 92–93; senators, terms of, 51, 141; legislature, 52, 68–69, 81, 83,

145–46, 193 (n. 37), 198 (n. 28), 201 (n. 75); constitutional amendment in, 57, 59; representation in, 68–69, 139; residency requirements in, 82, 185 (n. 78); patronage in, 116; separation of powers in, 118–19; veto in, 124, 146; privy council, 128–29; elections in, 138, 198 (n. 35); judges, 195 (n. 62)

New Jersey: provincial congress, 20, 22, 23, 37, 111–12; constitution making in, 20–22; declaration of rights, 37, 45; constitution of 1776, 37, 56, 158; church establishment in, 46, 49; officeholding in, 51, 82, 119, 137; constitutional amendment in, 56, 172 (n. 6); legislature, 72–73, 137; representation in, 72–73, 139; suffrage in, 91, 101, 105–6; patronage in, 116, 118–19, 121; judges, 123; veto in, 124; privy council, 126–27; elections in, 138; senators, terms of, 141

New York: committee of safety, 18; constitution making in, 21; provincial congress, 21, 23, 77, 115; constitution of 1777, 40, 125; church establishment in, 46; officeholding in, 47, 51, 119–20, 122, 136; elections in, 52, 88, 92, 138; constitutional amendment in, 55; representation in, 73, 139; right of instruction in, 77, 81; suffrage in, 91; separation of powers in, 115, 118–20, 122; patronage in, 117–20; council of appointment, 122, 129; council of revision, 125, 129; senators, terms of, 141; naturalization in, 179 (n. 120); judges, terms of, 195 (n. 62)

Nicholas, Robert Carter, 79

Nonelectors. *See* Suffrage

North Carolina: constitution of 1776, 16–17, 37, 39, 124; committee of safety, 19, 21; provincial congress, 23, 67, 95, 114–15; declaration of rights, 37, 39, 179 (n. 121); church establishment in, 46–48; officeholding in, 47–48, 51, 82, 119, 137; elections in, 52, 82, 92–93, 138; constitutional amendment in, 55; rep-

Rumsey, Benjamin, 134
Rush, Benjamin, 151
Rutledge, John, 56, 124

"Salus Populi," 145, 148
Separation of powers, 7, 14, 109–11, 160;
and provincial congresses, 111–16; and
officeholding, 116–23; and patronage,
116–23; and gubernatorial veto, 123–
26; in the English constitution, 124;
and privy councils, 126–30; M. J. C.
Vile on, 191–92 (n. 4). *See also individual states*
Septennial Act of 1716. *See* Elections;
Parliament
Seven Years' War, 4, 62, 65
Shalhope, Robert, xi
Shays's Rebellion, 108
Slaves, 89, 103, 106
Smith, William "Cato," 134
South Carolina: constitution of 1776,
2, 14, 16, 20, 122, 124; and declaration
of independence, 13–14; constitution
making in, 14, 16, 20, 55–56; constitution of 1778, 16, 46–49, 55–56, 122;
provincial congress, 20, 23, 126; declaration of rights in, 37, 173 (n. 9);
church establishment in, 46–49,
178 (n. 88); officeholding in, 47, 51,
97, 120, 122, 136–37; constitutional
amendment in, 55–56; legislature,
55–56, 70–72, 83, 136, 137, 138, 201
(n. 75); veto in, 55–56, 124; representation in, 71–72, 139; royal government
of, 72; elections in, 85, 138; suffrage
in, 92, 106; patronage in, 119–20, 122;
separation of powers in, 119–20, 122,
127; executive council, 126–27, 196
(nn. 80, 81); senators, terms of, 141;
judges, terms of, 195 (n. 62); nepotism
in, 196 (n. 80)
Sovereignty: popular, 6–7, 8, 15–16,
19–22, 25–26, 27–33, 40–41, 142; Parliamentary, 9–14
Stamp Act Crisis, 4, 10, 62, 65
Suffrage, 50, 159–60, 188 (n. 33); and

constitution making, 30–31; and tax-
paying qualifications, 43–44, 92–98; in
England, 63, 159–60; and the disfranchised, 63–64, 103–8, 160, 171 (n. 81);
and loyalty, 98–103. *See also individual
states*
Sugar Act, 62
Sullivan, James: and suffrage, 95, 188–89
(n. 43)
Sullivan, John: and the New Hampshire
constitution, 145–46

Taxation: parliamentary, constitutional-
ity of, 10, 62; legislatures and, 42–43;
and representation, 88, 159. *See also*
Suffrage
Term limits, 140–42. *See also individual
states*
Thoughts on Government. See Adams,
John
Triennial Act of 1694, 82–83

Unicameralism, 148. *See also* Legislatures; *individual states*

Vermont: constitution of 1777, 17, 37,
39; declaration of rights, 37, 39; taxation in, 43–44; church establishment
in, 46, 178 (n. 88); officeholding in,
48; council of censors, 57, 151; legislature, 81–82, 136–37, 149, 151; right of
instruction in, 84; representation in,
182–83 (n. 26); residency requirements
in, 185 (n. 78)
Veto: in English system, 133; gubernatorial, 133, 160; 195 (nn. 63, 69), 196
(n. 75). *See also* Governors; Separation
of powers; *individual states*
Vile, M. J. C.: on separation of powers,
191–92 (n. 4)
Virginia: constitution of 1776, 17, 20, 42;
provincial congress, 23, 112; declaration of rights, 37–38, 40; suffrage in,
41, 90, 92, 106, 188 (n. 28); officeholding in, 42, 47, 51, 119, 136; church
establishment in, 45–48; elections, 52,